Sethulego Matebesi
Civil strife against local governance

Sethulego Matebesi

Civil strife against local governance
Dynamics of community protests in contemporary South Africa

Barbara Budrich Publishers
Opladen • Berlin • Toronto 2017

All rights reserved. No part of this publication may be reproduced, stored in or introduced into a retrieval system, or transmitted, in any form, or by any means (electronic, mechanical, photocopying, recording or otherwise) without the prior written permission of Barbara Budrich Publishers. Any person who does any unauthorized act in relation to this publication may be liable to criminal prosecution and civil claims for damages.
You must not circulate this book in any other binding or cover and you must impose this same condition on any acquirer.

A CIP catalogue record for this book is available from
Die Deutsche Bibliothek (The German Library)

This book was subjected to a double-blind peer review process.

© 2017 by Barbara Budrich Publishers, Opladen, Berlin & Toronto
www.barbara-budrich.net
ISBN 978-3-8474-0578-8
eISBN 978-3-8474-0970-0

Das Werk einschließlich aller seiner Teile ist urheberrechtlich geschützt. Jede Verwertung außerhalb der engen Grenzen des Urheberrechtsgesetzes ist ohne Zustimmung des Verlages unzulässig und strafbar. Das gilt insbesondere für Vervielfältigungen, Übersetzungen, Mikroverfilmungen und die Einspeicherung und Verarbeitung in elektronischen Systemen.

Die Deutsche Bibliothek – CIP-Einheitsaufnahme
Ein Titeldatensatz für die Publikation ist bei der Deutschen Bibliothek erhältlich.

Verlag Barbara Budrich 🅱 Barbara Budrich Publishers
Stauffenbergstr. 7. D-51379 Leverkusen Opladen, Germany

86 Delma Drive. Toronto, ON M8W 4P6 Canada
www.barbara-budrich.net

Jacket illustration: Bettina Lehfeldt, Kleinmachnow, Germany
– www.lehfeldtgraphic.de
Technical editing: Anja Borkam, Jena, Germany – kontakt@lektorat-borkam.de

This book is dedicated in loving and eternal memory of my spiritual mother, Albertina Monare, for her extraordinary love unwavering belief that human beings can find courage in crisis, and faith in the most hopeless of situations.

Table of contents

List of Abbreviations — vii

Acknowledgments — ix

1. Introduction: The dynamics of community in South Africa — 1
2. A theoretical intersection of political trust, institutions, and actors — 24
3. Evolution of the local governance in South Africa: The triumph or failure of participatory governance? — 56
4. Schools and roads as bargaining power in community protests in predominantly black communities — 86
5. Ratepayers' associations and the "cheque book" protests in predominantly white communities — 124
6. Conclusions: The implications and future of community protests in South Africa and beyond — 144

References — 157

Index — 181

List of abbreviations

ANC	African National Congress
BLA	Black Local Authority
CDS	Centre for Development Support
CDE	Centre for Development Enterprise
COGTA	Department of Cooperative Governance and Traditional Affairs
COSATU	Congress of South African Trade Unions
DA	Democratic Alliance
DRA	Dullstroom Ratepayers' Association
EFF	Economic Freedom Fighters
EGGF	Emakhazeni Good Governance Forum
EGCO	Elgin Grabouw Civic Organization
ERA	Emthanjeni Ratepayers' Association
GRF	Ganyesa Residents' Forum
HLRA	Heilbron Landowners and Residents' Association
IDP	Integrated Development Planning
IEC	Independent Electoral Commission
JPI	Joint Planning Initiatives
LDC	Local Development Council
LGTAS	Local Government Turnaround Strategy
MCC	Meqheleng Concerned Citizens
MDB	Municipal Demarcation Board
NRF	National Research Foundation
RRA	Riviersonderend Ratepayers' Association
SABC	South African Broadcasting Corporation
SALGA	South African Local Government Association
SANCO	South African National Civic Association

SANFED	Sandton Federation of Ratepayers' Associations
SAPS	South African Police Services
SIBU	Sannieshof Ratepayers' Association
UFS	University of the Free State
WLA	White Local Authorities

Acknowledgements

The conception of Civil Strife Against Local Governance can be traced back to almost ten years ago when the Centre of Development Studies (CDS) of the University of the Free State (UFS) – where I am a Research Associate - was contracted by the Centre of Development Enterprises (CDE) to conduct a few case studies on community protests, two years after the outbreak of the first protests in South Africa. The CDE is an independent policy research and advocacy organization and one of South Africa's leading development think tanks, focusing on critical national development issues. Thus, my involvement in the CDE project piqued my interest in the broad field of social movements and in community protests, in particular. In this regard, I am grateful for the tutelage of my two good friends, Professors Lucius Botes (Dean of the Faculty of the Humanities) and Lochner Marais (CDS).

It would be remiss if I did not thank Professor Jackie Du Toit who encouraged me to apply for the Vice Rector's Prestige Scholarship Programme (PSP), led by Professor Jonathan Jansen of the University of the Free State towards the end of 2010. To Jackie and the PSP team, it is commendable that you managed to generously devote time to the advancement of other scholarships. I am very happy to have been part of the programme and feel a great sense of achievement.

Importantly, this book would not have seen the light if it was not for the generous funding from the National Research Foundation (NRF) in South Africa and Erasmus Mundus EU-SATURN (EUropean - South African programme in TUning for Regional Needs in higher education). The funding from the NRF enabled me to conduct the research and, together with the EU-SATURN funding, enabled me to spend four months at the Department of Peace and Conflict Research (DPCR) of Uppsala University, Sweden from August to December 2014. I would like to thank the staff of DPCR for the exceptional collegial environment during my visit. In particular, I feel great gratitude towards my hospitable host, Professor Ashok Swain, who took a passionate interest in my research. He has contributed much to the shaping of ideas and on drafts of the book.

Special thanks go to Professor Hussein Solomon (an internationally renowned scholar on conflict and conflict resolution in Africa, religious fundamentalism and population movements in the developing world), who had a great influence on the design of the study by suggesting the inclusion of the Western Cape Province in order to discern the different political dynamics of community protests. I also feel great gratitude towards my colleagues at the University of the Free State, Andre Pelser, Doreen Atkinson, and Lochner Marais, for their helpful and insightful feedback on earlier drafts of the manuscript.

With such a daunting project, there is often the likelihood of becoming disillusioned. I would like to express my sincere appreciation to all my colleagues at the Department of Sociology for affording me the space and time to accomplish this project. I am particularly grateful to Leane Ackermann whose constant words of encouragement have not gone unnoticed. I also owe a special debt to Malilimala Moletsane who ensured the consistency and completeness of the bibliography, Eleanor van der Westhuizen of the Research Directorate at UFS for her occasional guidance during the early stages of the study, as well as the current affairs teams of Motsweding FM (in particular David Magae), Motheo FM and various other radio stations and newspapers for the platform provided to share my ideas with their listeners.

I acknowledge the valuable contribution of officials of the Provincial Departments of Cooperative Governance and Traditional Affairs (or Local Government), the South African Local Government Association, leaders of civic groups and residents in the case study areas in the Free State, Northern Cape, North West and Western Cape Provinces of South Africa. In this regard, the contribution of a dedicated fieldwork team which, at various times, included Delsy Mashele, Keketso Raleie, Khotsofalang Makae, Thabo Kototsi, Pelonomi Tsoeu, Seipati Moleme, and Tshegang Maputle, is recognized.

I have been fortunate to have the help and advice of Professor Pumla Madikizela-Godobo (a Senior Research Professor in Trauma, Forgiveness and Reconciliation Studies) who helped me connect with my publisher and has supported the development of *Civil Strife*. Thanks to the Barbara Budrich team led by Sarah Rögl for their guidance throughout the process. I also thank the anonymous peer-reviewers for their invaluable comments and criticisms, as well as the Municipal IQ who gave permission to reproduce Figure 1 in Chapter 1 on the prevalence of community protests between 2004 and 2016. I also express my sincere gratitude towards Naledi Gouws of Star Language Services for the proofreading of most of the chapters.

Finally, I would like to express my appreciation to my family who supported me during both the fieldwork and the writing of the book. In this regard, special thanks to my wife, Lesego, daughter, Puleng, and son, Tshiamo. *Ke a leboga bagaetsho!*

Chapter 1: Introduction: The dynamics of community protests in South Africa

Introduction

In the twenty-first century, in which notions of a liberal, democratic nation-state thrive, protests in South Africa can be seen as the defining experiences and political apparatus of modernity, shaping public spaces, discourse, and popular culture. As an ongoing and pervasive phenomenon, protests have also redefined the economic, social and cultural dynamics of communities in South Africa. It was not so long ago that as a nation, South Africa moved from a political system concerned with racial polarization, to a nation concerned with truth and reconciliation, to the present nation concerned with the consolidation of constitutional democracy or the so-called rainbow nation. Thus, the current nation is geared towards promoting democratic values, a pluralistic political dialogue and an environment conducive to citizen participation. But notably, protests, which have been a prominent feature of black political expression in South Africa for many years, have taken on a striking resonance. These protests, which have been thrust to the forefront of mainstream politics, are no more apparent than in the realms of local communities.

Globally the rise of insurgent citizenship has not only grown in quantity, but has also evolved in terms of mobilization and protest tactics in both democratic and authoritarian political settings. Buoyed by a wider range of organizational networks and the use of technology to mobilize, protests transcend geographical borders. Global forms of mobilization aimed at facilitating economic, social or political change can be traced to, for example, the tremendous accomplishment of Occupy Wall Street in the USA, the generalized rise in various forms of political protests in Latin American countries, communal conflicts in Sudan, Arab Spring revolutionary tactics in Egypt and Tunisia, and the recent pro-democracy protests in Hong Kong. Scholars ascribe the rise of political protests in recent decades largely to the process of (post)modernization, which emphasizes how the individual's values have radically changed their way of interacting with the political system (Inglehart and Welzel 2009). This process triggered the reduction of political trust among citizens, while self-expression values gained priority, including the emergence of the so-called insurgent citizenship (Brancati 2014; Addler 2012; Inglehart and Catterberg 2002; Norris 1999).

The international discourse on sustained popular mobilization advances two competing views on the extent to which protests assist or impede democratization. In her book *From Protest to Parties,* Lebas (2011:14) argues that, to a large extent, scholars have viewed sustained popular mobilization as an impediment to democratization. Arguments advanced for this view are that popular demands can overwhelm weak states, reduce the "flexibility of the actors who have the power to form pacts and make compromises", or trigger authoritarian retrenchment. This perspective, however, is challenged by several scholars who purport that sustained protests advance democracy and transform the character of state-society relations (Machado, Scartascini and Tommasi 2009; Runciman 2014).

The focus of this book is on community protests directed against municipalities in both predominantly black communities *and* white communities in South Africa. These protests are a daily reality for many South Africans and involve communities going on the rampage over the perceived provision of basic municipal services such as water, electricity, sanitation and other municipal obligations. This, inevitably, devolved into what I refer to as a civil strife (a sustained collective advocacy to address a concern). This strife against municipalities cuts across geographic and demographic boundaries, but, in what has become a somewhat hegemonic account by scholars, is the considerable attention given to community protests that often turn violent and at times deadly in predominantly black neighborhoods in South Africa. In contrast, the nonviolent protest tactic of refusing to pay rates and taxes directly to municipalities by ratepayers' association in white communities, has received scant attention.

The book connects the critical issue of community protests to the equally precarious issue of political trust in local governance in South Africa by using comparative analysis of grassroots activism in predominantly black communities and predominantly white communities. Against this background, the book begins by asking several questions. Why, in an era of democratization, is South Africa experiencing such high levels of contestation between citizens and their local municipalities? In response to the question, this chapter provides a concise overview of the nature, prevalence and dynamics of community protests in South Africa since 2004.

Why this book?

My interest in pursuing this book was triggered by two main events. First, it was the prime time television news which covered an unarmed protestor in Ficksburg (a typical large town in the Free State Province) being murdered by a number of police officers without provocation in April 2011. While not being the first unarmed person to have been murdered by the police in post-apartheid South Africa, a decisive point was reached in respect of community protests in the country. This despicable act was rightly summed up Pithouse (2011:180) to conclude: "they murdered a man who had, with thousands of others, taken to the streets in protest at the unconscionable contempt with which the poor are treated in this country".

Second, a headline of a newspaper I read in 2012 stated, "*Children held to ransom for services*". The report stated that about 17 000 pupils in the Northern Cape Province of South Africa had been forced out of school for over four months (Nkosi 2012). The angry protestors from predominantly black communities cited a string of 'broken promises' by the government as their reason for protesting, and argued that the closing of schools was in the best interests of learners. I found it perplexing that parents could proactively prevent their own children from securing their future through education. Fast-forward to 2014, the so-called Northern Cape "*No Road, No School*" protest in Kuruman struck again and prevented learners from more than 50 schools from attending classes, thus, costing them a year of learning.

More specifically, the Olifantshoek/Kuruman cases represent some of the many intriguing cases of community protests in contemporary South Africa. These cases also represent a significant shift in community protests in the country: that public schools are being used as bargaining power in local struggles. For Jansen (2012), a key aspect of this shift is that such events had never happened before, even during the apartheid years. He further elaborates:

> What kind of society closes down its schools for months on end because of demands for a tarred road and for the ejection of a single person, the mayor? Think about this for a minute. I am not contesting, for the moment, the legitimacy of the community's

3

demands for better services or more competent officials. I am asking a broader question: why would a community sacrifice the one route out of poverty for rural youth in a socially and economically oppressed community like Olifantshoek and other areas of the Northern Cape? (Jansen 2012:2-3).

Another key shift in the nature of community protests involves their increasingly disruptive and violent character (Paret 2015). Scholarship has shown how community protest activists regularly move back and forth between institutional and non-institutional spaces of engagement and use violence to advance collective causes (Marais et al. 2008; Matebesi and Botes 2011; Steyn 2012). Furthermore, von Holdt (2013:590) provides another perspective on violence in South Africa by drawing attention to how inequality and economic exclusion, as well as the institutional challenges of a society in transition, produce a highly unstable social order in which violence is growing. He further argues that "democracy may configure power relations in such a way that violent practices are integral to them – producing a social system we may call violent democracy" (Von Holdt, 2013:590). As Tlhabi contends,

> It is not the first time we have seen property being damaged by protesters and to pretend that this has never happened in our lives would be silly. But there are certain experiences that the heart cannot get used to. Like death. The trauma of having lost and buried a loved one does not make the situation easier to bear the next time someone else dies. And so it was that I joined fellow South Africans in expressing our horror at images of bloodthirsty residents throwing bricks at a former ward councilor's house, ripping off the television satellite dish and, in the ultimate act of mob violence, setting a car on fire. These images were accompanied by angry voices threatening more violence and vowing to unleash further destruction. The visuals were not just reflective of residents who were fed up but rather, were a microcosm of the violent society in which we live (Tlhabi 2011:1).

As I was writing, a cursory glance at any article about protests in South Africa between the latter part of 2015 and early 2016 has been aptly dubbed the rise of "fallism". Fallism, in this context, refers to the nationwide student and worker activism against lack of transformation and colonial legacies in tertiary institutions (Pilane 2015), conducted under banners such as #RhodesMustFall, #FeesMustFall, and #EndOutsourcing. These protests, although vastly different, have two things in common with mainstream community protests: the return to revolutionary catchphrases and the eroding of the public education system in the country. Moreover, these forms of student activism are largely shaped by what typically constitutes "protest" and what might be seen as effective tactics to advance protest goals.

These illustrative examples broadly highlight the fact that the current wave of community protests in contemporary South Africa are as rampantly institutionalized and personally and socially detrimental to impoverished communities as apartheid was. There is a deeper issue here, however. Regardless of the explicit right to protest as enshrined in the South African Constitution (Republic of South Africa 1997), and regardless of the purported anger and frustrations of protest activists, a moral challenge remains for the country: Why have community protests not yet provoked, within the frameworks of a liberal-democratic society, any major moral outrage in South Africa?

The book is timely for three main reasons. Firstly, while the growth of international scholarly interest in protests has been substantial (Della Porta and Piazza 2008; Klandermans 1997; Lipsky 1965; Opp 2009; Swain . 2010), the upsurge in community protests in South Africa is matched by a growing, though limited, body of research investigating this phenomenon (Ballard, Habib and Valodia 2006; Booysen 2015; Booysen 2009; Brown 2015; Langa and von Holdt 2012; Piper and Nadvi 2010; Robins 2010, Tapscott 2010; Zuern 2011). While I applaud the insights and contributions of these studies, including the work of other leading private and university based research units, there remains a dearth of studies on the more "subtle" form of protest of withholding rates and taxes from municipalities, a tactic used by ratepayers' association in predominantly white communities in South Africa. Thus, the book informs the growing literature on community protests and also fills an empirical void by including protests by residents' associations both in predominantly black and predominantly white areas.

Secondly, with a few notable exceptions, the most striking and somewhat surprising revelation to emerge about studies on community protests in South Africa is the ignorance of the voice of municipalities. Therefore, the book also focus on the narratives of municipalities, the Provincial Departments of Cooperative Governance and Traditional Affairs (COGTA) and the South African Local Government Association (SALGA) (an independent organization mandated by the constitution to support local government).

Thirdly, the book seeks to make a modest contribution to the theory of political trust by drawing on an intricate three-dimensional theoretical framework of trust-institutions-actors, combined with insights from Karl-Dieter Opp's (2009) structural-cognitive model (SCM). The SCM emphasizes the implicit link between macro-level political institutions and micro-level motivations to participate in protest activities. For instance, the cognitive system of individuals, which includes identity and framing processes, is largely influenced by beliefs and attitudes towards formal political structures and processes. When relevant macro changes first enter the cognitive system of individuals, they set in motion cognitive processes that may create incentives to protest. These incentives include material as well as non-material costs (i.e. identity or identification with a group).

I use the metaphor of a swinging pendulum, where what I call a ravenous political trade-off between state and citizens, takes place along a continuum of political trust, with trust-building on the left end and distrust on the right end. The ravenous political trade-off constitutes the inherent conflict between the interests of politicians and citizens. To this end, the framework explicates how political trust, a cognitive function conceptualized as an individual's confidence in state institutions (a local municipality, in this context), influences actors (citizens) to engage in protest action. While political trust functions as a linkage mechanism between citizens and the political institutions that represent them (Kong 2014), the framework suggests that it is the structure of the community groups that motivates community groups with a fundamentally set of similar grievances to embark on miscellaneous protest tactics.

The book will also be centrally relevant to racially polarized post-conflict and post-liberation countries with longstanding and highly institutionalized states. Deepening our understanding of protests at community level may lead to a determination of how an effective trust-building intervention strategy should be approached. This will go a long way in repairing the ever-growing gulf of distrust between state and non-state actors and, as a result, halt the strife against local governance. To this end, three primary questions underlying the book are: How are community protests socially constructed and rendered meaningful at collective level? What elements of the "social fabric" enable communities to sustain mobilization against their local municipalities? What incentives motivate civic groups with a fundamentally similar set of grievances to embark on different protest tactics?

Community protests: some conceptual clarity

A large body of literature has been devoted to the concept of "protest" - a central aspect in the study of social movements. These studies have shown that protests are dynamic and characterized by great complexity. Broadly, protests are defined as a "resource of the powerless ... [who] depend for success not upon direct utilization of power, but upon activating other groups to enter the political arena" (Lipsky 1965: 1). In this regard, collective action is arguably the most defining characteristic that differentiates protests from other forms of political behavior such as voting. But a universal definition of the concept "community protests" is still elusive. The media, government and some scholars still use the term "service delivery protests" to illuminate the demands of residents. For example, Booysen (2007:21) described these protests broadly as being led "against both the quality of service delivery and public representation of grass-roots' service delivery needs".

But for others, the notion of "service delivery protests" not only blurs the debate, but also ignores the wider context of the issue (Friedman 2009; Pithouse 2011). For them, the issue encompasses much more than just the provision of basic services. A further linguistic challenge about the term is despite being pervasive in the political discussions of South Africa (Le Chen et al. 2014), "service delivery" is not universally defined (Stewart 2013). Furthermore, conceptions of the protest action as a way in which the use of violence is viewed as a natural and justified response by various actors (Von Holdt 2011), an effect of neoliberal economic policies in post-apartheid South Africa (Alexander 2010; Runciman 2014, Swart 2013), or "a rebellion of the poor" (Alexander 2010), are grounded in the precarious living conditions of black South Africans (Stewart 2013) and assist in understanding the dichotomy between community grievances and protests.

More recent scholarship, though, has also contributed much to the divergence in definitions of protest action. For instance, Powell, O'Donovan and de Visser (2015:4), describe the protest action as civic protests that refer to "organized protest action within a local area which directly targets municipal government or targets municipal government as a proxy to express grievances against the state more widely". The authors allude that the definition of the protest action as a form of civic conflict is useful in locating the South African experience within the broader field of comparative international scholarship on conflict in fragile and conflict affected countries. Conversely, others generally delineate the protest action as a form of "community protest". For example, Paret notes:

> Community protests refer to collective actions that take place within a highly localised geographic area, such as an informal shack settlement or a section of a township. They are popularly labelled as 'service delivery protests', in reference to common demands for services such as water and electricity... (Paret 2015:121).

The aforementioned conceptual innovations by Paret (2015) and Powell et al. (2015) elicit both similarities and differences. For instance, one key element in both definitions is the emphasis on the fact that the protest action typically takes place in a highly localized area. However, only Powell et al. (2015) mention municipalities as the target of the protestors, whereas Paret (2015) explicitly focuses on residents' common demands: water and electricity.

The definition by Powell et al. (2015) is a valid point of reference to shift from the focus on the term of "service delivery protests" to community protests. In this regard, I extend the two definitions by describing the protest action as collective action by residents in a highly localized area (community), which directly targets a local municipality over the provision of basic services such as water, electricity, and sanitation, including a wider spectrum of concerns such as housing, roads, government corruption, rampant crime, and unemployment.

It is this concept of community protests that underlies this book. It highlights one key broad aspect that characterizes the definition of community protests: that the protest action takes place within social contexts. Thus, community protests are defined on the basis of the often taken-for-granted dynamics of local government participatory governance. Furthermore, the concept embodies a new orientation toward the responsibility of municipalities in post-apartheid South Africa.

Tracing the inner logic of official state rhetoric on community protests reveals, in the words of the South African President, that "in some cases people protested against municipalities even if the issues at hand did not fall under their mandate" (News24 2014a). In hindsight, this seems to be an eminently sensible general analysis about the issue. However, this notion of community protests is highly untenable and may generate misguided policy and intervention responses. Such views are also not sensitive enough to the profound complexities of constructive engagement between municipalities (or broadly, the state) and local residents.

For instance, the emphasis on participatory governance in post-apartheid South Africa has been linked to substantive innovations in public participation. One such innovation included a set of requirements for public involvement in various decision-making processes similar to those in countries such as Argentina, Brazil and Mexico. These requirements, among others, include public consultation on the annual municipal budget, the integrated development programme (IDP) review process, and the service delivery contracting process (Barichievy, Piper and Parker 2005; Booysen 2009; Mubungizi and Dassah 2014; Piper and Nadvi 2010). This local participatory planning process, as in the case of Brazil, France and Spain (Ganuza, Nez and Morales 2014), is particularly prone to community protests. Evidence from several case studies in South Africa has shown that residents often identify a lack of housing, poor roads, and sewage systems as development priorities during IDP meetings (Botes et al. 2007; Johnston and Bernstein 2007). I contend that once the local municipality agrees to these priorities and includes them in the IDP, is it therefore not logical to assume that residents will approach municipalities should these needs and concerns not be addressed at a later stage? As I explain later in the book, IDPs (or participatory budgeting in international discourse) have become a contentious issue on whether municipalities implement them because it is normatively desirable to do so, or for the very practical reasons of achieving better municipal performance.

Local governance in South Africa

There is substantial literature on the local government system in general, and municipalities in particular, in South Africa. This sub-section is concerned, therefore, with an overview of the performance of municipalities, and not with providing an exhaustive account of local governance in the country.

Over the past few decades, many studies on the notion of democratic local governance were conducted in a variety of contexts in South Africa (Lobe 2008; Mohamed 2000; Patel 2006; Pillay 2001; Tshabalala and Lombard, 2009). The surge in the number of studies on local governance was largely as a result of the major reforms and new institutional mechanisms aimed at promoting the engagement of local elected leaders with their respective communities (Tshabalala and Lombard, 2009). Prior to the new political dispensation in South Africa, local government had little autonomy, and decisions were subject to judicial review by provincial and national governments (South African Local Government Association 2013). This period, characterized by wide-ranging popular mobilization against the apartheid government, was later followed by an era that coincided with the growing expectations of public consultation and articulation between popular needs and government action (Booysen 2009) from South African citizens.

It is perhaps important to pause here and provide a brief exposition of local government structures in South Africa. Broadly, there are currently three categories of municipalities in South Africa: metropolitan, district and local. Both metropolitan and district municipalities form the layer of government directly below the provinces. More specifically, while metropolitan (or metro) municipalities execute all the functions of local government for a city, on one hand, district municipalities execute some the functions of local government for a district, on the other hand. The district municipality comprises several local municipalities, with which it shares the functions of local government. Thus, local municipalities represent a subdivision of the district municipalities, and form the third layer of government (Department of Cooperative Governance and Traditional Affairs 2014). There are currently eight metropolitan municipalities, 44 district municipalities, and 207 local municipalities. All municipalities are governed by municipal councils which are elected every five years. In turn, municipal councils are managed by an executive committee consisting of an elected executive mayor (Electoral Commission SA 2016) - a political appointee who serves as the political head of the municipality – and a municipal manager who acts as the head of the administration of a municipality and the accounting officer (Surty 2010).

Historically, the administrative structure of local government was fragmented due to its duplication for each race group in South Africa. Since the advent of democracy, efforts to transform and develop municipalities into institutions of effective administration and service delivery LED to their newly found expanded and developmental role. To this end, the right of citizens to a basic level of services is enshrined in the South African Constitution. In this regard, municipalities are expected to deliver these services within the limits of their resources. However, this is an oversimplified means of evaluating municipalities. Too often are municipalities required to cross subsidise a number of national and provincial functions such as health services, roads, planning and land use management and transport being performed at the local level (South African Local Government Association 2015).

In response to the challenge of realizing the full role and potential of a developmental local government, municipalities in South Africa adopted largely technocratic processes. These processes focused "on ensuring service delivery and sustainability within legislated structures and systems" such as integrated development plans and budgets (Heese and Allan 2016). Thus, municipalities are often overwhelmed by rapid processes and approaches ranging from addressing past weaknesses to the process of consolidating the transformation of local government (South African Local Government Association 2015). This also include dealing with delicate, complex and multiple service delivery and governance problem areas: huge service delivery and backlog challenges regarding, for example, housing, water and sanitation; poor communication and accountability relationships with communities; problems with the political / administrative interface; weak civil society formations; intra- and inter-political party issues negatively affecting governance and delivery; and insufficient municipal capacity due to lack of scarce skills (Department of Cooperative Government and Traditional Affairs 2009).

One of the most recent approaches adopted in the local government sphere is the Back to Basics Campaign, initiated in late 2014 by the then Minister of Cooperative Governance and Local Government, Mr. Pravin Gordhan. The goal of this campaign was for municipalities to ensure that they get the core functions of providing services "to the right quality and standard" and ensuring "good governance and effective administration". The five pillars of the campaign are, i) putting people and their concerns first; 2) supporting the delivery of municipal services to the right quality and standard; 3) promoting good governance; 4) ensuring sound financial management and accounting; and 5) building institutional resilience and administrative capability (Department of Cooperative Governance and Traditional Affairs 2014). However, almost a decade ago, Thornhill (2008) argued about the elusive aspect of the lofty ideals of the so-called developmental local government in South Africa (Thornhill 2008).

In respect of the perception that citizens of South Africa have about local government, an elegantly written book edited by Muhammad Olimat – *Arab Spring and Arab Women,* is helpful. The book provides a detailed and carefully contextualized account of the death of Muhammad Bouazizi, a fruit vendor in a central Tunisian town. An important aspect of this story is that before setting himself on fire, Bouazizi went to the municipality to complain about a police woman. He was "told to leave and no one would talk to him". Needless to state, this later provided the spark for what has become known as the Arab Spring (Olimat 2014:14). What happened to Bouazizi at the municipality is all too common to many South Africans: an unresponsive local government system.

The foregoing discourse advocates a thesis of an unresponsive local government system. Increasingly, though, the peculiar juxtaposition of the local government character with unresponsiveness seems to have skewed any real discussion of several contextual factors: a system with devolved powers inhibited by centralizing tendencies; political expediency, compounded by the demand by communities for the provision of basic services, which were ancillary issues during the apartheid era. As such, many believe the criticism of municipalities has become unwarranted.

However, this does not dent my conviction that the performance of some municipalities in South Africa is questionable. Objective indicators such as the Auditor-General of South Africa (a chapter 9 institution that has a constitutional mandate to enable oversight, accountability and governance in the public sector) and the Municipal IQ (a specialized local government data and intelligence organization) reports contribute to this conviction. For instance, the report of the Auditor-General for the 2013-14 financial year took a decidedly more positive view of municipal financial audit results than previous audits. Still, only 40 of the 268 municipalities received financially unqualified audit opinions with no findings for the same financial year (Auditor-General of South Africa 2015). The Municipal IQ's annual set of results for 2014 reveals that municipalities in the Western Cape and Gauteng provinces of South Africa typically remain the best managed and most competitive. The findings suggest, nevertheless, that there are still "too many cases of individual underperformance, typically in areas that are the most developmentally disadvantaged; namely, former homeland and rural areas" (Municipal IQ 2014).

Meanwhile, the outcome of the Local Government Elections of August 3, 2016 in South Africa (see Table 1) has ushered in a new political era in South Africa and, in particular in the metropolitan municipalities won by the Democratic Alliance with the support of other smaller opposition parties (Letsoalo 2016). The Democratic Alliance, which only controlled the City of Cape Town metropolitan municipality, are now in control of four of the eight metropolitan municipalities. Given that five of the eight metropolitan municipalities (Cape Town, Ekurhuleni, eThekweni, Johannesburg, and Tshwane) accounted for half of all community protests between 2007 and 2014 (Municipal IQ 2014; Powell et al. 2015), issues relating to municipal service delivery and the administration of municipalities will be under the constant scrutiny of citizen in these metros. While it is too early to evaluate the impact of the coalition-led municipalities on service delivery and governance, the possibilities that they open for local governance is monumental. It remains to be seen whether these municipalities will become more responsive and extend purview of democracy at local level, or become a space where the ostensibly ideological and doctrinal differences among the newly-found political allies take centre stage.

Table 1: Leading political parties in the metropolitan municipalities of South Africa, 2016

Metro	Leading political party	%
Buffalo City	African National Congress majority	58.74
City of Cape Town	Democratic Alliance majority	66.61
City of Johannesburg	Hung council led by the Democratic Alliance	38.37
City of Tshwane	Hung council led by the Democratic Alliance	43.11
City of Ekurhuleni	Hung council led by the African National Congress	48.64
eThekweni		56.01
Mangaung	African National Congress majority	56.52
Nelson Mandela Bay	Hung council led by the Democratic Alliance	46.71

Source: Adapted from Independent Electoral Commission SA

South Africa can find some general lessons and also some specificities from countries with longstanding and highly institutionalized local government systems such as Australia, Japan, and New Zealand, as well as parts of northern Europe and the United States. But, notwithstanding the progressive nature of local governance in these countries, numerous studies have commented on the challenges faced by the political democratization and decentralization at municipal level in several Latin American countries (Nickson 2011), Ghana (Okuru and Armah-Attoh 2015), Pakistan (Ahmad and Abu Talib 2013), Uganda and South Africa (Chulu 2015). Thus, any attempt to understand local governance needs to consider how political institutions and processes work, as well as the different mechanisms of interaction between the state and non-state actors. This may explain the influence of these factors in exacerbating the incongruence between municipal local government obligations and the lived experiences of communities. The most critical question observers and analysts have since debated in this regard, is whether the gulf between municipalities and residents will be narrowed to halt the protracted contestations and indifferent relationship between the two actors. The structure and mobilization tactics of the civic groups are discussed in the next section.

Civic groups in contemporary South Africa: A racial gulf

Over the last decade, there has been a significant increase in the number and prominence of civic groups involved in fomenting community protests in South Africa. Although new social movements emerged consistently in the period after 1994 (Ballard et al. 2006), the dramatic eruption of community protests in Diepsloot (a densely populated area in Gauteng Province) and Harrismith (a typical town in the Free State Province) in September 2004, represents a defining moment in the history of what has been known as service delivery protests (Alexander 2010; Booysen 2009) and currently community protests. Then, the protests were labeled as being "spontaneous" (Ngwane 2011), but since then, South Africa has witnessed unrest of significant proportions at local government level across the country.

Figure 1 depicts that these protests increased substantially from about ten in 2004 to more than 100 in 2009 and 2010, and subsequently reached unprecedented levels, with 173 protests in 2012. Since then, the annual incidence of community protest activity has remained within the high range recorded in 2012, with 2014 representing the highest peak at 191 protests (Municipal IQ 2016). Service delivery protests constituted 80% of all violent conflict events in South Africa in 2012 (Armed Conflict Location and Event Data Project 2013:10).

I acknowledge the limitations inherent in the Municipal IQ Hotspots Monitor. The Hotspots Monitor is only concerned about "a protest involving more than 100 people ... [and] that pertains to local government service delivery issues" (Municipal IQ 2014).

Figure 1: Major community protests, by year (2004-30th April 2016)

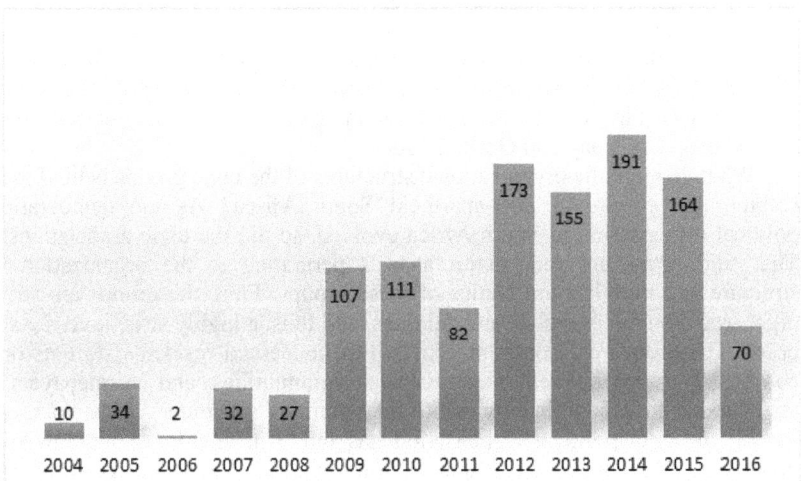

Source: Municipal IQ Hotspots Monitor (2016)

Historically, the South African local government system was also the target of civic groups (also referred to as neighborhood or residents' associations throughout the book) during the apartheid era. Similar to the emergence of urban movements in Europe and Spain during the 1970s (Castells 1983), in what is well-documented elsewhere, black civic associations in South Africa spearheaded the boycott of rent, electricity and water bills during the 1980s. This was an effective protest tactic against the apartheid government, but no one could predict that the culture of non-payment in black communities would continue unabated (albeit in a less organized manner) in post-apartheid South Africa. These groups were highly politicized, while civic groups, in the form of ratepayers' associations in predominantly white areas played a somewhat instrumental role in local governance by contesting local elections (Seekings 2000).

Ironically, starting in 1996 with the rates dispute in the affluent predominantly white area of Sandton in Johannesburg, 24 ratepayers' associations, led by the Sandton Federation of Ratepayers' Associations (Sanfed), adopted the tactic of boycotting rates and taxes. Although relatively unsuccessful in achieving their goals, ratepayers' association have, undoubtedly, not only presented major challenges to the new black-led democratic local councils, but inadvertently brought to the fore the ongoing racial polarization in the country as well. There have been strong sentiments from various sectors, including the South African National Civic Association (SANCO), which represents black communities, that ratepayers' associations are small groups of white elites concerned exclusively with their own interests, who aim to undermine local municipalities led by democratically-elected blacks (Camay and Gordon 2000).

What then are the organizational structures of the civic groups behind the community protests in post-apartheid South Africa? As the democratic political dispensation in South Africa evolved, so did the civic associations. That said, there are four major aspects pertaining to the organizational structure and mobilization tactics of these groups. First, the groups are still organized along geographic societal lines, and thus, a highly structured racial order. The groups are commonly known as concerned residents' forums or concerned groups in predominantly black communities, and as ratepayers' associations in predominantly white communities in South Africa. In this regard, the new political dispensation has failed in creating a window of opportunity for new forms of social group and mobilization at community level to compel municipalities to provide what should be common basic public goods that are accessible and publicly provisioned. Second, both groups have an ambivalent relationship with the state (or municipalities, which serve as proxies for the state). However, these groups have unequal access to resources and, as Monaco (2008) argues, this implies that some actors are more influential than others. As such, this explains the titles of the empirical chapters: Schools and roads as bargaining power in predominantly black communities (chapter 4), and ratepayers' association and the "cheque book" protests in predominantly white South African communities (chapter 5).

Third, and closely linked to the first two issues, is that while community protests in both predominantly black *and* predominantly white communities neighbourhoods are organized around and motivated by basic municipal service provision, the lived experiences of activists in black areas expand much more broadly than this narrow focus. More fundamentally, black citizens in South Africa are rigid with tension, partly as a result of a sense of entitlement created by years of unfulfilled political promises of a "better life" for all.

Consequently, with some notable exceptions, notable traits and mobilization tactics of civic groups in predominantly black communities are that they are highly fragmented and spontaneous, with intimidation, destruction and violence serving as indicators of the overt manifestation of the strife against local municipalities. These civic groups lack internal democracy, discourage debate and are led by individuals who are eager to establish local hegemony.

Fourth, ratepayers' association in predominantly white communities are highly structured and linked to a national organization: the National Taxpayers Union (NTU). The NTU is an umbrella body with more than 300 community ratepayers' associations across South Africa. As stated earlier, these ratepayers' associations withhold rates and taxes from municipalities and, in some places, provide particular municipal services themselves.

The associations seem to follow four common steps to establish their grievances. Firstly, they document their efforts to resolve the problem through engagements with the local municipality in the form of meetings and grievance letters, amongst others. Secondly, if these efforts fail, they declare a dispute with municipalities in terms of legislation. Thirdly, they withhold rates and deposit their payments into an interest-bearing account. Fourthly, they provide detailed accounts of these deposits to the municipality (Multi-Level Government Initiative 2011).

For the reasons given above, community protests have presented a diverse set of outcomes. But a common theme that emerges from the literature is that the civic groups have a fundamentally similar set of grievances. These grievances are varied and complex. However, it is widely acknowledged that the reasons for the protests can be divided into three broad categories: systemic (maladministration, fraud, nepotism and corruption); structural (healthcare, poverty, unemployment and land issues); and governance (limited opportunities for civic participation, lack of accountability, weak leadership and the erosion of public confidence in leadership) (Matebesi and Botes 2011; Ngwane 2011). At this juncture, questions that I answer later in the book are: what happens to the leaders of civic groups in predominantly black communities in the aftermath of protests? What incentives motivate community groups with a fundamentally similar set of grievances to embark on different kinds of protests? What are the implications of the increasingly common trend to disrupt schooling or destruct schools during community protests?

The evidence

The research question was empirically investigated between May 2011 and August 2015 by comparing community protests in predominantly black communities and white communities in four of South Africa's nine provinces: the Free State, Northern Cape, North West, and Western Cape. In order to account for the different protest tactics, two case study sites were selected in each province: a predominantly black community and a predominantly white community.

The provinces and case study sites were selected for several reasons. Firstly, the different provinces illustrate a significant variation regarding the

Source: Author

In addition, a survey of 1200 residents was also conducted in the four predominantly black communities across the four provinces. Prior to the community survey, I had already built rapport with community leaders during several visits to the case study areas. These community leaders played a prominent role in informing community members about the study. The primary purpose of the sampling design was not to yield a probability sample, but to ensure that broadly representative neighborhoods in each study area were included. To identify individual residents, a multistage cluster sampling strategy was applied. Firstly, the study areas were divided into clusters (enumeration areas). Secondly, each enumeration area was narrowed down by randomly selecting a number of blocks within the cluster. The number of households selected was determined by the required sample size. Any adult household member who was available and who had resided in the community for 36 months at the time of the interviews was eligible for inclusion.

The survey data was collected by means of face-to-face interviews conducted by trained fieldworkers between March 2013 and June 2015. In total, 1200 residents participated in the survey: 200 (16.7%) in Ficksburg, 250 (20.8%) in Ganyesa, 350 (29.2%) in Grabouw, and 400 (33.3%) in Kuruman. The statistical analyses were performed using the SPSS software programme version 23. Broadly, more males ($n = 731$, 60.9%) than females ($n = 469$, 39.1%) participated in the survey. In addition, three out of four of the residents had lived in the study area for more than 15 years at the time of the survey.

Since there is a dearth of studies on ratepayers' association in South Africa, data was also obtained from an additional 30 of the 220 active ratepayers' associations in the country.

Plan of the book

This book is largely written from a social science perspective and aims to contribute both to the development of theory as well as to empirical, field-based research in the field. The book's main focus is on the central role of political trust, state-civil society relations, and local governance in community protests. These are topics that garner interests from academics of various social science disciplines, including sociology, political science, political geography, and political psychology.

Through a critical, but uplifting tone as well, the book holds an important policy and practical implication which extends beyond scholarly contributions. This involves the recommendation of procedures relating to minimum uniform norms and standards for municipalities in dealing with community grievances and community protests. This aspect may be of interest to academics who are, broadly speaking, interested in collective action and local governance in racially-polarized settings. The book proceeds as follows.

Chapter 2 extends the research problem introduced in chapter 1 by focusing on the theoretical framework that will guide the discussions in chapters 4 to 6. To this end, the chapter seeks to make a modest contribution to the study of the link between what I call an intricate three dimensional framework of trust-institutions-actors and community protests. It does so using a metaphoric swinging pendulum to explicate how political trust increases or decreases, depending on a peculiar combination of institutionalized and non-institutionalized mechanisms, as well as drawing on Opp's (2009) structural-cognitive model. In this regard, trust not only serves as a mechanism to regulate and enforce equilibrium, but also as a reservoir that the state (or municipalities) draw on to return to a normalized environment.

The chapter further demonstrates how a common identity is created within civic groups during the identity formation stage and the construction of the so-called "constituting other". This constituting other refers to local authorities and other political institutions. Whilst interacting with municipalities, the chapter argues, civic groups construct alternative channels of political expression such as protest action as a direct response to the distrust of local authorities. The next part of the chapter will show that the mantra, "when formal institutions are weak, actors are more likely to participate through alternative arenas", holds true if one assesses the actions of civic groups in South Africa

Chapter 3 seeks to contribute to current debates on the dialectical relationship between the state and civil society in post-apartheid South Africa. By tracing the historical roots of local governance and, in particular, participatory governance - defined as a set of structural and procedural requirements to realize public participation in the operation of provincial and local governments – the chapter outlines central features of the development of state-society relations in South Africa. In so doing, the chapter further deepens the background and theoretical issues discussed in the first two chapters. The chapter enables readers to situate the study of community protests within the context of state-civil society relations at local level. It also reveals that the widely-observed commitment in South Africa to participatory local governance at all levels of government is reflected in a multitude of laws and policy documents. However, concerns remain regarding the effectiveness of these institutional mechanisms for participatory local governance. A pertinent question asked is to what extent participatory governance - as envisioned in the South African Constitution – has triumphed or failed. Throughout the chapter an appraisal is provided of how citizens and the groups that represent them are influenced by the performance of local governance structures. The chapter ends by describing some challenges facing local governance and the extent to which participatory governance has triumphed or failed in South Africa.

Chapters 4 and 5 contain the presentation, analysis, systematization and interpretation of the case studies. The first half of both chapters focuses on the socioeconomic and political context of the case study areas. In the second half of the chapter 4, I present evidence of how the tension between actors – the municipality and residents – becomes antagonistic due to the trust deficit. The trust in local governance is largely influenced by unresponsive municipal officials, as a paper trail of evidence illustrates the attempts made by residents in the different provinces to engage with the state. More specifically, I outline how the spontaneous, highly fragmented civic groups with weak authority structures in predominantly black communities fail to constrain intimidation, violence, and the mass destruction of public property.

The chapter then accentuates how the variation in patterns of protests in predominantly black communities across the four case study provinces can be explained by localized factors such as in-migration and racial disparity in the Western Cape, and the demand for proper infrastructure in the other three provinces. For example, an enduring legacy of separate development in the 224 rural villages in the Northern Cape has led to demands for tarred roads. Sadly, though, the residents led by the so-called Roads Forum, forcefully closed down schools in 2012 and again in 2014, each time costing more than 16 000 learners a year in learning. The chapter ends by concluding that, while many community protests in South Africa are founded in fundamental constraints such as deep-seated backlogs in rural areas, the level of trust in political institutions remains a significant determinant of protests. Since the dynamics underlying protests differ, it is important to respond to individual protests to prevent the trend - of blocking national roads and using learners as bargaining power - from spreading to other parts of the country.

Building on the preceding chapter, and consistent with the proposed theoretical framework, the chapter helps claim that community protests in predominantly white communities are led by highly structured ratepayers' association. Here, the leaders and members of the ratepayers' association meet regularly to discuss activities. Thus, collective action is organized through a sanctioning system consisting of strict norms requiring cooperation. Unlike residents' forums, ratepayers' association do not believe in the efficacy of violence and prefer to challenge the hegemony of the state through peaceful and legal means.

Together with the other three case studies on ratepayers' associations, the chapter also explores one of the most enduring associations in South Africa: the Sannieshof Residents and Ratepayers' Association (SIBU). SIBU is based in the North West province and its strife against the local municipality was primarily about water supply and sanitation services. Readers will note that the white town of Sannieshof has no reticulated water or sewerage system, with residents relying on a municipal tractor to extract sewage at least once a week from their septic tanks. SIBU was formed in 2005 after the tractor broke down and residents spent more than seven weeks without this essential service. The sewage system disintegrated and, consequently, sewage bubbled from septic tanks and even toilets. Since then, SIBU has been boycotting the paying of rates and taxes to the municipality and, instead, uses the money to provide services to residents on behalf of the municipality. The chapter concludes that the protest tactic of ratepayers' association – namely the withholding of municipal rates and taxes from the local municipality (or the refusal to pay) – is a highly contentious issue.

In Chapter 6, the concluding chapter, is a summary and general discussion of the major arguments provided in the book and some recommendations are offered. The chapter raises fundamental questions about the state's response to community protests in a country with structural pathologies such as ingrained inequality, poverty, and growing unemployment. The chapter demonstrates how several macro-political opportunities and advancements made by the continued democratization of South African society have been favorable for the development of protests in the country. The chapter further underscores some of the challenges faced by participatory local governance in maintaining the stability of state-civil society relations. Accordingly, the effects of community protests have been tangible and visible in South Africa, with almost daily reports of violent confrontations with police, extensive damage to property, looting of businesses, and at times, the injuring or even killing of civilians. This is largely influenced by the diverse, fluid and multifaceted nature of protests in both predominantly black and predominantly white communities.

The chapter argues that in order to halt the strife against local governance in South Africa, the state should invest in the capacity of municipalities to provide services to citizens. In addition, a normative question about the values of protestors in predominantly black communities is posed: does the lack of service provision warrant the destruction of public facilities and the closure of schools? It asks whether these are these the norms and values South African parents want to permeate into the future. It concludes that participatory governance systems that are context-specific and accountable, as well as the adoption of minimum uniform norms and standards for municipalities in dealing with community grievances and community protests, will go a long way in arresting the strife against local governance.

Chapter 2: A theoretical intersection of political trust, institutions, and actors

> Plants don't flourish when we pull them up too often to check how their roots are growing: Political, [and] institutional ... life too may not flourish if we constantly uproot it to demonstrate that everything is transparent and trustworthy (O'Neill 2001:19).

Introduction

Citizen attitudes towards political institutions and actors have been examined from various perspectives. Existing research on political trust broadly focuses on international institutions (Brewer et al. 2004), established democracies (Nye, Zelikow and King 1997; Pharr and Putnam 2000), and theoretical traditions (Duvsjö 2014; Kong, 2014; Shaleva 2015). The primary purpose of this chapter is to explore the intricate link between political trust, political system (consisting of political actors and institutions), and non-state actors (citizens).

Drawing on former scholars, Kong (2014) confirms that cultural theories and institutional theories are the two theoretical traditions that dominate the discourse about the origin of political trust. Cultural theorists, Kong argues, maintain that political trust is rooted in social capital and, thus, is exogenous to political institutions. The origin of the cultural thesis lies in deeply-rooted beliefs, values and long standing norms that have been transmitted through the process of socialization (Inglehart 1997; Putnam 1993). A central focus of the proponents of this thesis is on the time lag between culture and institutional change. This is based on the point that changes in political culture do not occur at the same time as changes in institutions. In this way, cultural theorists conclude that the individual's orientations could affect the performance of institutions (Shaleva 2015). For example, studies in six Asian societies found that the effects of cultural factors such as post-materialism, traditionalism, and authoritarianism are either insignificant or weak (Wong, Hsiao and Wan 2011).

Conversely, institutional theorists argue that political trust is endogenous as it is the outcome of the perceptions of citizens about institutional performance. The institutional matter thesis is a consequence of satisfactory institutional performance and is developed by a cluster of perspectives:

institutional/modernization theory, rational choice and experiential theory (Shaleva 2015). Studies by Wong et al. (2011) of six Asian countries; Misler and Roise (2001) of 10 post-communist countries in Eastern and Central Europe and the former Soviet Union, Shi (2001) of China and Taiwan, and Duvsjö (2014) of 27 European countries, reconfirm the superiority of the institutional approach over the cultural approach by emphasizing that institutional factors such as the economic and political performance of government, are powerful determinants of political trust. Despite this dominance, the logic underpinning the institutional thesis has been questioned:

While intuitive and appealing as a policy recommendation, the 'institutions matter' argument appears problematic on two accounts. First, the theoretical and empirical model from which it was derived suffers from inferential and evidential shortcomings. Second, a closer scrutiny of the literature, covering a broad range of countries over a significant timespan, shows that outside the world of mature democracies, the presumed dividends of implementing democracy have rather mixed empirical support and generalizability, vary by type of institution, and depend very crucially on the country's specific circumstances (Ahmadov and Guliyew 2016:36).

However, what remains largely undisputed is that trust in political institutions or the state is a critical element of the state's ability to mediate between the demands of competing groups within society (Hutchison and Johnson 2001). Broadly defined, trust refers to elements of interpersonal relationships and is central to the ability of individuals to act collectively (Fukuyama 2001). Trust helps us to understand the benefits as well as the threats of promoting social capital within and across organizations (Laser and Leibowitz 2009). What then is political trust?

Before answering this question, I share Christensen's (2011) concern that, despite forming a uniform dimension, it is important to consider different types of political trust. This, she argues, may have different implications for the object under study. In that sense, examples of the growing importance of the variants of trust are provided by Fukuyama (1995) and Levi and Stoker (2000). The former maintain that trust is an efficient means of lowering transaction costs in relationships, while the latter argues that a person, group or institution that trust another party will worry less about the party's conduct. Both constructs presuppose the holding favorable perceptions by the parties to the relationship.

A useful outline of trust measured in political terms is provided by Blind (2006). Political trust, Blind notes, refers to the appraisal of government and its institutions, policymaking in general, and the individual political incumbents as keeping promises, and being fair and honest. The two main variants of political trust are macro-level or organizational trust and micro-level or individual political trust. On one hand, organizational political trust involves citizens' appraisal of the government and is largely based their satisfaction or dissatisfaction with policy alternatives. This variant of political trust is therefore an issue-oriented perspective. Here, organizational trust is further subdivided into two components: diffuse or system-based trust (citizens' evaluation of the performance of the overall political system and the regime) and specific or institution-based trust (directed towards certain political institutions, such as the local police or local municipality). On the other hand, micro-level or individual political trust is a person-oriented perspective whereby the level of trust is determined by the approval or disapproval of individual political leaders.

Some scholars, however, question to what extent political trust is directed towards the incumbent leaders or the political regime. Scholars such as Bean (1999), Newton (1999), and Worthington (2001) aptly deal with these challenges. While I acknowledge that varying gaps in trust among actors continue to permeate political relations (Monn and Plott 2013), this chapter is not concerned with a nuanced discussion on the challenges of defining trust.

I define political trust broadly. In this regard, political trust can relate to a cognitive function involving an individual's confidence in state institutions or the subjective interpretation of the environment (for example, institutions), including what Tonkiss (2009) refers to as the assurance held by one actor that another actor will behave in an appropriate manner to ensure that expected outcomes are reached. This notion of political trust has two particular resonances. First, it explains it as a key micro-determinant or framing process acting as an agency to examine a condition. Thus, the level of political trust may determine the extent to which individuals participate in or respond to political actors, institutions, and processes. Second, the determinants of political trust are nurtured by real events or genuine grievances, whilst others are rooted in imaginary or perceived phenomena. For Christensen (2011), lack of political trust is one of the main reasons for the dissatisfaction with existing institutions in established democracies. Such dissatisfaction ushers in the rise of alternative forms of political participation.

In the South African context, a direct consequence of the high levels of political distrust is indicative of the ways citizens engage with institutions of representative democracy and their ability to access them or act in relation to them (Khanna et al. 2013). For those living on the socio-economic margins of society (Runciman 2014), or relatively powerless groups (Scott 1985), or those facing the unequal structure and distribution of power by democratic institutions (Burawoy and Von Holdt 2011), social movements provide a non-institutional space (Dawson and Sinwell 2012) or a fluid space (Langa and von Holdt 2012) outside of the state.

As such, insurgency has created a political space in which the meaning of citizenship is daily extended and power relations challenged (Friedman 2002; Holston 1998). This enables community-based organizations to move regularly back and forth between institutional and non-institutional spaces to advance collective causes (Steyn 2012). This way, the meaning of citizenship is daily extended and power relations challenged (Friedman 2002; Holston 1998). As the South African Public Protector puts it, "If there is water, electricity, it is unlikely that people will follow whoever says let's go to the streets, but if there isn't people are likely to take to the streets" (*News24* 2014b). Therefore, community protests can be seen as a conscious way of engaging the state, as well as an overt manifestation of the new insurgency.

This chapter builds on Opp's (2009) structural-cognitive model (SCM) to explain the intricate link between political trust, political institutions, and actors. The chapter begins by providing a brief outline of the SCM theory. This is followed by the outline of the theoretical framework of political trust. I utilize the metaphor of a swinging pendulum to illustrate how political trust plays a central role in community protests. Trust building and trust take place along a swinging pendulum, moving forth and back between the two extremes, depending on the success of the ravenous political trade-off between state actors and citizens. Under this view, the two extreme opposites are trust on the left and distrust or trust deficit on the right side of the swinging pendulum. The focus later turns to the contexts in which community protests arise, proceed and end. To this end, I therefore propose a four-stage analytical framework in which I combine the notion of political trust with ideas such as political opportunity, mobilization structures, and framing (that are well confirmed by empirical research), which are central to contentious theories. These stages are the following: 1) grievance formulation; 2) mobilization; 3) action; and 4) the aftermath. This analytical framework, however, does not provide all the answers to the questions and polemics raised by community protests. Rather it serves as a useful tool to shed light on the deep-rooted and multifaceted community protests in both black communities *and* white communities. In the next section, I provide the context of the cases discussed in chapters 4 and 5.

Overview of the Structural-Cognitive Model

Collection action theories provide a rich analytical foundation for the study of community protests. Models of collective action are diverse, representing attempts to capture different kinds of problems (Ostrom and Ahn, 2009). These theories can be classified into three broad categories. First is the earlier group of theorists such as Bentley (1949) and Truman (1958). These theorists expressed that individuals with a common interest would voluntarily act to achieve common interest. Second is first-generation theorists which include Olson (1965) and Hardin (1968). Broadly, first-generation collective action models assume homogeneous, selfish individuals. For example, Hardin (1968) and Olson (1965) concluded that individuals could not achieve joint benefits when left by themselves. The third category is the second-generation theorists such as Ostrom (2005), Henrich (2004), and Gintis (2000). At the core of these theories is an image of an atomized, selfish and fully rational individuals. However, in reality individuals do not live in an atomized world and, notably, a significant proportion of individuals do have non-selfish utility functions.

Drawing on Opp's (2009) SCM, a link between macro-level political institutions and micro-level motivations to participate in protest activities is theorized. Opp highlights the implicit and under-theorized links between micro and macro level collective action perspectives, and argues that current theoretical approaches should be integrated to gain a better understanding of protest actions. Such integration can be achieved by adopting a SCM.

Opp (2009) highlights eight shortcomings of extant theories of social movements and political protest such as the resource mobilization, political opportunity, collective identity, framing, and dynamics of contention perspectives. First, he suggests the first major obstacle is to find out what the problems of the theories are or what exactly their propositions are. This argument suggests that it is difficult to indicate what exactly the dependent and independent variables are and what the concepts mean. Second, most of the approaches have little explanatory power. Third, it is not clear what the relationships are between the social movement theories. Fourth, the approaches have no explicit theoretical foundation. Fifth, Opp argues that the macro (or structural) approaches neglect the micro level. For example, Corcoran's (2011) resource mobilization theory emphasizes the effects of organizational and institutional environments on social movement dynamics while often ignoring individual-level considerations. Sixth, the approaches that are primarily micro-oriented do in general not engage in relating the micro variables to the macro level. Seventh, Opp's analysis shows that all the perspectives implicitly apply a micro model. However, none of these perspectives specifies the micro model in detail. Lastly, the empirical validity of most of the approaches is questionable.

In proposing conceptual extensions to overcome the weaknesses of the major theoretical perspectives guiding collective action research, Opp's (2009) SCM fills the dearth of integrative models in the protest literature by yielding a synthesis that links the macro and micro levels. At the macro level, the political opportunity and resource mobilization perspectives focus on propositions that increasing political opportunities (such as the right to vote and participate in governance structures, for example) lead to political action. This hypothesis, Opp maintains, is not a causal, but a correlational statement. Other theoretical perspectives, such as the identity (van Zomeren et al. 2008) and framing perspectives (Oberschall 2008; Benford, 1997), focus on the micro level. These models claim to explain protest behavior on the micro level by applying general psychological theories.

How do we connect the micro and macro levels then? Firstly, Opp (2009) argues that the macro-micro relationship indicates how macro variables (e.g. new technologies, including movement activities) affect factors on the micro level (individual protest behavior) that lead to individual collective action. He further maintains that the procedure to connect the two levels is to "explain macro relationships by invoking processes on the micro level". While other theories (Klandermans 1984) fail to explain the proposition that increasing political opportunity raises collection action, Opp (2009) uses what he terms a top-down bridge assumption (macro-to-micro relationship) to explain such a relationship. Thus, "political opportunities affect collective action because opportunities change individual incentives" (Opp, 2009: 329). This is confirmed by Machado et al. (2009) who argued that the strength and relevance of formal political institutions are key determinants of the individual and collective choice of channels of political participation. As stated before, they hold that when institutions are strong,

actors are more likely to participate through institutionalized arenas.
Second, Opp (2009) explains the relationship between individual protest behavior (micro level) and collective action (macro level). He argues that the proposition that a repressive government increased (and did not deter) political action (a macro proposition) does not explain why the unexpected effect occurred. He further contends that collective action is not a summary of individual protests, but a result of the aggregations from individual to collective action. For example, if the incentives for many individuals to participate in a protest are strong, individuals will convene at a certain place at a certain time and, thus, forming a demonstration.

Opp (2009:330) explains that the "cognitive" suggests that "one major variable on the micro level is that individuals perceive (or recognize) the macro changes". This implies that the definition of the situation (i.e. ineffective client-interface and poor service delivery in the case of South Africa) is an important determinant of collective action. Thus, the cognitive system of individuals, which includes identity and framing processes, will be influenced by beliefs and attitudes towards formal political structures and processes. When the relevant macro changes first enter the cognitive system of individuals, it sets in motion cognitive processes that may create incentives to protest. According to Opp (2009), incentives include material as well as non-material costs (i.e. identity or identification with a group).

Theoretical framework of political trust-institutions-actors

Connecting to the main assumptions of the SCM, I propose an intricate three dimensional theoretical framework of political trust-institutions-actors to analyze community protests in South Africa. I do so by using a metaphoric swinging pendulum to explicate how political trust in political institutions matters in community protests. I define the swinging pendulum in terms of a dichotomous trust/distrust categorization. A left swing is synonymous with a path of trust-building, including its antecedents such as trust consolidation; and civic trust in state institutions and political actors. A right swing, on the other hand, represents a move towards a path of increasing distrust, political malaise, and ultimately protests. It should be noted the notion of political trust is discussed from the perspective of non-state actors or citizens.

Broadly, there are four primary assumptions that underlie the theoretical framework. First, is that individual and collective citizen trust in political institutions and actors is largely impacted by micro and macro level factors; the current and historical experiences of the political system serve as a basis for understanding and relating to political institutions and actors; the fickleness and complexity of the swinging pendulum of trust is impacted largely by framing processes; and the swinging takes place along a four-stage continuum of protest formulation: grievance formulation, mobilization, action, and the aftermath.

Figure 3: Theoretical framework of political trust

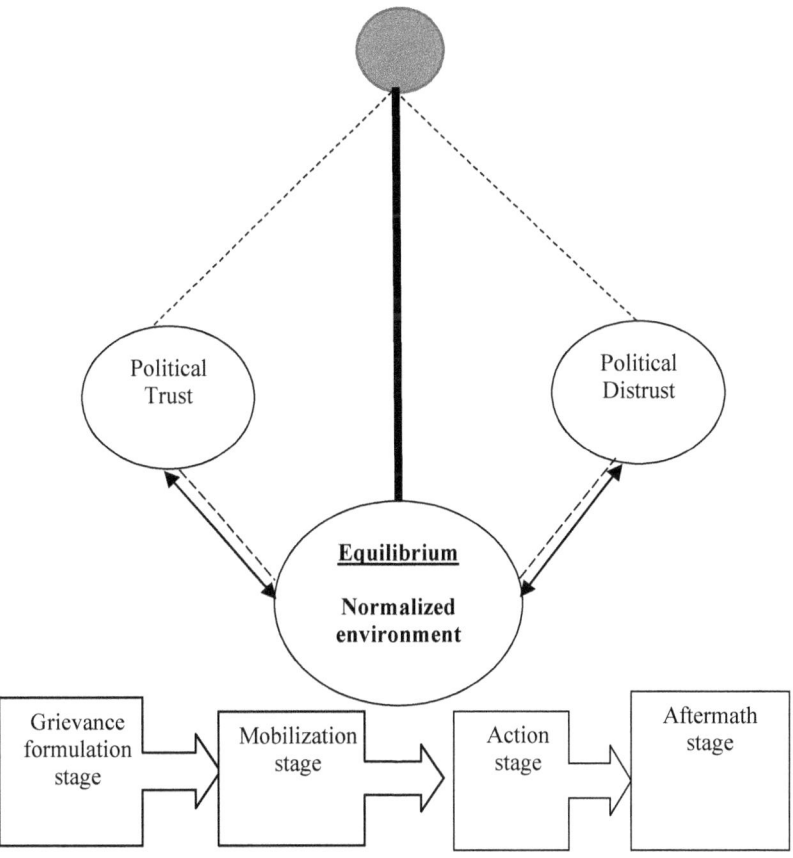

Source: Author's material

Political trust, Shaleva (2015) contends, is an essential ingredient for the functioning of democracy. As stated earlier, cultural theorists trace the origins of political trust in political institutions to deeply rooted and long standing cultural norms, whereas institutional theorists view political trust as a direct consequence of institutional performance. This institutional focus is closely linked to what Bains and Hicks (1998) regard as the structural component of social capital. This component includes the "composition and practices of local level institutions" (Krishna and Shrader 2000). Generally, since the levels of social trust are based on the social circumstances in which citizens find themselves at a given time, similarly, political trust is based on the political circumstances in which citizens find themselves at a given time (Gormley-Heenan and Devine 2010). The central thesis of this statement is that the networks that people build help them form trust in other people. This trust serves as a base for a wider understanding and social confidence (Duvsjö 2014) in the political systems and political actors (Putnam 2001). The cognitive ability of people to assess their circumstances is rooted in their beliefs, attitudes, and social norms, and in turn, is influenced by national contexts like a country's institutional organization, policy, or socioeconomic circumstances and level of general economic development. These elements predispose people toward mutually beneficial collective action (Krishna and Shrader 2000).

Broadly, the metaphorical swinging pendulum of the proposed theoretical framework of political trust-institutions-actors begins to swing from equilibrium (a normalized environment). In this regard, trust not only serves as a mechanism to regulate and enforce equilibrium, but also as a reservoir that the state and non-state actors draw on to return to a normalized environment. When trust is consolidated, the pendulum tilts off the center towards the left, moving towards an increasing path of trust building. When trust is lacking (caused by real and imagined expectations of macro and micro factors), the equilibrium tilts and veers off (as a display of the fickleness of the pendulum) the center towards the right, along a path of escalating distrust. The pendulum is largely tilted by the ravenous political trade-off between the interests of the state and non-state actors. Thus, in sum, local communities are a living space that represents an asymmetric mosaic of trust or trust-deficit.

Political institutions here refer to the state institutions, which include national-, provincial-, regional-, and local government. The municipality is the embodiment of local government and is regarded as a vehicle for service delivery (Walker and Andrews 2013). This role of the municipality creates many potential traps that unwittingly ensnare it. This undermines the municipality's effort at trust-building. Conversely, the actors consist of state and non-state actors. The state is a distinct structure that is independent of society and, therefore treated as a unitary actor, with specific focus on local political actors. Political institutions are in the custody of these political actors (Gormley-Heenan and Devine 2010).

There is an array of actors on the non-state side including, for example, citizens and civic organizations. Borrowing from Opp's (2009) SCM, individual citizens cognitively assess core political institutions and, depending on their level of trust in them, will determine whether they become politically active, comply with decisions made by political actors, or whether they favor policy reforms undertaken by elected leaders. In established industrialized democracies like the USA, citizens are the ultimate source of power (Jacobsen 2011).

By extension, during elections (a key component of any democratic system), public opinion exerts influence on citizens to choose political actors that can express a political view with which they agree (Jacobsen 2011). But there is an inherent dichotomy and conflict between political theory and political reality: election promises are seldom, if at all, translated into tangible policy changes that enhances democracy and governance practices. However, Guo and Neshkova (2013:342) note:

> An engaged citizenry has the potential to solve a range of problems related to widespread distrust in government and to generate some important benefits for the participants in the process, such as educating them about the intricacies of policies and increasing the understanding on where both citizens and administrators stand on issues.

Left swing of the pendulum – path of trust building

At local government level, a left swing of the pendulum of political trust also signifies that political actors recognize the existence of different civic actors, interests, and opinions. These different actors are often seen as a barrier to effective municipal-citizen engagement. However, these actors can serve as a resource. The issue during this left swing of the pendulum is to determine what incentives are required to maximize the trust consolidation potential of these civic actors. Without trust, Hetherington and Rudolph (2015) argue, consensus to development and compromise does not occur. In this regard, communication is a vital first step towards compromise and moderation of the interests and opinions of citizens, which are largely dependent on historical or current experiences of the local political system.

In the context of South Africa, Brown (2015) contends that citizens tends to have higher levels of trust in national democratic institutions such as the constitutional court. At local level, there is a set of rules and an array of local participatory governance mechanisms enshrined in the Constitution that are helpful tools to assist municipalities reach a balance between its own obligations and the interests of citizens (Matebesi and Botes 2011; Runciman 2014; Smith and De Visser 2009).

Still, political trust at local government level significantly increases, for example, when political actors are willing and able to deal with residents' grievances in a more proactive and transparent manner. This counteracts the perverse framing potential that such grievances create (Amaechi 2013). However, several studies have shown that peaceful citizen-state engagement has not always achieved desired outcomes (Epstein 1991; Nepstad and Kurtz 2012). Conversely, there is evidence that a truly representative and accountable governance system based on sharing information with citizens about programs and providing citizens the opportunity to actively participate and demand good governance, tends to enhance public confidence in the political system (World Bank 2009).

It is one of the fundamental principles of democracy that people's interests must at all times remain supreme. But let us remember that, in reality, politics is a muddled activity and no issues are ever really settled. The irony undergirding this lies in the parochial nature of municipalities, involving the constant straddling between the responsibilities of a decentralized developmental-oriented sphere of government, and the demands of central government and political expediency. Consequently, municipalities are under constant pressure exerted by the top-down hierarchical directives from central governments (Sotarauta and Beer 2016), hence the fickleness of the pendulum (Parkison 2015).

Right swing of the pendulum – path of trust deficit

Swinging gradually or rapidly back and past the center to the right, the metaphorical pendulum veers towards a path of escalating trust deficit. This swing acts like a rapidly descending fog engulfing the relationship between the municipalities and residents. An extreme right swing represents a higher deficit of trust in the political system and, thus, a higher probability for communities to engage in what Machado et al. (2009) and Runciman (2014) call alternative channels of political engagements such as protests. This political trust malaise, Opp (2009) contends, is largely framed by macro and micro level determinants of collective action. For example, different civil society actors may act together in a curious constellation of highly unlikely allies to challenge the state's unresponsiveness. However, such attempts will be constrained largely by political opportunities, the mobilization resources, and the presence of previously unresolved aspirations (Swain 2010).

What are some of the potential factors that could affect such a left swing of the pendulum? Internationally, public concerns about immigration have undermined public confidence in democratic political institutions in many parts of the world, as will be seen later in the chapter. Ironically, immigration not only tilts the swinging pendulum of trust towards higher levels of distrust, but also presents a more serious challenge in instigating the rise of the far-right in affected countries (Eierman 2016; Smith 2016; Visser 2016).

Furthermore, lack of confidence in local participatory governance structures in South Africa are caused by many factors. First, ward committees and other local participatory channels are highly politicized. As a result, more than often, citizens use alternative means of engaging with the state. As in the case of Cambodia, power in the South African local government system as well at national level, tends to be personalized instead of institutionalized. Such personalized governance systems are inherently influenced by patron-client relationships (Langa and von Holdt 2012; World Bank 2009). Similarly, high levels of distrust are further engendered when "there is little notion of citizen rights, citizen empowerment or the obligation of government officials as duty-bearers" (World Bank 2009:32).

Thus, when dissatisfied with the state, citizens could act collectively through local civic organizations to mobilize support by arranging an array of activities and public events: writing of letters, petitions, demonstrations and protests. Such periods of tension generally entail more constraints, less consent, and higher stakes for the actors involved (Arjun 2009). And as the mood of hopelessness, unemployment and poverty pervades the life of ordinary citizens, compounded by poorly managed public institutions, combined, these forces weigh heavily down on the right-hand side of the pendulum.

Political trust in national institutions and political leaders

At the macro level, central political institutions are largely removed from the everyday realities of citizens (Brown 2015). Established democracies are not immune to this anomaly. For example, there has been widespread distrust of democratic representative institutions and politicians in Western Europe as a result of the significant economic changes in the 1980s and 1990s, as well as political changes stemming from the furthering of European integration. In that respect, governments became more and more engaged in international cooperation. Some citizens attributed this move to attempts of government to transfer political power to a more central arena, with less democratic accountability (Held 1999).

Other factors that contributed to low levels of public confidence are illustrated by international immigration in Europe and the United Kingdom (Gormley-Heenan and Devine 2010), the intensifying public debt crisis in Greece (Exadaktylos and Zhariadis 2013), and the big demonstrations by Catalans in Spain over their alienation from Spanish central institutions (Moreno 2015). A study by Christenssen (2011) on political trust and political consumerism found that political consumers tend to have higher degrees of trust in democratic institutions such as the Supreme Court, Ministry of Justice, and the State Council's ability to redress grievances (Tong and Lei 2014).

Recently, the integrity and, thus the confidence of citizens in political leaders from around the world have been called into question on an almost daily basis. This relates to a spate of perturbing cases in which safeguards against the abuse of state power face the stiffest test ever and constitutions are being shredded by the very same people who are supposed to guard them. Undoubtedly, the decline of trust in political institutions and incumbents coincides with the release of the Panama Papers, which show heads of state, criminals and celebrities in more than 200 countries using secret hideaways in tax havens take centre stage. Though being an issue of tax avoidance, and by extension, corruption, traditional Marxists would capture this moment as the continued injustice by the wealthy in an era of global income inequality. Just two days after the revelation in the Panama Papers, Iceland's Prime Minister Sigmundur Gunnlaugsson resigned, following concerted calls and huge protests for him to do so. Gunnlaugsson's resignation should also be seen in the context of a country with strong press freedom and progressive tax structures. Mauricio Macri, the president of Argentina, is thus far the only sitting Latin American leader mentioned in the Panama Papers (Erlanger, Castle, and Gladstone 2016)

In 2008, Mr. Ilkka Kanerva, the then Finnish Minister for Foreign Affairs, was compelled to resign because of the sensation arising from the enormous number of suggestive text messages that he had sent to a young female erotic dancer (Isotalus and Almonkari 2014). In the Phillipines, presidential frontrunner, Rodrigo Dutere, cultivated an image as a crime-busting politician and a no-holds barred campaign that has endeared himself to the Filipinos. Yet at the time of writing, a tragic twist based on one bad error of judgement quickly cascaded Dutere's campaign into a sea of trouble and he was facing the potential of losing the presidential race due to a statement in which he trivialized rape. And in Serbia, far right nationalists lost confidence in Prime Minister Aleksandar Vucic because of his pro-European and austerity policies. These nationalists are advocates of the so-called "Great Serbia" ideology, and are pro-Russian, but anti-Nato (Reuters 2016). Brazilian President, Dilma Rouseff, was also facing a similar challenge, though of a much more serious nature. Senators approved in a vote to impeach her for allegedly running the country's finances into the ground and broke the law by trying to fill the budget deficit with illegal state-run banks (Watts 2016).

In accounting for the peculiarities of these international experiences of the dynamic of political trust, it is evident that trust tends to run low when the political elite insulate itself against public scrutiny (Eiermann 2016). This is especially the case when assessing the impact of longstanding pressures such as international immigration, which has become the most potent and prominent contemporary issue posing challenges to policy-makers around the world. Recent anti-immigrant sentiments spreading across Europe and elsewhere as a result of the huge number of refugees fleeing conflicts in the Middle East and Africa have reached unprecedented levels. This perhaps explains the success of right-wing political parties in Austria, Finland, France, UK, and Sweden. There seems to be greater civic trust in these right-wing parties that maintain that European countries should assist the immigrants in their home countries (Visser 2016).

Furthermore, in the US, controversies over Mexican immigrants and undocumented aliens in Arizona have been at the centre of immigration issues. Using the notion of "the principle of constituted identities", Smith (2011:545) argues that there is a dichotomy between the coercive shaping of the social identities and aspirations of immigrants and the obligations of the immigrant-receiving country. These anti-immigration views in general and anti-Mexican immigration views in particular, may arose from the nineteenth-century nation-building called the American Dream – an ideology about the socioeconomic possibilities of the free market (Barvosa 2011). The failure of the DREAM Act in 2010, which would give legal status to illegal immigrants (Smith 2009), and the continued failure of American President Barack Obama's administration to enforce the nation's immigration laws have led to a Supreme Court challenge by more than a dozen U.S. states. The states claim that the president's deferred programs are nothing but an abuse of executive authority (Masters 2016).

Similarly, low levels of political trust in the UK and Europe are driven not solely by distress at economic downturn, but also by wider concerns over immigrants and the failure of the political system to control it. This issue, McLauren (2016) insists, underlies the tensions between citizens and states and presents potentially a much more serious challenge in that it undermines public confidence in institutions and elites in contemporary representative democracies.

In South Africa, contrary to Christenssen (2011) finding about higher degrees of trust in national institutions, Brown (2015) correctly emphasizes that there is high levels of trust for the national parliament and the legal system, but high levels of distrust for the police and politicians in South Africa. Likewise, the Chinese also have much more confidence in their presidency while their national parliament seems to be the furthest removed from ordinary citizens. Generally, though, local institutions such as municipalities, schools, labor courts, magistrate courts and local police stations, are key spaces for state-citizen engagements that shape citizen's experiences and the views of the state (Brown 2015).

The rule of law, in particular strong legal systems and more capable state apparatuses, are central to modern democratic society (Tong and Lei 2014). In the same vein, negative views of elected officials are hardly a new phenomenon (Pew Research Center 2015). In South Africa, for example, there is no doubt that a series of scandals involving President Jacob Zuma, have been a lightning rod for public opinion about the government and governance in the country. Since his appointment, President Zuma's tenure is characterized by questionable interventions in the judiciary and the Scorpions, a multidisciplinary agency that investigated and prosecuted organized crime and corruption under the auspices of the National Prosecuting Authority. The South African Public Protector has also endured vicious attacks from the ANC-led tripartite alliance, as Makhanya (2016a:13) sums it up: "the folly of disrespecting one of the key institutions that today stands between our constitutional order and descent into a tinpot dictatorship".

In order to understand the link between these scandals and political trust, this assertion needs a little further elucidation. During late March 2016, the South African Constitutional Court found that the President has failed to comply with the public protector's remedial action to pay back a portion of the approximately R250-million (18 million USD) (The exchange rate used throughout the book is 1 USD = 13.6182 ZAR.) spent on non-security features at his private rural homestead in Nkandla. The court also pronounced that both the President and the National Assembly failed to uphold, defend and respect the Constitution as the supreme law. Attempts by the country's leading opposition parties to impeach the President five days later failed.

Interestingly, this judgment - widely regarded as the triumph of constitutionalism in South Africa - was read by the Chief Justice Mogoeng, whose fitness for judicial official was questioned by the media and civil society before his appointment. The judgment comes at the backdrop of a litany of scandals that started with the indictment and 700 charges of corruption and a charge of rape against Zuma in 2005, but acquitted in May 2006 when he was the deputy president of the ANC. This was followed by the media revelation about the Nkandla saga in 2011, then the landing at the Air Force Base Waterkloof of the wedding guests of the Gupta family - his influential friends - in 2014, the sudden dismissal of the Finance Minister in December 2015 (a decision that negatively affected investor confidence and caused a market turmoil), and the persistently widespread criticism, condemnation and demand for the President to resign over allegations of state capture by his friends (Masondo 2016).

The mainstream media pointed out a deepening crisis of loss of confidence in the government. For example, when the saga of Nkandla emerged in 2009, several supporters including the ANC alliance partners' battle cry was "Hands-off Zuma". This tune has recently shifted to calls that "decisive action is now imperative", otherwise "the continuing loss of moral authority, political paralysis and fragmentation of our movement will continue" by the South African Communist Party (SACP) (Nhlabathi 2016:4). Furthermore, in an open letter to the President, ANC stalwart Ahmed Kathrada, writes:

> The position of President is one that must at all times unite this country behind a vision and programme that seeks to make tomorrow a better day than today for all South Africans. It is a position that requires the respect of all South Africans, which of course must be earned at all times.... The unanimous ruling of the Constitutional court... has placed me in an introspective mode and I had to ask myself some very serious and difficult questions. Now that the court has found that the President failed to uphold, defend, and respect the Constitution as the supreme law, how should I relate to my President? (TimesLive 2016).

This profound statement is significant because political elites such as Ahmed Kathrada are in a particularly important position considering their standing in society. More importantly, Jacobsen (2011b) suggests, elite views can be perceived as representing the prevailing opinion of a given society. Similarly, mainstream newspapers captured the sentiments of South Africans: "Zuma is the antithesis of democratic values" (Mguni 2016); "New plan to fire Zuma" and "ANC – versus the people" (Sowetan 2016).

Tracing the statements and actions of the ANC in response to the judgement and the subsequent public outcry, an absolute affirmation and support for the notion of "party first and country second", can be discerned. The key problem with the vehement tone of the ANC's response to the Constitutional Court judgment about the President and the National Assembly is that it dogmatically asserts the power structure, including efforts to pacify the dominant faction within the ANC. Amidst this period of low trust in the government, it is difficult to grasp to what extent national issues in South Africa, the scandals surrounding the President, as well as the manner in which the ANC responded to them, contributed to the poor performance of the ANC in the August 3, 2016 Local Government Elections. The ANC has lost key metropolitan municipalities such as Johannesburg, Nelson Mandela Bay and Tshwane to the Democratic (Letsoalo 2016).

Also of significance are the allegations of state capture by the Gupta family. The allegations have been explosive revelations in South Africa and a major test for public confidence in governance and political incumbents. Ramphele (2016) provides some provocative insight by describing state capture as a network structure in which actors cluster around certain state organs and functions. These captured institutions are often linked to each other and are controlled by elites at national level. Such acts, however, are not immune to public scrutiny and heavily influence how political incumbents are perceived. Nowhere else are these dynamics more evident than with the differing views of the South African public and the ANC over the alleged state capture by the Guptas.

Several current and former senior government officials have publicly revealed about the Gupta family's influence over state decisions such as informing senior ANC members of their impending appointment as ministers. Both the Gupta family and the President have explicitly denied these allegations. Above all, the President has also won the backing of the ANC's top-decision-making group, dominated by his loyalists (Shabalala 2016). However, any reasonably diligent and vigilant person would weigh this denial against the business interests of the Guptas that perfectly fit into the ministry portfolios mentioned in the allegations.

Think of this saga in business terms. It does not take a long time for major corporations to withdraw sponsorship of athletes or cut ties with other corporations embroiled in public controversies. Similarly, in an unprecedented move in South Africa's history it took several leading South African financial service companies such as First National Bank, ABSA, Sasfin and an auditing firm, KPMG, less than two months to sever ties with the controversial Guptas' Oakbay Investments and its listed entity, Oakbay Resources (Matsilele 2016). I leave it to you to decide whether the step taken by the financial service companies are what the Guptas regard as "part of a carefully orchestrated political campaign which, tragically, involves some of the country's most senior institutions and individuals" against the wider Gupta family" (Donnelly 2016:1). But even in the absence of detailed explanations from the financial service companies about their decisions (except for the standard line: "due to the confidential nature of our customer relationships, we cannot provide further details"), it is not hard to believe that the decisions were based on the risk of association principle. Simply put, the reaction of these companies that operate in a highly regulated environment (Matsilele 2016) is, though not expressly intended to, a victory for ethical business conduct at one level, and the nascent role of public trust in companies, at another.

In the realm of politics, the very same saga had a different outcome. But unless we forget, politics are politics. The revelations about the state capture kind of feed into the narrative of what Cathorers (200:4) described as the "standard lament" about political parties in new democracies across the developing world. The lament, which also has some resonance in South Africa (O'Really 2010), depicts political parties as corrupt, self-interested organizations dominated by power-hungry elites who pursue their own interests or those of their wealthy backers, and not those of ordinary citizens (Cathorers 2006). Past experiences are instructive: the President and the ANC can afford this reputational risk because of the dominant partisan support for the ruling party. The issue of partisanship is discussed next.

Political trust, partisanship and collective action

Existing perspectives on partisanship make important contributions to the study of collective identity theory and, subsequently, party identification. Partisanship is the struggle to enact a fixed course of action, and involves the factional exercise of rhetorical manipulation or raw power (Lodge 2000). It should be noted that partisanship is often incorrectly equated with party identification. Party identification narrowly describes an individual's self-identification with a certain political party. This concept, however, largely fails to acknowledge the general behavioral attributes of partisans. In addition to being short-lived given individual social and political experience, party identification must also converge with core values, beliefs, and preferences over issues. Conversely, partisanship is a broader construct with multiple facets. For example, it involves developmental learning and intergenerational transmission, including a complex transition to general consistency in an individual's loyalty to a party, political preferences, and expectations (Smirnov et al. 2010).

Partisanship is a fundamental aspect of politics in democracies as it clarifies choices and provides cues to voters. It involves developmental learning and intergenerational transmission, including a complex transition to general consistency in an individual's loyalty to a party, political preferences, and expectations. The process of socialization has a huge effect on how individuals form partisan attachments early in adulthood. These political identities, Smirnov et al. (2010) note, tend to persist or change only slowly over time. They further contend that party identification is greatly affected when the "social imagery" of the party changes - as when African Americans became part of the Democratic Party in the South after the passage of the Voting Rights Act – but not by scandals, economic recessions, and landslide elections. Let it be noted, though, that while economic voting studies have diverse findings, they tend to agree that the economy is a significant predictor of vote choice (Lewis-Beck, Nadeau and Elias 2009).

Montgomery, Smith and Tucker (2015) took a markedly different tone in that they argue that, historically, studies in long-standing democracies postulate that party identification is a dynamic psychological phenomenon that is influenced by short-term political forces. These forces could include short-term evaluations of the parties, the president, and the economy. For example, in America, individual-level party identification changes over time to ensure correspondence with views about the role the government should play in the economy and society of the country. Similarly, a Brazilian study found that the wave of massive protests in Brazil in June 2013, while attributed to the significant decline in support of the governing Worker's Party, is indicative of how partisanship is responsive to government performance in the short term (Winters and Weitz-Shapiro 2014). But partisanship is more flexible to short-term political events in young democracies (Winters and Weitz-Shapiro 2015).

In stark contrast to the view of protest politics as seditious radicalism, the surge in protest activity has also been linked to the normalization of contentious politics in countries like Argentina and Bolivia. Adherents of this view claim that individuals who protest are generally more interested in politics and likely to engage in community-level activities, seemingly supplementing traditional forms of participation (such as elections, for example) with protest. Interestingly, the difference in protests between Argentina and Bolivia has been ascribed to the degree to which demonstrations are led by actors within government (the governing political party, the MAS) in Bolivia and non-government actors (the piquetero movement and various trade unions) in Argentina (Moserley and Moreno 2010). Another contribution is adept at highlighting the complex nature of movement of individuals between parties and social movements. In this context, activists move between the two spaces to advance their goals (Arce and Mangomet 2012). Thus, individual activists often engage in activities (such as protests) that are rewarding and instrumental to the attainment of a particular goal.

The efficacy of political systems depends on creating relationships of trust. Such reciprocal commitments create a framework of predictability, whereas a culture of competitive ethos undermines trust and maximises insecurity (Marris 2008). Central to this trust building exercise are political parties, which within government, seek to implement their identified policy choices, and by extension, enables the electorate to assess the performance of a ruling party on the performance of government. Accordingly, political parties have what O'Regan (2010:7) refers to as "a direct interest in ensuring that government works efficiently in implementing its policy choices" and other basic tasks to ensure a stable and successful state.

However, a common feature of post-liberation politics and democracies is the dominant role played by liberation movement leaders who use state resources to reward themselves. Political crises and trust in government in Africa are partly attributable to leaders that seek to reinforce their support among loyalists and at the expense of national interests. This challenge is not unique to Africa though. For example, Barr's (2016) research on contemporary Latin America suggests that weakly institutionalized party systems present party leaders an opportunity to be self-serving. In Ireland, one of the many European countries that have been facing an economic crisis, the financial crisis of 2008-2011 met with widespread low levels of political trust in representative institutions and the political elite. The issue of political distrust in Ireland goes back to a twenty year period between 1990 and 2010, in which 32 public inquiries have been initiated to examine matters of ethical concern within, among others, politics. It is thus not surprising that the pillars of democracy have become weakened, as evident by low voter turn-out and participation in elections in Ireland (Byrne 2013).

In representative democracies such as South Africa, political parties are key agents that shape citizens' opinions and behaviour. This is because of their capacity of providing a source of identification and attachment; their ability to frame the debate across specific issues; by providing a powerful informational cue; and by setting the levels of political and ideological polarization of party systems (Druckman et al. 2013). Therefore, partisanship could be a powerful informational cue to other people's trustworthiness (Carlin and Love 2013). For instance, an online survey-experiment carried out on national samples in Spain and Portugal found that citizens' interpersonal trust is heavily affected by partisan identities favoring the so-called in-group members' trust over that of the out-group identifiers (Torcal and Martini 2014).

The South African public's trust in the government is at historically low levels currently. This trust deficit is wrought, among others, by the government's neoliberal policies, and its neoliberal governance practices. Instability is thus produced through the dialectical relationship between government policies and practices and grassroots resistance to their exclusionary and marginalizing effects (Langa and von Holdt 2012). The foregoing argument generally characterizes the nature of collective behavior of South African citizens outside the realm of the formal political arena. What, then can be ascribed as the potential reasons why individuals who identify with the ruling ANC continue to participate in protests against the South African government? One possible explanation for this phenomenon offered by South African scholars is that it has to do with the dual nature of protest movements: factional struggles on the part of some of the protest leaders to shift power within the local ANC, and the struggle of the masses to attain socioeconomic rights (Langa and von Holdt 2012; Thwala 2014).

Furthermore, a paradox exists for ANC supporters: A dominant ANC is necessary and desirable to protect democratic rights and accelerate the fight against poverty, but the party is also known for its long history of exhibiting anti-democratic features in the conduct of its own internal affairs and in relation to the South African society as a whole. And thus far, the party has been struggling to address the sources of the party's structural decline, the erosion of trust in the party, as well as recurrent internal party controversies: Hostile intra-party leadership factions, internecine strife, and countless corruption scandals. In relation to this, the decrease in electoral support of the ANC during the 2014 South African National Elections, which was more evident in Gauteng (Greffrath and Duvenhage 2014), could be ascribed to the fact that the ruling party ignored the widespread call by numerous socio-economic and political forces, including party members, to abandon e-tolls in the province.

At the level of practice, partisanship is a complex phenomenon with many cross-cutting considerations. In a country such as South Africa, where the social identities of 'party member' and 'civic activist' are often intertwined and inseparable from each other, partisan protest activists are able to successfully navigate between the party and social movement. This is because the loyalty of partisan supporters is not only a valuable asset to political parties, but also holds great rewards for loyalists. In the case of a ruling party, the government often becomes susceptible to the demands of concessions from interest-group pressures. It is precisely for this reason that it is necessary to consider the potential impact of these community protests.

Trust in local governance and the stages of protest behavior

Against the foregoing discussions, this section provides an overview of the relationship between trust in representative political institutions and protest behavior at local government level. For several decades, scholars regarded distrust as a major determinant of protest behavior (Blind 2006; Fitzgerand and Wolak 2016; Newton 2001), while the main narrative of recent studies is that protest behavior has normalized over time (Hutter and Braun 2013). The account given here represents only a part of the many dimensions of the stages each protest go through, and is not necessarily an attempt at espousing the mixed and inconclusive results of empirical studies on the link between distrust and protest behavior.

Studies have shown that trust in local authorities does not simply translate into generalized trust in national political institutions or government. For example, Fitzgerald and Wolak (2016:130) found that "When opportunities for voice in local government are high, as in decentralized systems, people report greater trust in local government". They continued that "when opportunities for voice in national government are limited, as in majoritarian systems, people report lower trust for national government and higher trust in local government" (Fitzgerald and Wolak 2016:130).

There are three primary assumptions that underlie the proposed four-stage model of political trust. First, each stage involves the interaction between the state and non-state actors. Second, these interactions, in combination with various other factors, play a significant role in the extent to which individuals trust or distrust political actors or political institutions in representative democracies. A third assumption is that political trust is not static, but rather constantly changes, or should I say swings in the case of the pendulum, from a normalized environment to either a trust-building path or a path of increased trust deficit.

Grievance formulation stage

Today, there is hardly any society in the world that does not have any form of experience in engaging with its government. The first proposition, to put in Blind's (2006:5) words, is that "political trust does not emerge, nor does it operate, in a vacuum". The level of political trust of citizens is largely a response to circumstances, knowledge and experience (Newton 2001). I contend that all three factors are shaped by the historical legacy of the state in socialist (Dimitrova-Grajzl and Simon 2010), postwar (De Juan and Pierskalla 2014), and post-liberation African societies. Thus, I propose that in the racially polarized South African society that went through a painful transition period, ideas about the inability of the state to improve the living conditions of blacks, on one side, and deal with concerns of political and minority rights of whites, on the other, have been shaped over many years into democracy.

The second proposition during the grievance formulation stage relates to the existing social networks, both formal and informal ones. As unresolved grievances of individual actors at local municipal level accumulate, existing social networks provide a significant platform to the aggrieved to share their frustrations. The availability of dense social networks with frequent interactions allow individual residents to share their grievances with relatives, friends and colleagues, among others (Swain 2010). Additionally, associational communal life not only further permits residents to influence others (Blind 2006), including strangers, but may elicit renewed concerns and give credibility to notions of distrust in the political system. These residents can only remain patient with their local municipality for so long.

Broadly, citizens who distrust representative political institutions are more likely to engage in political participation through alternative extra-representational channels. Hutter and Braun (2013) caution that such micro-level interpretations should be viewed within the broader cultural or institutional context faced by protestors. They further note that citizens are more likely to engage in protest behavior in culturally more open political environments. Other micro-level factors include a critique of representative democracy, influenced largely by unfulfilled expectations (Della Porta and Reiter 2012).

In the context of South Africa, macro-level factors such as the fragility of the rand, increasing unemployment, and a growing youth populace faced with daily challenges and inaccessible higher education or the realization that education will not necessarily lead to a world of employment, may influence how citizens evaluate and act on their perceptions of government performance. This resonates with the youth of Tunisia who view themselves as deeply marginalized actors in a context dominated by secular regimes. In fact, the political significance of youth movements in Tunisia provide history with a clear example that once "suddenly imposed grievances" are raised to such a high level that a "generalized belief" is created, the mobilization process sets off (Opp 2009:89).

Mobilization stage

For several decades now, scholars have been analyzing the growing mobilization power of communities across the world. These studies chronicled an interesting view of how communities respond to grievances, which include the gap between local authorities and citizens and the paternalistic character of elected representatives. The lack of public confidence in local authorities is reinforced by the lack of public consultations and transparency in local decision-making (Aulich 2009).

During the mobilization stage, what happened at the micro-level is now transferred to the meso-level of society. I take it for granted that most scholars agree that mobilization and political opportunities are much more central to the success of civic collective action than the actual grievances of citizens. And as Eiermann (2016) puts it, "stunted social aspirations" alone are insufficient to explain political engagement on a mass scale. Individuals have to be deeply aggrieved about some condition before engaging in collective action (Snow 2013). Similarly, mobilization receives much more impetus when individual grievances are revealed as shared frustrations, and when the dispersed activities of powerful elites or charismatic community members are coaxed and channelled into collective action (Eiermann 2016).

It is important to note that a vibrant civil society and the strategies deployed by citizen groups are the hallmark of this stage. Thus, the network structures of civic organizations is important in terms of understanding the power of civic mobilization, as well as the existence of pressure groups and organizations that could pursuit the interests of residents that could make mobilization easy (Chan and Lee 2005). In the absence of established groups, small scale, sporadic, and localized groups may emerge driven largely, but not exclusively by the distrust in the political system.

Organizers of protests are a large spectrum of groups like social movements, and citizen initiatives. This group is a collectivity of individuals with a common goal to realize their interest. The group leaders coordinate action and suggest what is to be done, how and where (Opp 2009). This could however only happen once the group has successfully mobilized individuals. According to theories of collective action, three factors contribute to positive mobilization of individuals: strong discontent; personal influence and social incentives (Swain 2010; Pichardo 1988; McAdam 1982; Olson 1965). In the literature, the motivational aspects of participation are dealt with using different concepts such as framing, emotions, grievances, and networks (Van Stekelenburg, Klandermans, and van Dijck 2009).

Meanwhile, as the decline in trust of political actors escalates, existing and newly established groups now need to actively promote the collective interests of their members. Such a promotion needs a collective identity. As a result, the leaders of these local groups act like inverted pendulums: the creation of a common identity within the groups (Swain 2010; Opp 2009) and the construction of a contrast with a "constituting other" (Silvo 2014:12), which is the state.

In order to reach and recruit large numbers of potential participants, groups may employ various communication methods to share information and messages about (Chan and Lee 2005), once again, the lack of trust in political actors and the purported benefits of joining the group. As the group leaders mediate between the citizenry and the government through meetings, letters and other means of communication, the feedback given to the group members is then further shared during interpersonal interactions and online communication platforms like Facebook, Twitter and YouTube. But the dissemination of news about the persisting low levels of political trust among the participants is further buoyed by the media in the form of television, newspaper, and online coverage. How the group act afterwards will, among other things, be shaped by their perceptions of depleted levels of trust in the political actors. This period refers to what Della Porta (2015) label "intense times":

> Intense times are described by the activists as times in which crucial decisions have to be made quickly, in the heat of the moment. While strategic approaches assume at least constrained rationality, with relations based upon some information and expectation about others' behavior, in intense times decisions are based more on clues than on knowledge, as the identities, preferences, and interests of the involved actors shift and change. Predictability is radically reduced by constantly moving targets and lack of routines. Time is in fact accelerated because of the breaking down of previous institutions, rules, and norms, and the capacity of movement actors to occupy these spaces, changing them in the process. In a sort of hydraulic system, empty spaces are filled in by mobilized citizens (Della Porta 2015:1).

If the decision to protest is taken, the flight into the next stage largely depends on the political opportunity and cost of participation (Opp 2009).

Action stage

During the action stage, the non-state actors put their plans into action by actively engaging in protests. The protest action chosen to reach their goals will vary from group to group, according to their social, economic, political, and organizational contexts (Della Porta 2015). The protest can be expressed in a number of ways: demonstrations, boycotts, petitions, and gatherings

(Camaerts 2012). These protests could either be violent or peaceful. The question here thus is, what incentives motivate community groups with a fundamentally set of similar grievances to embark on either violent or peaceful protest?

A few studies noted that much of the answer regarding protests lies within the structures of community groups (Aghajanian 2012; Opp 2009; Rustad et al. 2011) Firstly, peaceful protests require coordination and restraint, which only a highly structured group can provide. This kind of structure makes communication, mutual encouragement and sanctioning easy. Conversely, spontaneous and highly fragmented groups have weak authority structures and, thus, fail to constrain violence (Opp 2009). Secondly, in highly structured groups, meetings are regularly held to discuss activities. Thus, collective action is organized through a sanctioning system consisting of strict norms requiring cooperation (Heckathorn 1989). Thirdly, in highly structured groups violence may be regarded as not efficacious or morally unacceptable. Those in less structured groups may, however, see the efficacy of violence differently and accept the common justification of engaging in violent actions (Opp 2009). This is particularly true for groups from poor and under-resourced communities which are at a distinct disadvantage when attempting to challenge the hegemony of the state through peaceful means. For such a group, therefore, recourse to protest action with the latent potential for violence remains the only viable option (Tapscott 2010).

Protests are not static and initial protests objectives can change over the duration of the conflict (Miethe 2009). Similarly, the conflict may spread over time and space (Kalyvas 2008; Bohara et al. 2006), and also be influenced by neighboring conflict (Rustad et al. 2011). At the same time a great deal is at stake for the group during this stage. First, some protestors and non-participating residents may doubt the efficacy of the protest tactic. This will be particularly the case when the impact for residents is negative, for example, in the case of a defiance campaign, stayaway, blocking of roads, and damage of public facilities. Second, the reaction of the state could either further diminish the purported objectives of the protest group or reignite anger and more radical actions from the protestors. In this respect, states often take a swipe at both protestors and the media by labeling them as anti-democratic elements. The state is also likely to harness its power through the security forces that are tasked to maintain order. The presence and reactions of police during protests have been found to encapsulate and produce new conflict (Brown 2015; Langa and von Holdt 2012; Runciman 2014). Often protest leaders will make an assessment of the level of impact and suggest alternative plans.

The aftermath

The outcomes (aftermath) of political violence are rarely theorized or studied empirically. The dominant focus of research on protests in general is often directed towards understanding who takes part in protests, their motivations, and their attitudes towards politics more broadly (Braun 2016). The aftermath of protests are marked invariably by an assessment of the impact of the action stage. As noted by Langa and von Holdt (2012 90), `the aftermath of … protests is as important for understanding the protests and the social forces that shape them as the origins and dynamics of the protests themselves'. The state may follow the participatory negotiation route or adopt a radical reactionary stance against protestors. In the case of the former, the state can undertake symbolic or substantive initiatives to mitigate the trust-deficit, at least for some time, or guarantee long lasting political trust from citizen groups.

If the action stage degenerated into violence or looting during this time, state violence (Johnston 2012) or state repression (O'Connell 2008) can limit political opportunities for or fuel more daring acts from non-state actors (Johnston 2012). It is also natural that when political institutions fail or manifest injustice themselves, people will direct their anger to those who hold official positions (Beerbohm 2012).

Generally, the effects of protests are tangible: extensive damage to property, looting of businesses, and at times, the injuring or even killing of civilians (Goebel 2011; Besada 2009; Haider 2009; Paffelholz 2009). Another aspect of the impact of conflict and violence often overlooked by researchers is that conflict is either caused by, or brings about, drastic changes in the underlying social relationships between the protestors themselves (Aghajanian 2012). For example, Langa and von Holdt (2012) aptly demonstrate the role of the dual nature of protests in South African black communities: factional struggles on the part of some protest leaders that turn into leadership battles within the ANC. This has perennially been at the center of many protests in the country. However, protests not only weaken the social fabric of societies, but also negatively affect trust in the state. Thus, political trust can be considered particularly relevant (De Juan and Pierskalla 2014) in post-liberation contexts. There remains is great potential that, even years down the line, unresolved and new grievances, could again set off the first stage.

Conclusions

Political trust is a valuable currency for both political actors and civil society. For many decades, the long-standing issue of political trust resulted in the redefining of state-society relations around the world. This can be seen in the number of resignations by the political leaders over issues ranging from the collapse of economies, treatment of immigrants, corruption, to scandals that typically involve sex, money and power. Broadly speaking, the distrust of political institutions and actors can derive from a range of sources, including the effectiveness in their performance of various functions, such as service delivery, and their degree of representation and accountability. Such distrust may be viewed as being intangible, but if the wave of insurgency in the contemporary world is taken into consideration, tangible outcomes such as citizens who are killed or injured, and derelict infrastructure seem to have become entrenched features of modern politics.

In a political environment that are based on patronage and lack of accountability, and where dishonesty and corruption are now sought-after political capital, fractious identity politics reign supreme. This flawed situation used to characterize the political landscape of many fragile and conflict-affected states. However, it is safe to conclude that representative democracies have consistently failed to provide the requisite safeguards against the factors that engender political distrust. In South Africa, the scandals of President Zuma, which have been intensely followed by the media, have rigorously tested the trust of South Africans in him as an individual, as well as the government and the ANC. These scandals, which are largely seen as ostensibly trivial by government leaders and party loyalists, have wider implications about the values of political credibility and the reputation of the country.

The evaluations and descriptions of political institutions and political actors should be understood in the context of the power rhetoric. It has long also been thought paradoxical that post-apartheid South Africa, which is celebrated for its liberal tradition, should have witnessed an increasing adoption of mechanisms of bureaucratic expansions and the absolute exercise of political power. Any evaluation of both the complexities and the undisputable nature of political power in the country will reveal that democracy has unintentionally created a democratic social order in which certain attitudes have become deeply ingrained: a politically-engaged public and elites, which are intolerant to opponents. This situation is further perpetuated by the newly-created elitists who have positioned themselves as purveyors of a specific set of moral values. It is therefore perfectly understandable, if not indeed inevitable, that mainstream political debates either trigger outrage or retaliatory threats from the politically-engaged public based on their political affiliation. This tendency has imbued a siege mentality in South African citizens, which is most telling in the forceful removal from parliament of parliamentarians; the continued vitriolic attacks on the Public Protector and the judiciary by politicians, demolishing of statues, xenophobic attacks, and violent community protests including the ill-fated tactic of using school learners as bargaining power.

The theory of trust also helps us understand the implications of international confidence in a country. The credit rating assigned to a country by credit rating agencies such as US-based Moody's Investors Services (Moody's) – one of the world's top three rating agencies – is widely regarded as an indication of a debtor's ability to pay back debt. The recent Moody's stay of execution on South Africa's rating (at two levels above sub-investment or junk grade) has brought a huge relief to the country. The decision by Moody's comes after a 4-month intense and closer collaboration between the South African government and social partners such as business and labor. Certainly, the recent Constitutional Court judgment against President Zuma and the high court in Pretoria which set aside the decision not to charge the president for 783 charges of corruption also played a role in affirming the country's institutional strength (Brown 2015). But these ferocious efforts between the state and civil society, which I consider exemplary of the country's resilience and capability, call into question the will of South Africans to deal with the challenges facing local governments. How else are we to explain the annual adverse audit findings on municipal finances by the Auditor General that are not met with the same level of intervention? Or are we first waiting for a similar situation like our weakened national economy to hang like an albatross around municipalities before a political seismic shift directed towards more prudent fiscal control at local level?

As noted in the chapter, the process of trust building and trust deficit takes place along a pendulum, moving back and forth between the two extremes. The pendulum is largely tilted by the perceptions citizens hold about political actors and political institutions. I contend that citizen distrust and outrage at local government level arise because of defaults on trust building. Fitzgerald and Wolak (2016), for instance, have outlined how trust in local government finds a basis in the social fabric of communities, by offering a reservoir of public trust that will persist even if the performance of local government stumbles. Using the metaphor of a swinging pendulum of political trust, the chapter has shown how trust swings from a normalized environment to either full-throated trust in which citizens exude high levels of trust in political institutions and actors, or to an environment characterized by a ferocious amplification of distrust. Once embedded, such distrust forms a powerful frame that discourages and prevents citizens (Fitzgerald and Wolak 2016; Opp 2009) from believing that efforts to remedy the situation by municipalities or any other actors are genuine.

Over time, South Africans, as elsewhere, have realized that the best strategy to engage the state, particularly regarding service delivery at municipal level, is to embark on protests. Protest activists have taken advantage of political instability caused by partisanship, cronyism and patronage, and weak local institutions to manipulate popular grievances for public ends. In a context of a widening gulf between municipalities and residents, coupled with macro-level conditions of unabated poverty, unemployment, and political polarization, municipalities face enormous challenges. But the apparent weaknesses of municipalities should be understood in the context of the intergovernmental relations and concessions they have to make in respect of service delivery, and contributing and promoting inclusive participatory structures. Thus, municipalities that are accountable and responsive to the needs and expectations of its residents have a better chance of veering off the path of trust depreciation, but more towards a path of trust consolidation. Conversely, those that are not realistic about the challenges facing local residents will have little capacity or the requisite leadership acumen to deal with the escalating trust deficit.

Intensifying the focus on state-citizen engagement at local government level is likely to reveal several themes that are implicit in trust in government. The first is that citizens in representative democracies that place a high premium on the principle of the rule of law should more readily embrace an attitudinal endorsement of democracy and guard against a cyclical trap of violent engagement when in response to grievances.

The second is that the consolidation of democratic institutions and processes at municipal level could serve as an important feedback loop that reverses the political distrust malaise. Trust is inscribed into the very fabric of political participation, which, I contend, creates new opportunities for reform, reconciliation and partnerships that would play a role in structuring future discourse on local governance and democracy in a more rational fashion among researchers, politicians, political parties, bureaucrats, the media and general public.

The third is a narrative that calls for a new trust calculus that should be engineered by both state and non-state actors in order to recognize and, subsequently, understand modern anxieties and the intersection of citizen needs and expectations vis-à-vis municipal obligations and challenges.

Borrowing from O'Neill (2001) in the opening quotation of this chapter I contend that local governance and municipalities, in particular, will flourish if we constantly uproot it to demonstrate that it is the level of government most seriously affected by a variety of (partly contradictory) pressures, including conflicting reform objectives.

Chapter 3: Evolution of local governance in South Africa: The triumph or failure of participatory governance?

A wise saying goes: "all politics is local". It reflects the wisdom that those issues that really matter in people's daily life – water, sanitation, primary health care, primary education, year-round access to affordable and nutritious food, access to markets and employment opportunities, basic safety and social justice – must be resolved locally. This requires responsive, effective local governance (The Hunger Project 2014:5).

Introduction

The 21st century citizen is widely described as a confident, frustrated, connected and lonely non-state actor who distrusts state actors and institutions. In addition, citizens have become increasingly assertive, effective, and technologically adept at a rate that their reach in respect of mobilization is phenomenal. This should be understood in the context of a world that views democracy as one of the ultimate ideals that modern civilizations strive to create, or preserve. Democracy, in turn, is a system of governance that is supposed to allow extensive representation and inclusiveness of as many people and views as possible to feed into the functioning of a fair and just society (Nabatchi and Leighninger 2015).

Similarly, the notion of citizenship has been catapulted to the forefront. This has led to the redefinition of spaces of politics, ruptures in the aesthetic regimes of power, and the creation of imaginaries of power beyond the state. The elevation of citizenship, particularly state-citizen engagement is in large part the overt manifestation of citizens' response to the state's complicity in dealing with their demands. This is succinctly captured in several events around the world, including established democracies, that challenge the status quo and illustrating that things do not always seem what they be. These events range from the widespread protests in the Arab world in 2011, the middle-east, protest movements demanding "real democracy" in Greece and Spain, and widespread movements against pushing for policy reforms and normative change on a variety of social, political, and economic issues other parts of the world (Khanna et al., 2013).

Local authorities such as municipalities form the cornerstone in effective and efficient service delivery. However, evidence shows that unless there is effective civic participation and mutual respect between local authorities and citizens, the capacity for service delivery is severely undermined (Pandeya 2015). There has, therefore, been a global shift towards more participatory forms of decision-making at local government level over several decades (Belle and Cupido 2013). This shift entailed the departure from traditional frames of public participation in *government* that assert that people first become informed, then become politically involved, to participation in *governance,* or participatory governance. The latter involves different principles and methods for public engagement including, for example, developing transformative partnerships; establishing system-wide information exchanges and knowledge transfers; and decentralizing decision making and inter-institutional dialogue (Aulich 2009).

Over the past few decades, many studies on the notion of democratic local governance have been conducted in a variety of contexts in South Africa (Booysen 2009; Lobe 2008; Mohamed 2000; Patel 2006; Pillay 2001; Tshabalala and Lombard, 2009; Vivier et al. 2015). The surge in the number of studies on local governance was largely as a result of the major reforms and new institutional mechanisms aimed towards promoting the engagement of elected local leaders with their respective communities (Tshabalala and Lombard, 2009). Prior to the new political dispensation in South Africa, local government had little autonomy, and decisions were subject to judicial review by provincial and national governments (South African Local Government Association 2013). This period, characterized by wide-ranging popular mobilization against the apartheid government, was later followed by an era that coincided with the growing expectations of public consultation and articulation between popular needs and government action (Booysen 2009) from South African citizens.

The emphasis on participatory governance in post-apartheid South Africa has been linked to three substantive innovations in public participation. First, was the redefinition of the term "municipality". This led to the inclusion of the local community alongside councillors and administrators in the legal definition of municipality. The second innovation included a set of requirements for public involvement in various decision-making processes. For example, these requirements included public consultation on the annual municipal budget, the integrated development programme (IDP) review process, local economic development planning, and the service delivery contracting process (Mubungizi and Dassah, 2014; Piper

and Nadvi, 2010; Booysen 2009; Barichievy et al. 2005). The third innovation is the establishment of ward committees chaired by the ward councillor and consisting of up to ten people from diverse interest groups in the ward (Piper and Nadvi, 2010).
Concern has been raised in both the South African and international literature about the means and extent of participatory governance. In the context of South Africa, scholars have been skeptical about the collaborative effort in decision-making at local government level. For example, Mubangizi and Dassah (2014: 275) argue that the increasing involvement of the courts in enforcing correct public participation procedures is indicative that public participation processes followed by the state "are not commensurate with existing policy and legislation". In addition, ward committees and IDP processes have been filled by loyal partisan supporters (Nyalunga 2006; Reddy and Maharaj 2008; Steyn 2007) and, thus, are exclusionary (Smith and De Visser 2009), with the public merely acting as "endorsees of predefined planning programs" (Williams 2006: 197). Ward committees in particular, are simply rubber stamps of whatever the majority party decides.

Furthermore, for the past few decades, research on public participation has been grappling with the decline in conventional participatory behaviors in formal political institutions and the new emerging participatory behaviors that have bypassed political institutions and thus escaped the conventional measures utilized to analyze political activity (Skocpol 1999; Zittel and Fuch 2007). These behaviors are the declining levels of civic engagements and party membership, declining voter participation, loss of faith in institutions of representative democracy and the escalating levels of distrust of politicians amongst citizens (Ekman and Amna 2012).

It should be noted that despite this bleak picture of participatory governance and the fact that the civilized world today is beset as much by terrorism and conflict as it is by peace, states possess remarkable capacity to address the daunting problems they face. And one primary source to address these problems is the expectation on the part of public leaders to transform political systems to tap into citizens' full, democratic, problem-solving potential. However, there remains skepticism on the side of public leaders and citizens about the virtues, capabilities, and good senses of each other. In this regard, Nabatchi and Leighninger (2015) enlighten us about the most common mistake made by people who try to facilitate citizen participation: the failure to first trying to understand citizens and their needs. According to

Nabatchi and Leighninger (2015:3):

> The official, conventional processes and structures for public participation are almost completely useless for overcoming this divide between citizens and government; in fact, they seem to be making matters worse. In large part, that is because the infrastructure for participation is inefficient and outdated; it does not recognize citizen capacity and it limits our collective problem-solving potential.

This chapter aims to provide a critical review of participatory governance at local government level in South Africa. It begins by outlining a conceptual framework of participatory governance, following by a brief international overview of participatory governance at local government level. Next, the focus is on participatory governance in post-apartheid South Africa, with particular emphasis on the past decade (2006-2016). The issues of public participation and participatory governance, in the South African context, have been well articulated in many texts and do not need to be repeated.

I specifically focus on the following channels of public participation: local municipal communication; Integrated Development Plans, and municipal demarcation – issues that play a central role in citizens' trust of the political system and, ultimately, community protests in South Africa. I then turn to the fundamental question of whether participatory governance in the local government arena triumphs or has failed. I further consider the implications of these discussions for normative debates and citizen attitude and opinions towards political actors and institutions.

At the outset, I would like to point out that the main insights of the chapter are drawn against a local government system that has to fulfill its perceived developmental role, including dealing with an array of challenges. These challenges, among others, include inter-governmental relations, budgetary constraints, and lack of adequate support. But above all, I argue that in an era of hyper-informed citizens that are constantly making claims to resources and justice, municipalities that move beyond merely engaging local citizens in local government activities to a more participatory governance approach, will have a much different type of currency than others to deal with the various social tensions, frictions and conflicts that naturally arises over the provision of basic services.

Public participation versus participatory governance: A conceptual framework

An inherent function of local government spheres anywhere in the world has always been to provide services to local citizens. Therefore, fostering dialogue between the state and citizens remain a huge challenge for this sphere of governance. Buoyed by the radical transformation of local governments, deeply-rooted local civic society organizations are now occupying a public sphere which is based on the expansion of deliberative democratic practices within civil society, in contrast to traditional representative practices. Deliberate democracy is a "school of thought in political theory that claims that political decisions should be the product of fair and reasonable discussion and debate among citizens" (Eagan 2016). These deliberate practices help to establish and enhance democratic processes and practices at grassroots level. These practices include universal franchise, periodic elections, civic participation, accountability, transparency (Islam 2015), urban renewal, development, the environment, and health/social services (Bifulco 2013).

The main theme emerging from the evolution and development of citizen-state engagement at the local government arena has been the shift from "public participation" to "participatory governance". These two concepts are often used interchangeably (as the case in this book), however, they represent divergent perspectives on state-citizen engagement. I explicitly recognize that there is value in both in that they focus on what Vivier et al. (2015) regard as the substantive engagement in service delivery. Similarly, Bifulco (2013) regard both as an integral part of the changes in public action which have taken place over the past few decades.

The literature is replete with methods of measuring public participation including; among others, Arnstein's (1969) seminal theoretical work and her notion of the ladder of citizen participation. Here, Arnstein focuses on power structures in society and how they interact. In short, a key narrative of this framework is to determine who has power when important decisions are being made. Since Arnstein's original theory, various scholars have adapted her work by adding new terminology (see for example, Bovens 2003; Burns, Hambleton, and Hoggett 1994; Harvey 1989; and Wilcox 1999). However, most of these measures of participation are not explicitly based on a theoretical model but a mere checklist of behaviors.

A more useful framework is the participation typology of Ekman and Amna (2012). The typology analyses four distinct dimensions of participation: formal participation, activism, civil participation and disengagement. The typology presents all forms of civic and political behavior and their distinctions in a unitary framework. The typology is regarded as being more innovative compared to other typologies for the three main reasons. Firstly it includes all forms of civic and political behavior, emphasizing the importance of latent (or pre-political) participation, in its turn divided into social involvement (attention) and civic engagement (action). Secondly it incorporates the category of ''non-participation'' (distinguishing between those who are a-political and those who are partisan) which may not necessarily be classified in the absence of participation. Lastly, it is a classification that defines various concepts and avoids conceptual confusions (Talo` and Mannarini, 2014).

The term 'public participation' is often interchangeably used with community-, civic-, citizen- and popular participation (Mubangizi and Dessah 2014). A broad conception of public participation implies providing ordinary people with opportunities to influence decisions that may have far-reaching consequences for their lives and livelihoods (Osmani 2008). Guwa (2008:6) refers to public participation as "a democratic process for engaging people in decision-making, planning, and generally allowing them to play an active part in their development and service delivery". This is premised on the principle that ordinary people, especially those of a democratic country such as South Africa, have the right to be involved and engaged in the decision making processes of matters that directly affect them as well as being involved in developmental programs, governance and planning at a local level.

In the same vein, Nabatchi and Leighninger (2015:6) regard public participation as "an umbrella term that describes the activities by which people's concerns, needs, interests, and values are incorporated into decisions and actions on public matters and issues". This notion of public participation emphasizes its power to achieve problem-solving, civility, and community. Interestingly, Nabatchi and Leighninger's (2015) argue that for this happen regularly, it must be sustained by a robust participation infrastructure. The latter refers to the laws, processes, institutions, and associations that support regular opportunities, activities, and arenas that allow people to connect with each other, solve problems, make decisions, and be part of a community. I therefore, operationalize public participation as the practice of consulting and involving members of the public in the agenda-setting, decision-making and policy-forming activities of the state (Matebesi and Botes, 2011; Osmani 2008; Rowe and Frewer 2004).

Closely linked to the concept of public participation is the concept of "participatory governance". This concept gained prominence during the third wave of democratization, which was characterized by widespread incorporation of citizens' voices into policymaking processes. This implies involving citizens in incremental decision-making processes, including the allocation of public resources and state authority, and for local governments to become more responsive to local needs (Montambeault 2016, Wampler and McNulty 2011). For Wampler and McNulty (2011), participatory governance consists of state-sanctioned institutional processes that allow citizens to exercise their voice and vote, and thereby, ensure the implementation of public policies that somehow changes their lives. This way, citizens are engaged in public avenues at a variety of times throughout the year, thus allowing them to be involved in policy formation, selection, and oversight.

Placing emphasis on the constant contact of citizens with elected representatives and state officials illuminates how participatory governance differ from more well-known alternatives of direct democracy or deliberative democracy, beyond the fundamental mechanism of turning up once in a while to participate in referendums or elections. Broadly, participatory governance mechanisms generate new forms of interactions among citizens as well as between citizens and government officials and, more specifically, allow interested citizens the right to reshape local policy outcomes.

Recent research conducted in various contexts such as Australia (Holland 2015) Brazil (Vitale and Lavalle 2014) Finland (Opu 2014), Japan (Tsubogo 2014), and U.S (Mossberger and Wu 2012) have suggested the significance of social networks for explaining community participation practices. These studies show how participatory governance is not static, but emerge and evolve through contingent innovations, structures, and practices that value the collaborative dialogue and problem-defining capabilities of social networks.

In the light of the foregoing discussions, I use Gaventa's (2006:26) definition of participatory governance: "[democratic spaces of] opportunities, moments and channels where citizens can act [constantly] to potentially affect policies, discourses, decisions and relationships that affect their lives and interests".

For Gaventa, participatory governance represents "invited spaces" - those where the state offers citizens the possibility of participation in decision-making processes and may be institutionalized and permanent or transient - as one of the three types of interrelated participatory spaces. The other two types of participatory spaces are closed- (citizens are not allowed any say in decisions taken by the state) and claimed spaces (citizens come together as autonomous agents to create opportunities to influence the state) (Patel, Sliuzas, and Georgiadou 2016). Therefore, when scholars refer to participatory local governance, they refer to a governance practice where the state "is but one actor, along with civil society and citizens" unlike in traditional practices where "local government is the sole actor in providing decisions and services" (Waheduzzaman and Alam's 2015:262). The focus now moves to how the spaces of participatory local governance is produced, perceived, and experienced in the world and South Africa, in particular.

International perspectives of participatory local governance channels

Participatory local governance is gaining traction all around the world. The story emerging from the combined narratives of research conducted over the last two decades on local governance is one which indicates how decisive it has become in shaping local politics and state-citizen engagement. But more importantly, is the two parallel developments that could be observed in many countries, which are a so-called "democratic deficit" and the proliferation of participatory democracy experiments. According to Schugurensky (2016), the democratic deficit refers to a general dissatisfaction with the institutions of representative democracy, whereas the second is about the proliferation of democratic innovations to engage residents in local affairs.

On the global stage, the United Nations (UN) recently adopted the Sustainable Development Goals (SDGs) – a declaration of aspirations for improving various aspects of human conditions. The SDGs build on the eight anti-poverty targets of the Millennium Development Goals adopted in 2000. SDG 16 explicitly deals with participatory governance in that it requests all member states to "ensure responsive, inclusive, participatory, and representative decision making at all levels (United Nations 2015). Thus, the SDGs may serve as a lever for citizens to ensure that local authorities are more accountable and inclusive.

In most countries, progressive right-based participatory governance already exists, but this has recently gained traction in the US. For example, major cities in the US such as Boston, New Hampshire, Portsmouth and St Louis all experience new innovations in respect of participatory local governance. The launch of the first youth participatory budgeting process in January 2014 in the City of Boston allowed the youth a direct say in developing, among others, parks, playgrounds, streets and safety. In essentially similar terms, a new system of parks and trails were the outcome of city officials-citizen engagements in St. Louis (Schlesinger 2015). These innovations are exemplary and should be replicated everywhere or scaled-up where they already exist.

In Asia, despite most countries following the global trend in participatory governance since the 1990s, there has been an uneven pattern of implementation attributed to the approaches of individual countries. In the Phillipines, Barangay Assemblies at ward level and Local Development Councils (LDCs) at city level act as invited spaces for participatory governance space. The LDCs were mandated to formulate development plans, public investment programs and annual investment plans (Patel 2016). In practice, though, research found that less than one-third of the local governments were found to have development plans with meaningful citizen participation. This can possibly be attributed to the elite capture of the participatory governance structures (Yilmaz and Venugopal 2013). Other Asian countries, like Cambodia, Vietnam and India among others, experienced several challenges in the implementation of effective and meaningful participatory local governance due to what I call a political blackspot: the obsession of states to keep power at centralized higher tiers of government (Patel 2016). In the UK and Canada, the principles of subsidiary, citizen empowerment and community engagement have been much greater entrenched features of the local government landscape than in, say, Australia (Aulich 2009), where there is limited evidence of a willingness to engage with citizens rather than merely consult them as consumers of public services (Aulich 2009; Herriman 2011).

The Hunger Project's 2014 State of Participatory Democracy Report – an insightful and valuable report - provides some interesting lessons on the scope of participatory local democracy in areas where democracy is most fragile in Africa, the Middle East, the Balkans and Central Asia, as well countries the MENA region (Middle East and North Africa), Arab countries and Western Asia. Broadly, the report illustrate that in many countries where national-level democracy and respect for human rights may be fragile, participatory local democracy is premised on democratic values, which led to the rapid improvement in public services in these areas. As expected, the developed countries scored best as a region and the MENA region the lowest in respect of citizens' perception of the implementation of participatory local governance. The report further provides a glowing account of Sub-Saharan Africa's attempt to discard some of the rigid conventional approaches to planning and replace them with legislation that facilitate community participation in local governance by placing it just behind the most developed countries (The Hunger Project 2014).

While a revolution in participatory governance is underway in many parts of the world, the move towards this approach has been carried much further in African countries such as Zimbabwe and Kenya. For example, the Zimbabwean citizens have numerous ways to influence policies and practices, and are given space to have a say in institutional issues in the Zimbabwean local government system (Chikerema 2013). In Kenya, the Local Authorities Transfer Fund – an inter-governmental transfer system which provides resources to local authorities to supplement the financing of services and facilities required by the citizens - sought to strengthen participatory development by involving stakeholder participation in local authority activities. Ironically, the Local Government Act, which provided for public access to council budget information, was silent on citizen participation in decision-making processes at local authority level and did not guarantee access (Kanyinga 2014).

To some degree, I contend that citizens in developing countries need the implementation of effective and meaningful participatory local governance approaches the most. Take the case of Bangladesh, one of the developing countries where democratic institutions have yet to be strongly embedded. Consequently, the local government in this country is characterized by the lack of a democratic culture. For example, the major challenges of participatory local governance remain the practice where each new leader who ascends to power attempts to nullify the efforts of previous leaders (Fox and Menon 2008). Thus it is tempting to quote at some length the findings of Waheduzzaman and Alam (2015:275) that potentially also illustrate the practice in other developed countries:

The Bangladesh experience reveals that successive governments have focused on changing functional and structural elements in local government with limited financial autonomy. However, none of these focuses on strengthening collaborative activities, which we term the 'congregational element', in local government. One of the main reasons behind this failure is attitudinal readiness: neither the central government nor policymakers have positive mindsets about the practices and procedures of collaborative functions at local levels. The central government has taken initiatives to reform local governance without strengthening local government institutions and allowing genuine democratic engagement of citizens and community groups. This article reveals that the political party in the central government exercises considerable power over local governments, destroying the fundamentals of accountable and participatory governance architecture. The strong presence of patron-client relationships also creates barriers to establishing a collaborative process that can enhance participation of a broad range of stakeholders.

Notably, however, some of the best documented and well-known experience is from the city of Porto Alegre, Brazil. The participatory budgeting, which is a year-long decision-making year process, was created by the local government in Porto Alegre in 1989. This process enabled citizens, through neighborhood-based forums, to negotiate amongst themselves and with government representatives over the allocation of municipal funds for capital improvements (Abers 1998). Since then, participatory budgeting has spread to several other cities around the world, albeit in varied formats with a broader set of principles that are adapted by local governments. In this regard Wampler (2012) notes that participatory budgeting should be conceptualized as a set of principles that can generate social change. These principles are active citizen participation; increased citizen authority; improved governmental transparency; and reallocation of resources to improve social justice (Wampler 2012).

Participatory local governance channels in South Africa

Participatory local governance in at local government level in South Africa needs no introduction. A wealth of insightful scholarship exists on the paradigm of participatory governance, albeit with different orientations (see, for example, Piper and Nadvi 2010; Smith and de Visser 2009; van der Walt 2014; Vivier et al. 2015). During the previous political dispensation, the apartheid government systematically excluded blacks and colored people from meaningful participation in the country's economy, let alone local governance.

Generally, though, the local government system was characterized as one with little autonomy and, as a result, decisions were subject to judicial review by provincial and national governments (South African Local Government Association 2013). It was therefore not surprising that popular mobilization against the then government became embedded within the psyche of the majority of black South Africans. Since then, South Africa emulated the global shift towards more participatory forms of decision-making, including playing a developmental and transformative role at local government level (Belle and Cupido 2013).

It is worth noting, though, that municipalities were also vibrant before 1994 (although for whites only). The apartheid local government system was established in the early 1920s with periodic reforms aimed at making the system more acceptable. While the White Local Authorities (WLAs) that governed and administered white areas "were fully-fledged municipal institutions with a political council and, administration to carry out the functions of the council and taxation powers" (Nyalunga 2006:1), colored and Indian areas were governed by Management Boards and Local Affairs Committees and black areas by Black Local Authority (BLAs) (Nyalunga 2006).

The fact that public participation is a widely recognized aspect of democracy and governance, and entrenched in the South African system, played a significant role in shaping participatory governance. South Africans today enjoy much more abundant and vibrant participatory governance opportunities than most other African or developing countries. For example, Booysen (2009 and Vivier at al., (2015) note that participatory governance in the country is captured in various institutional, policy, and law-making processes, including the establishment of statutory bodies, structures and programs. These conditions fast-tracked the creation of more constructive engagement between the state and local communities (Piper and Piper 2010).

The emphasis on participatory governance has been linked to three substantive innovations in public participation. First, was the redefinition of the term "municipality", which included the local community alongside councillors and administrators in its legal definition (Piper and Nadvi 2010). The second innovation included a set of requirements for public involvement in various decision-making processes. These requirements among others included public consultation on the annual municipal budget, the integrated development programme (IDP) review process, and the service delivery contracting process (Mubungizi and Dassah 2014; Piper and Nadvi 2010; Booysen 2009; Barichievy et al. 2005).

The third innovation is the establishment of ward committees chaired by the ward councillor and consisting of up to ten people from diverse interest groups in the ward (Piper and Nadvi 2010). The common issue of these range of participatory processes is that the involvement of citizens in actual decision-making, the co-production of services, or oversight of service delivery and government performance must take precedence over one-way communication channels where a municipality either provides or obtains information (Vivier et al. 2015).

In my opinion, the nature and extent of participatory local governance in South Africa, whether viewed from the so-called democratization angle or other frameworks such as the public management ideals and neo-liberal governmentality (Tahvilzadeh 2015), reaffirms the government's relationship with the country's well-established civil society. It is also comforting that the aspiration of empowering South African citizens "to become their own governors" is coming from the ruling ANC. For instance, Strategic Task 4 – the mobilization of the masses of the people to govern themselves in the context of the objective that "the people shall govern" - of the National Democratic Revolution (ANC 2007) notes:

> The empowerment of the people to participate in the process of governance, expressed in the concepts of a people-centred society and people-driven processes of transformation, indicates the centrality of the concept of popular and participatory democracy to our understanding of the functioning of the democratic state. We should therefore leave no stone unturned to mobilise our people to participate in the fight against major problems confronting them such as crime through their Community Policing Forums, the HIV/AIDS pandemic through their Community Health Committees or to transform education through their School Governing Bodies.

It is against this backdrop that this section examines the nature and extent of participatory local governance in South Africa in relation to two local planning frameworks - integrated developments plans (IDPs) and local development plans (LEDs) – as well two independent institutions supporting constitutional democracy: the Independent Electoral Commission (Electoral Commission) and the Municipal Demarcation Board (MDB). There is an intricate link between the Electoral Commission and the MDB in that they both manage complex and interrelated processes (Electoral Commission 2015). For instance, the issue of jurisdictions has electoral consequences.

As we have seen in recent months in South Africa, serious questions are being raised about these two institutions that underpin the very basis of local government. I acknowledge that these issues are not necessarily conclusive and do not fall in the scope of community protests, but they remain useful in understanding some of the factors and dynamics that intersect political trust and the strife against local governance, or other forms of extra-representational participation in South Africa.

Local planning through Integrated Development Plans and Local Economic Development strategies

The implementation of IDPs and LEDs was thrust into the local government arena after the post-apartheid government, following international trends, realized the importance of devolution of economic functions to municipalities (Davis 2006). The adoption of IDPs and LEDs also came as a result of the philosophy of developmental local government (Atkinson 2007), which is committed towards finding "sustainable ways to meet their social, economic and material needs and improve the quality of lives " of citizens (White Paper 1998). At the very least, now that these channels for participatory local planning are embedded in the contemporary local governance in South Africa, it seems appropriate to ask what current challenges remain in respect of the meaningful participation of local citizens.

There is an intricate link between IDPs and LEDs in South Africa. Broadly, an IDP serves as the principal five-year "strategic planning instrument which guides and informs all planning and development, and all decisions with regard to planning, management and development, in the municipality" (DPLG 2008:4). Thus far, IDPs are heralded as one of the most progressive policy initiatives of the South African state to promote accountability, inclusion and participation through decentralization (van der Walt 2014). In sum, IDPs are expected to focus on the broader development priorities and objectives of each municipality, including LED strategies (Koma 2014).

An analysis of the practical implementation of IDPs is a good entry point into a discussion of participatory governance. During the early stages of the IDP, there was considerable confusion as it competed with other instruments such as the Land Development Objective (Parnell and Pieterse 1999). Similarly, later reviews also reveal widespread dissatisfaction among South Africa citizens that the IDPs do not respond adequately to the needs of communities (Idasa 2010). From a management perspective, responsibilities for the drafting of IDPs lie with the municipality, executive committee or the mayor. This arrangement, Hlongwane (2011:16) notes, ensures that the implementation of the IDP receives top priority within decision-making structures in municipalities. There is truth in Hlongwane's account. However, it does not consider the implications of patronage networks that are dependent on government largesse. The issue of patronage is not a new phenomenon in the South African political landscape, but it has now reached new heights. In sum, entrenched patronage-based practices at local government level prevent political leaders from adopting transparent and accountable practices. When the interests of these patrons become more embedded in local governance practices and processes, it is logical that they will seek greater exemption from following acceptable practices. And, in the long run, this will have serious implications for citizen trust in IDP participatory forums.

In respect of LEDs, the inherent expectations that such strategies should be rooted most firmly upon the developmental and participatory responsibilities that have been given to municipalities in South Africa (Bond 2001; Mbontsi 2010). Such an approach stimulates and affirms the entrepreneurial spirit in communities by enabling the economy to grow the bottom up (Mngoma 2012), and allows communities to identify, implement, monitor and evaluate local projects (Nyaguthii and Oyugi 2013). At the core of this paradigm shift was the growing inability of macro policies to effect desired economic developmental effects at local level (Rogerson and Nel, 2008: 4). This has led to a new policy paradigm for LED from a national top down approach, to a locally focused approach, as captured in a report titled *Strategic Review of Local Economic Development in South Africa* (Rogerson 2009). A major advantage of such an approach is that it caters more broadly to knowledge creation and innovation that meet local needs and demands (Komito 2012: 198).

Rogerson (2004; 2006; 2008; 2010; 2011; 2014) – an established and leading scholar on LED in South Africa – further deepens our theoretical understanding of LED, and expands its relevance. For example, he contends that few municipalities are conscious of how their LED strategies can be designed, structured and monitored, so as to ensure a systematic strengthening in the assets of the poor and the reduction in their vulnerability. In addition, Rogerson laments the lack of capacity within local government structures. He is of the opinion that despite the considerable policy support for LED and interest being expressed, few municipalities have established functional LED units. Consequently, the positive results are limited, as rural areas in South Africa often do not appeal to external investors (Rogerson 2010).

A study of LED in small towns in the Free State Province of South Africa emphasized that "LED is about people working together at the local level to improve the local economy" (Human, Marais, and Botes 2008:66). The scholars further lament that well-intended LED strategies will fail to effect any change as long as municipalities use them as a means for election campaigning. A fundamental shift needed, according to the scholars, is:

> Involving the local business community in identifying possible areas where the municipality could make it easier for businesses to operate might be of much more value than strategies that are not practical or require extensive human and financial resources, while only providing short-term employment benefits (Human et al. 2008:64).

Other areas of concern about LED have been about public participation. For instance, the view of various scholars (Cheema 2011; Mngoma 2012; Rogerson 2014), including development mainstream agencies such as the World Bank and United Nations Development Programme, that promote the pervasive belief that public participation in LED initiatives is intrinsically good, has evoked diverse view.

Critiques maintain that participatory development interventions do not always empower local communities and might actually contribute to the perpetuation of exclusionary practices (Sibisi 2009). Others contend that promotion of LED strategies without actively engaging a range of local stakeholders, and particularly the business community, in the planning and implementation processes, are bound to fail (Klenk and Hickey 2011). A critical barrier in this regard, from a community perspective, is the lack of understanding of the LED policy process, lack of community resources, lack of community access to information, the absence of community representation in the decision-making process, and the attitude of local municipalities towards community participation (Leduka 2009; Reddy and Maharaj 2008).

At the heart of these challenges, is that while community participation mechanisms are in place at municipal level, they are currently dominated and reduced to participation by the political elite, organized civil society in the form of mainly non-governmental organizations, business and other interest groups with access to resources. This, in turn, has created a crisis of legitimacy and accountability and, thus, negatively affected municipal-community relations (Reddy and Maharaj 2008). Such barriers and challenges to community participation also threaten the value of local decision making for LED.

There have also been numerous reported cases of IDP or LED success in South Africa. For example, the metropolitan cities of Cape Town and eThekwini (in Durban) demonstrate the usefulness of integrated development planning, beyond its traditional role. In trying to find best practices to achieving long-term development, the two cities are among the first to include climate change in their IDPs. This ultimately led to the mainstreaming of climate change and ensuring that the cities build climate resilience (Parramon-Gurney, Gilder, and Swanepoel 2012). However, it is not clear whether these municipalities are doing this on their own initiative – without any guidance from COGTA.

Other instructive cases of participatory governance are presented by the ANC-led Emthanjeni Local Municipality in De Aar in the Northern Cape, and Knysna Local Municipality, located in the Western Cape Province of South Africa. According to the Government Performance Index, which ranks South Africa's 234 municipalities on the basis of quality of administration, financial soundness, economic development and service delivery achievements, Emthanjeni is among the top ten best performing local government institutions in the country (Good Governance Africa 2016).

In respect of the IDP, the successful implementation of projects is ascribed largely to the vigorous monitoring process involving the active participation of local citizens. In addition, all IDP projects are not only outlined in the Service Delivery Implementation Plan, but communities can track projects and programs that are to be implemented per Key Performance Indicators within the IDP in the current financial year (Emthanjeni Municipality 2015).

Concerning Knysna Municipality, it was through the public participation process during the review process of the IDP for the 2015/2016 that the municipality became aware that approximately 40% of the issues raised and the projects suggested by communities, relate to competencies which fall outside of the ambit of local government. Rather than ignoring such valuable feedback, the municipality acknowledged that integrated planning is increasingly becoming a cornerstone for intergovernmental planning and budget alignment by establishing strategic partnerships between the different spheres of government, sector departments, as well as local business groups (Knysna Municipality 2015).

What further further distinguishes Knysna Municipality from many others in the countries is the support it receives from the Provincial Western Cape Government in respect of fostering partnerships with sector departments. For instance, the Department of Local Government in the Western Cape facilitates annual IDP engagements, which focus on strategic alignment between all the municipalities and the different sector departments in the province. A major outcome of these engagements has been the identification of Joint Planning Initiatives (JPIs). These JPIs require collaborative planning and pooling of resources between the relevant government departments and municipalities in order to maximize the impact on the socio-economic and infrastructure challenges faced by local communities (Knysna Municipality 2015).

These stories emphasize one of the most important lessons of all: South Africa has pockets of success stories due to local initiative in the implementation of IDPs and LED strategies that need to be replicated throughout the country. In this regard carefully and thoroughly benchmarking processes, including the political will for participatory governance at the local level, offer developing countries such as South Africa a way out of the current crisis of the perceived or real crisis of meaningless public participation.

Municipal Elections – the role of the Independent Electoral Commission

As stated earlier, the IEC is one of the Chapter 9 institutions supporting constitutional democracy in South Africa. These institutions are presumably "independent, and subject only to the Constitution and the law, and they must be impartial and must exercise their powers and perform their functions without fear, favor or prejudice" (Gutto 2001:321). However, since their establishment, most of the Chapter 9 institutions have been dogged by one controversy after another. A decade ago, Murray (1996) cautiously pointed out the diverse nature of the critique against these institutions: are insufficiently independent; led by partisan Commissioners, and ineffectively managed. Today, there is still much debate (and widespread concerns) in South Africa about the independence and extent to which Chapter 9 institutions fulfill their constitutional mandate. This provides a good entry point in to the discussion of the IEC and participatory governance in South Africa.

It is widely accepted that elections represent the traditional means of citizen participation in government. This is one form of citizen participation is congruent with Aulich's (2009:45) articulation of the notion of the "shift from government to governance", which involves the provision of means to involve citizens in matters that affect them. Broadly speaking, municipal elections in South Africa serve to encourage the involvement of civil society in the matters of local government. More particularly, they enable communities to elect councillors who will be responsible for governing a municipality, as well as ensuring that basic services, including the provision of water, electricity, sewerage and sanitation services, waste removal, are delivered to residents (IEC 2015).

What is remarkable of the South African IEC is its ability to deliver free and fair elections. Unsurprisingly, then, this electoral body is lauded internationally and has become the benchmark for best practice for similar institutions around the world (Runji 2016). For instance, since Since December 2000, municipal elections in South Africa have been held in every five years. Likewise, the South African IEC is also very active in monitoring and assisting elections elsewhere in Africa (IEC 2015).

The rather recent controversies surrounding the IEC in South Africa have revealed that this world-renowned electoral body is not above reproach (Runji 2016). A critical analysis of the IEC in respect of municipal elections reveals three challenges the electoral body face. These challenges are potentially major barriers to civil society's ability to influence and shape the discourse, practice, and process of service delivery at municipal level.

The first major challenge relates to the low voter turnout at local elections. A low voter turnout at local elections is a typical worldwide phenomenon. For example, voter turnout at local elections ranges from 12% to 65% with averages in the low 30s in Australia (Aulich 2009) and about 64% in Norway (Kleven 2016). In comparison, the highest turnout in a municipal election in democratic South Africa is 58%, achieved in the most recent poll of 2011. This represents a 10% increase from the previous municipal elections of 2000 and 2006 that both yielded an overall turnout of 48% (Municipal IQ 2016). Of concern is that voter turnout is one measure of citizen participation in politics (Pintor, Gratschew, and Sullivan 2012). In addition, election results are supposed to reflect the preferences and, above all, the considerable capacity of civic actors to bring about change through election outcomes.

Boulding and Brown's (2015) study explored the influence of the number of parties in an election on voter turnout in two very different local electoral systems: Bolivia and Brazil. These scholars argue that the effect of the number of parties on turnout must be understood in the context of the electoral rules. In addition, voter turnout often increase in contexts where voters have a wider range of choices combined with a good chance their favoured party will win some representation, as in the case of proportional representation (PR) system followed for local elections in Bolivia. Conversely, Boulding and Brown note that in Brazil, where local elections are run according to majoritarian rules, voter turnout decreases as the number of parties rises.

The second is the question about the appropriateness of various electoral systems and the desire to change them. South Africa is currently utilizing a system of PR for national elections and a ward/proportional representative system for local elections. The Electoral Commission SA (2015) cautions about attempts to find a perfect electoral system. The IEC highlights two advantages of these two systems which are also confirmed in extant literature on electoral systems. First is that the PR system affords voters an opportunity to choose from a wide range of parties and this creates room for smaller parties to get representation in the legislative structures. Second, the PR system has the potential to promote gender and special group representation in structures of governance, ultimately promoting participatory governance. The Electoral Commission SA (2015) conceded that the PR system cannot ensure the accountability of public representatives to their constituencies.

Although this is not a comprehensive debate on the vexed matter of electoral system, the current PR electoral system in South Africans - with its inherent limitations – is exemplary and has a much better chance of solidifying representative democracy than in other African countries. According to outcome Essoungou (2011), other African countries with independent electoral bodies and competitive political environment are Benin, Botswana, Ghana, Mali, Mauritius, and Senegal. Sadly, Essoungou continues, there are about ten sub-Saharan countries where their leaders have been in power for more than 20 years. This is perhaps indicative of the weakness in the electoral processes of these countries, and resonates well with the admission of the former president of the Republic of Congo, Pascal Lissouba, who once stated that "one does not organize elections to end up on the losing side" (Essoungou 2011:15). And at the rate at how electoral systems are generally being transformed in Africa, elections that are inclusive, transparent and accountable to citizens will remain a far-fetched dream for many Africans.

The third challenge is the issue of independent ward candidates, which thus far have been receiving scant attention from researchers. Generally independent candidates do not belong to any political party and only appears on the ward ballot, unlike political party which are eligible for both ward and PR seats in municipal councils. An important hallmark of the South African local elections is that "any registered voter in a municipality may stand for election as a ward councillor in that municipality" (IEC 2015). This practice gives citizens an opportunity to stand as candidates or field others. According to Letsoalo (2016), the proliferation of independent candidates in South Africa is perhaps the manifestation of dissatisfaction with the candidate lists of political parties. This is a matter that is particularly haunting the ANC if the current wave of protests across South Africa over ANC councillor candidate lists (Letsoalo 2016). But the willingness of independents to stand for election should be considered as a very positive feature: Firstly, it shows that not all people believe that municipalities should be beholden to party politics. Secondly, it shows a general lack of intimidation in South Africa's elections. Hence, ordinary South Africans have the courage and confidence to stand for elections.

Ironically, the greatest challenge to the credibility of the IEC South Africa to run free and fair elections comes from six of the 14 former ANC councillors in Tlokwe Municipality (situated in Potchefstroom in the North West Province of South Africa). The former ANC councillors were expelled from the party in 2013 after taking part in a vote which ousted the ANC Tlokwe mayor in favor of an opposition candidate of the Democratic Alliance (Nandipha 2013). After their expulsion, the former independent candidates decided to contest the by-elections in their respective wards. According to law, municipal by-elections have to take place within 90 days after a municipal ward council seat becomes vacant due to death, expulsion or resignation of a ward councillor (IEC 2015).

The first challenge from the independent candidates came when the Electoral Court ruled in favor of the independent candidates by reversing the Electoral Commission's decision to disqualify them ahead of the by-elections held between in September 2013 (Nandipha 2013). Subsequently, the by-elections were postponed. This court ruling was to be followed by an even much more damning one by the Constitutional Court in November 2015. The Constitutional Court ruled that the Electoral Commission has breached its own statutory obligation by having allowed more than 4000 voters without addresses to vote in the by-elections in Tlokwe. In nullifying the outcome of the by-elections, the Constitutional Court further lamented that the constitutional right of the independent candidates to participate in the elections was impaired and the Electoral Commission is obliged to obtain sufficient particularity of the voter's address to enable it to ensure that the voter is at the time of registration a legal resident in that voting (Runji, 2016; Williams 2015).

At the time of writing, the Constitutional Court was hearing the Electoral Commission's urgent application for leave to appeal the Electoral Court decision compelling the commission to furnish political parties with addresses of all registered voters on the voters' roll. The ruling has serious implications for all future elections in South Africa.

Broadly, the action taken by the independent candidates in Tlokwe, in many respects, is revealing. I contend that the court ruling provides conclusive evidence about the implications of the conduct of institutions most central to the nature of representative democracy. To prevent citizen trust from eroding and dissipating, electoral bodies have to uphold their statutory obligations. Again, the bold act of the independent candidates indicates the power of ordinary citizens when confronting powerful opponents of all kinds in their quest to claim their rightful place in spaces of participatory governance. However, this is possible because of the quite tolerant political order in South Africa.

The Municipal Demarcation Board –contentious demarcation of municipal boundaries

In this section I try to explore the issue of municipal boundary demarcation as well as reviewing the response of South African citizens which has shown some worrisome trends. What emerges from this discussion of the demarcation of local municipalities, as I shall explain later, is an unprecedented, brazen and calculated public agitation using public schools as a means to protest the decisions of the MDB. This is an interesting contrast to protest during the erstwhile apartheid period in South Africa. This evolution has generated a concern with morality and ethics in community protests in the country.

The process of redrawing ward and voting district boundaries before a municipal election is quite complex. The Municipal Demarcation Act, No 27 of 1998 (Demarcation Act) as well as the South African Constitution of 1996 provides for the established of the Municipal Demarcation Board (MDB). The MDB is an independent body that follows in the steps of the discontinued Provincial Demarcation Boards. The primary purpose of the MDB is drawing up municipal boundaries for the purposes of local government and the election of municipal councils – a process known as demarcation in South Africa (Electoral Commission 2015).

There is often talk about the role of the MDB in the demarcation of municipal boundaries. But in practice the process is much more cumbersome in terms of the number of agencies and government units involved, including the rigorous steps to follow. According to the Electoral Commission (2015), the first step in determining municipal boundaries for municipal elections is the prerogative of Minister of Cooperative Governance and Traditional Affairs (COGTA). The Demarcation Act provides sole powers to the Minister of COGTA to define the formulas for determining the number of councillors for the various municipal councils. The formula for the 2016 municipal elections was determined by the former Minister of COGTA, Mr Pravin Gordhan, after consultations with various stakeholders. This process effectively reduced the number of councillors by about 2% (Electoral Commission 2015).

In what becomes a high-stakes numbers' game, it is on the basis of this reduced number of councillors, for example, that a decision is taken to split current boundaries of voting districts. It is only once the provincial Members of the Executive Council have applied the formulas and determined the number of municipal council seats in each municipality that the baton is handed over to the MDB. At this stage, the MDB has to fulfil its ultimate legal responsibility: implementing a lengthy public participation process. It is only afterwards that the MDB then hands over the final wards to the Electoral Commission (Electoral Commission 2015).

Since public participation only takes the form of comments and objections to the MDB's decisions, this raises questions about the authenticity of this process. In fact, scholars such as Duncan (2010); Matebesi and Botes (2011), and Ngwane (2010) provide a thought-provoking portrait of how the unilateral decisions about the demarcation of municipal boundaries have led to widespread community protests across South Africa. These anti-incorporation protests were initially directed against the provincial demarcation process, which entailed the incorporation of a number of cross-border municipalities from their existing provinces into others (Alexander 2010). It was a decision which ended in violence in several localities.

The idea of cross-border municipalities can be traced back to a year before the new political dispensation, a time when political difficulties prevented the adjustment of some provincial boundaries. This left seven provinces with the responsibility to co-administer the 16 cross-border municipalities. The process of abolishing these municipalities was only completed in December 2005, meaning that the assets, rights, obligations, duties and/or liabilities that resided within the cross-border municipality were subsequently wholly excised from one province and transferred to the receiving province (Matebesi and Botes 2011). Since then, this process unleashed a series of community protests across South Africa over a considerable period of time. Some of the most notable of protests occurred in Khutsong (located in the Merafong City Local Municipality, Gauteng, but incorporated into the North-West province, and later back into Gauteng), Matatiele (located in KwaZulu/ Natal but relocated to the Eastern Cape) and Moutse (located in Mpumalanga but relocated to Limpopo) (Duncan 2010).

As expected, the same ferocious community protests have now spilled over to municipal border demarcations. Thus far, the violent protests the first in the second quarter of 2016 in Vuwami (in the Limpopo province of South Africa) mark the strongest challenge yet to the controversial demarcation of municipal borders. The residents of Vuwami has been demanding the MDB reverse its decision to include the area in the new Malamulele municipality, but without success. They next launched a high court bid, where they argued that they were inadequately consulted. This also failed. Next was an unprecedented, brazen, organized campaign to burn down the public schools. The results have been chilling: more than 27 schools have been burned down (Municipal IQ 2016).

The Vuwami protests follows sharply after Malamulele residents embarked on a six-week protest action, demanding a separate municipality from Thulamela Local Municipality (also in Limpopo province). The main claim of the predominantly Xitsonga-speaking Mulamulele community was that the municipality prioritizes services to Tshivenda-speaking sections – a claim the municipality denies (Municipal IQ 2016).

As outrageous as these cases seem, they are far from isolated. There have been many others, for example, Zamdela (near Sasolburg in the Free State province) and Sterkspruit (in the Eastern Cape Province). The concerns of residents in these diverse settings in South Africa share a common narrative: logistical concerns with the headquarters of the new municipalities, which often are far away; the fear that municipal satellite offices would not be able to provide the necessary basic services, and relative deprivation on the basis of tribal identities and the fear that they will be excluded from patronage networks.

Notwithstanding these concerns of communities, a substantial part of the problem is that procedures for public participation in demarcation matters are highly restricted. A key question remains: Why does the MDB insist on overriding local views? This is evident in the growing practice by South Africans to resort to courts of law to force the state to comply with its legal obligation to ensure meaningful participation. That many courts have already ruled in favour of communities affected by municipal demarcation is indicative of the need for local government agencies, including the MDB, to thoroughly follow statutory demarcation procedures. This resonates with the call by Mubungizi and Dassah (2014:282) that "What South African society should avoid, is the process of the courts becoming the established conduit through which key administrative processes are dealt with". This suggests that the MDB does not set a high priority on its own consultation mechanisms. The impression is created that the MDB is implementing decisions taken somewhere else (possibly in political party headquarters), and then rammed through the consultation process.

Generally, though, there are still worrisome trends regarding the reaction of communities towards the issue of municipal demarcation. For example, during the height of the Vuwami protests, the MDB chairwoman urged residents to engage peacefully and noted, "We appeal for calm to be restored and for peaceful dialogue amid the protests that will ensure that the rights of others are not violated in the process ... Citizens need to understand that this was not about winning or losing, it was about constitutional democracy being the winner" (Magubane 2016). However, the community leaders did not hold this view. In displaying the community's continued dissatisfaction with the demarcation process, one community leader retorted, "they are insisting on taking us to a place we never desire, and we will insist on remaining in

Makhado [municipality]" (Mail & Guardian 2016).

Still, I contend that what occurred in Vuwani is not surprising. There seems to be no inkling that the MDB is prepared to reconsider its decisions through the process of "peaceful dialogue". Somehow, this dialogue is conducted simply as a formality, and not as a genuine give-and-take compromise between the views of the MDB and the views of the residents in affected localities. There is little further insight to what the demarcation process of municipal boundaries will hold. But there is a crucial advantage of this matter that the MDB cannot concede: it serves as a subtle way, beyond its statutory obligations, in which any threats to the political hegemony of the ruling party can be muted in highly contested municipalities.

Conclusions

In this chapter I have outlined, by means of selected strategies and governance agencies, how the notion of participatory governance has taken shape in the South African. This discussion was done against the backdrop of various participatory governance processes and practices found in other regions of the world. In this contribution the concept participatory governance refers to democratic spaces of opportunities, moments and channels where citizens can act constantly to potentially affect policies, discourses, decisions and relationships that affect their lives and interests (Gaventa 2006:2). By this definition, we are now in an era where citizens with a large space for agency in Della Porta's (2015) words, have in principle became a key micro- and macro-determinant of the destiny of participatory governance processes across the world.

Scholarly contributions are replete with evidence about the well-entrenched challenges in designing, implementing and monitoring participatory local governance policies and practices. The somewhat dominant themes that emerge from these contributions are that most citizens across the world have entrusted political parties to protect and advance their needs (Piper and Nadvi 2010). In the context of South Africa, Williams (2006:198) notes, public representatives "are determined to impose their own truncated version and understanding of "community participation" on particular communities". This constitutes a very real threat to the participatory local governance, particularly in most developing countries, where the norm for public officials is to approach public participatory processes with indifference.

But this participatory anomaly is widespread in Africa – a situation which reinforces the notion that the concentration of power in a few political elites who benefit from patronage often have little incentive to engage with citizens - thereby limiting public participation (Haider 2011). In fact, to be able to understand the complacency of African governments in respect of participatory governance, and the rule of law, more broadly, one should not look further than the current tensions within Africa over the role of the International Criminal Court. Such attitudes at the national level ultimately lead to weak local state institutions and threaten the principles and values that underpin any democratic state.

But has participatory governance at local government level *triumphed* or *failed* in South Africa?

There are often implicit standards that can be utilized to determine whether one judges participatory local governance to have triumphed or failed. I am not proposing any answer to this question, but there is no doubt that the effective implementation of evidence-based participatory local governance demands a good blend of explicit and tacit knowledge forms possessed by public officials. In addition, although tainted by an all-too-familiar instance of being highly politicized, participatory governance have won some praises.

Thus, the call by the Gauteng Premier, David Makhura, for more proactive governance to tackle protests, is welcoming. In what has been described as a stark contrast to the characterization of community protests by the previous provincial administration and national government, the Premier emphasized that:

> The idea that we must just focus on economic freedom because we have achieved political liberation ignores the fact that the institutions of state require deep and thorough-going transformation fundamental. [Community protests is a] fundamental expression of governance failure … Governance is more than delivery. If the state delivers and the people are not involved they are alienated. That is why, when they protest, they burn things down. So an activist government approach is about changing the relationship, the way government must involve people from the beginning to the end (Marrian 2015).

The discussion of the triumph or failure participatory local governance will not be complete without mention being made of the actual beneficiaries of the process: the citizens. The preceding chapter has shown how, what I call a ravenous political environment, enabled citizens to gain both greater trust as well as lose trust in public actors and institutions. Despite the expectation that elected representatives and institutions such as the South African Independent Electoral Commission and the Municipal Demarcation offer, in principle, the most direct mechanism for representing citizens and their interests, the widespread protests relating to the decisions of these statutory bodies suggest otherwise. When questions are asked about the independence of these institutions, as the Economic Freedom Fighters (the second major opposition party in South Africa) did during its election manifesto, it raises serious questions (Makhanya 2016b).

At a recent celebration of the twentieth anniversary of the adoption of the South African Constitution at the University of the Free State's Centre for Human Rights and the Faculty of Law, Judge Azar Cachalia of the South African Supreme Court of Appeal reflected on his role in the realization and upholding of the constitution, from his days as a student activist, then as an attorney representing detainees during political turmoil, and currently as a judge. In concluding, Judge Cachalia emphasized that the need to respect the Constitution. He noted: "Constitutions are drafted in moments of calm. It is a living document, and we hope it is not torn up when we go through social conflict, such as we are experiencing at present" (University of the Free State 2016).

But we should understand that in order to deal with the negative perceptions spawned by the generally declined confidence of citizens in democracy and manipulative participatory local governance structures and procedures, distressed citizens do not have the luxury of what is widely known as a "sandbox" environment. Simply put, at the peak of the tension between citizens and the state, citizens usually develop and deploy mobilization and protest tactics in a highly sporadic and coordinated (through the possible help of social media) manner to respond to the political system. This perhaps explains the outbreak of violence during community protests. However, no civilized society can condone the pervasive trend of burning down or destructing schools and other public facilities each time there communities feel aggrieved.

Returning to the opening statement, I have no doubt that the Hunger Project (2014:5) envisioned a direct and more expanded role of participatory governance: that citizens should meaningfully participate in those issues and decision-making processes that really matter in their daily life. In this regard, a vast body of scholarship shows how the power of citizen participation and involvement in their own democracy leads to better decisions and outcomes. A more pragmatic outcome of this approach is that it has somewhat played a great effect in accelerating sustainable development in communities.

But policymakers should guard against a stimulus-response approach: participatory structures mechanically lead to meaningful participatory governance. Too often, local governance decisions are made without the involvement of those most affected. Furthermore, a major flaw of public representatives – as we is to assume that they are entitled to think on behalf of citizens once elections have been held. For example, Schlesinger (2015) concludes:

> We think of "democracy" as the thing that people do when they vote. And once they vote, we leave it to the elected officials to make the best decisions. This inevitably means that communities with less political influence will be consulted less when the decisions that determine the opportunities and constraints of their lives are made. This inevitably means that the divide between people and their government representatives will continue.

A possible explanation for the conduct of local councillors in respect of participatory governance in general and the demarcation of municipalities in particular is the central role taken by state-party relations in South Africa. Currently, party political interference in institutions such as the judiciary, the police and several state-owned enterprises is at an all-time high, premised on the tendency towards micromanagement of the bureaucracy, fraught executive management relations, and what Netshitenzhe (2016:5) refers to as the "regular and acrimonious departures of senior managers, and the like". It is thus not surprising that in the desire to protect the exercise of full personal control over resources – that can be political and financial – local public representatives have taken a personal interest in the conflict between municipalities and communities. For example, that a local councillor is among 21 people facing charges of arson, damage to property and pubic violence following violent community protests over the relocation of Vuwami village into the new municipality of Mulamulele that left 26 schools damaged, certainly acknowledges what public officials would do to protect their perks (Tau 2016).

Whether the implicated councillor is found guilty or not is another matter, but it is important to point out that the effects of municipal demarcation, often occurring in a highly-contested political terrain characterized by state capture by privileged elites and populism, are profound for some councillors for two reasons: a potential loss of power and influence and, subsequently, a pervasive lack of the requisite support for activities at local government that inhibits overall efforts directed towards institutional development.

I contend that for as long as participatory local governance mechanisms are inefficient, and disconnected from the needs, goals, and capacity of local citizens, the various tensions and conflict between citizens and local municipalities in South Africa will continue unabated. Similarly, any local governance infrastructure that do not align with the realities of democracy and citizenship in the 21st century, are bound to fail. This is more so if one considers the post-apartheid context in which the majority of South Africans explicitly exert and express their existence.

The case studies in the next two chapters encompass the variety of ways in which trust in the representative political system and meaningful participation in local participatory governance mechanisms have significant meaning for civic actors. Thus, exploring the relationship between political trust and participatory governance deepens our understandings of their role in community protests.

Chapter 4: Schools and roads as bargaining power in community protests in predominantly black communities

Introduction

Why are South Africans so matchstick happy? What explains the long, recurring and somewhat violent community protests spreading across the length and breadth of predominantly black communities in South Africa? Recent research on community protests in South Africa converges around the view that the protests are characterized by violence (Runciman 2014), rebellion of the poor (Alexander 2010), a dual nature (Langa and von Holdt 2011), and insurgency (Brown 2015; Zuern 2011). Broadly, both this literature as well as many other commanding voices on the subject, are useful in that they provide a trajectory of the evolution of community protests, which have now reached a scale previously unimaginable. Recent extant studies on community protests in the country further reveal a profound shift towards violence (Runciman 2015; Brown 2015), driven largely, but not exclusively, by unresponsive political actors and ineffective local institutional arrangements.

The theoretical explanations in chapters 2 and 3, although fairly general, reveal that political actors and local institutions are fundamental in explaining community protests. These two chapters highlighted several important factors as causes of community protests in the South African context. One of the essential insights emanating from these chapters is that, before any protest could take place, a degree of trust or trust deficit has already begun to exist, depending on the lived experiences of that particular community (as discussed in chapter 2 in relation to the swinging pendulum of trust). Citizen perceptions of the actual functioning of political actors and institutions are key, because the more citizens view the output of political actors and institutions as unsatisfactory, the more distrust is generated.

Studies by Denters (2002), Fitzgerald and Wolak (2016), and Miller (1998) on the roots of political trust in local government reflect how trust reflects political performance. The distrust of the political system is further fostered by both traditional media outlets and news spread on social media which often report on repeated political scandals or the perceived or real inefficacy of the political system (Shaker 2014).

Interestingly, the profound shift of protest towards using violence as a tactic also seems to have an impact on the media. For instance, towards the end of May 2016 the South African Broadcasting Corporation (SABC) took a decision not to publicize any content displaying violent community protests in South Africa. More specifically, the SABC's decision involves not showing footage of people burning public institutions like schools in any of its news bulletins, heralding it as an act to halt "to provide publicity to such actions that are destructive and regressive" (Pather 2016). This controversial editorial decision of the SABC drew widespread condemnation, most significantly from opposition parties who labelled it as a ploy to protect the ruling ANC.

Notwithstanding the current political malaise of community protests, South Africa has been both blessed and cursed by its abundance of participatory governance channels. To better understand the challenge of building mutual trust between local municipalities, it is important to understand the nature and extent of participatory local governance in the country. As an example, consider how democracy as a system of governance is practised in reality. With all its known weaknesses, democracy remains the best system of governance to fight the challenges faced by citizens around the world (Lekvall 2013).

Thus, wherever democracy is practised, the expectation is for the state to be a non-partisan instrument of society, pursuing national interests. In practice, however, the relationship between the South African state and the ruling party is largely premised on the form of democracy adopted by the ANC (Netshitenzhe 2016): the state is the provider of employment to partisan supporters. Partisanship and intraparty conflict are some of the core factors related to community protests in predominantly black communities. Despite a growing awareness, the skewed democratization process in which the party comes first and the country last, continues unabated.

Another insightful explanation for the eruption of community protests is provided by the Civic Protest Barometer. In this regard, Powell et al. (2014) categorized the grievances behind community protests into six categories: 1). municipal services (basic services like water and electricity), 2), municipal governance (issues such as mismanagement and corruption), 3) non-municipal services (services which are the responsibility of other organs of the state), 4) party political (intra- and inter-party matters including competition for public office), 5) socio-economic (broader issues related, for example, to jobs and land distribution), and 6) unspecified services (grievances not reflected in the records). Interestingly, the authors further noted that for the seven-year period of the study (2007-2014), municipal services (45%) were the single foremost category of grievances cited by the respondents (Powell et al. 2014).

The main objective of this chapter is to better understand the strife of civic forums against local municipalities in predominantly black communities by utilizing the theoretical framework of political trust introduced in chapter 2. More specifically, the empirical findings are presented according to the four proposed stages of protest: grievance formulation; mobilization; action; and the aftermath. In addition, the structural-cognitive model (SCM) of Opp (2009), which emphasizes the implicit link between macro-level political institutions and micro-level motivations to participate in protest activities, is a useful tool in contextualizing the data. Taking my cue from Fitzgerald and Wolak (2016), my main argument is that the levels of political trust, and thus the propensity to engage (or not engage) in protest action, depend on the character of South Africa's political actors and institutions.

In the following section, I provide a brief but meaningful overview of the social, economic and political context in case studies in order to contextualize the lived overview of the selected cases. I then go on to present the empirical findings in the main body of the chapter. Some issues of design have already been discussed in chapter 1. In the context of this chapter, the design, to repeat, is based on in-depth interviews with representatives of the civic groups that led the protests in predominantly black communities, community members, and municipal managers in case study areas. In addition, a survey of 1200 randomly selected residents was conducted in order to gauge the views on community protests from a much wider pool of community members. This approach is distinct from previous South African research on community protests, which primarily follows a qualitative research approach. Furthermore, mainstream media (conventional newspapers and online) coverage of the protests in these cases has been included.

For reasons that will become clear later on, I question whether this conspicuous role of civic groups is applicable in the South African context, where violence and the burning down of schools has become an ominous trend. This leads us into the discussion of the social, economic and political context in the case study areas.

Overview of key socioeconomic and service delivery indicators of the cases

Ficksburg is situated in the Free State province of South Africa, at the national border between South Africa and Lesotho. It is part of and an administrative centre of the Setsoto Local Municipality, which has a collective executive with a ward participatory system. The town's economy is based mainly on mixed agriculture, concentrating mainly on asparagus, cherries and deciduous fruit (Setsoto Local Municipality 2015). It has a total population of 5,400 people, with a dependency ratio of 41.5, and the entire municipal area has an unemployment rate of 35.7%. In respect of service provision, 97.7% of the households have a flush toilet connected to sewerage, 94.9% have weekly refuse removal, 94.1% have piped water inside their dwellings, and 97.7% have electricity for lighting (Statistics South Africa 2011).

Ganyesa is located in the North West province of South Africa, in an area that was formerly part of the homeland of Bophuthatswana. It hosts the head offices of the Kagisano-Molopo Municipality, formed after the merger of the municipalities of Kagisano and Molopo in 2011. The 30-seat council is dominated by the ANC with 24 seats. The municipality is completely rural, consisting of 77 villages under the leadership of a single paramount chief and seven local chiefs who operate from seven areas/villages. Ganyesa has the second highest dependency ratio of 76.1. With the exception of electricity for lighting which stood at 86.6%, other municipal service provision is appalling: flush toilets connected to sewerage (5.2%), weekly refuse removal (0.7%), and piped water (13.9%) (Statistics South 2011).

Grabouw, a town well known for its apples, is based in the Western Cape Province of South Africa and is part of the Theewaterskloof Municipality, led by the Democratic Alliance. It is the most populous of the towns in the municipality ($\pm$ 40 000 of the 106 000 population), and has the highest number of informal settlements and influx of people. This influx is mainly from foreigners and people from Eastern Cape Province who are mostly unemployed, unskilled and homeless. It also has the lowest collection rate and the highest service backlogs. The town is further home to several agricultural processing firms including Appletiser and Elgin fruit juices. The Municipality has an unemployment rate of + 40% and high seasonal employment (semi-indigents) due to the highly agricultural economy (41%) (Theewaterskloof Municipality 2016). According to Statistics South Africa

(2011), Grabouw has a dependency ratio of 45.9, flush toilet connected to sewerage (85.3%), weekly refuse removal (90.4%), piped water inside dwelling (63.8%), and electricity for lighting (89.1%).

Table 2: Comparison of key socioeconomic and service delivery indicators of the cases

Indicator	Case study area			
	Ficksburg!.	Ganyesa	Grabouw	*Kuruman
Local municipality	Setsoto	Kagisano-Molopo	Theewatersklo of	Joe Morolong
Community-based advocacy group	Meqheleng Concerned Citizens	Residents' Forum	Elgin Grabouw Civic Organization	No Road No School Forum
Leading political Party	ANC	ANC	DA	ANC
Total population	5,400	19,290	30,337	89,530
Dependency ratio	41.5	76.1	45,9	84.6
Unemployment rate	*35.7%	*30.2%	*14.9%	38.6%
Youth unemployment rate	*46.1%	*38.8%	19.8%	49.5%
Flush toilet connected to sewerage	97.7%	5.2%	85.3%	6%
Weekly refuse removal	94.9%	0.7%	90.4%	6.1%
Piped water in dwelling	94.1%	13.9%	63.8%	9.1%
Electricity for lighting	97.7%	86.6%	89.1%	81.8%
Voter turnout 2011 Local Elections	45.3%	52.90%	59.77%	57.47%

*Data for entire municipality

Source: Statistics South (2011) and Electoral Commission SA (2014)

The fourth case study site is Kuruman and surrounding villages, based in the Joe Morolong Local Municipality in the Northern Cape Province of South Africa. According to Statistics South Africa (2011), the population of the municipality was 89,530, dependency ratio 84.6%, unemployment rate 38.6%, and youth unemployment 49.5%. The villages are predominantly rural and underdeveloped areas, situated in the former Bophuthatswana homeland (COGTA 2013). As in the case of other former homeland areas, these villages are extremely poor, underdeveloped, and are still characterized by low incomes and high rates of infant mortality, malnutrition and illiteracy (South African News Agency 2013).

The case studies that follow are a microcosm of protests in South Africa and are presented separately for ease of exposition. Furthermore, to provide for a better understanding of the protest events, the discussions only follow after each case has been presented.

Ficksburg – "a hungry stomach knows no allegiance"

If there is one image that reflects the brutal outcome of community protests in post-apartheid South Africa, it would be the one of a dying Andries Tatane broadcast during the prime time evening news of the national broadcaster, the SABC. Tatane, a community activist in Meqheleng Township (Ficksburg) was shot and killed by members of the South African Police Service (SAPS) during a community protest on April 13, 2011. Following his death, six policemen were charged with his murder and another two with assault with the intention to cause grievous bodily harm. Two years later the Ficksburg Regional Court acquitted all the police officers accused of the death of Tatane (City Press 2011).

Mobilization in Ficksburg

Tatane's death occurred less than two months after the death of another community protestor in Ermelo (Mpumalanga Province of South Africa). Unlike the Ermelo case, the Tatane murder provided a stark reminder of police brutality and abuse against black South Africans, or what the ANC described at the time as "resembling apartheid-era police strong arm tactics, showing total disregard for human rights" (Ndabeni 2015).

But what was the central grievance of the Meqheleng residents? How was the community mobilized? Who were the protest organizers? What was the final precipitating factor that shifted the metaphorical pendulum of political trust towards complete distrust of the municipality and political actors?

The protests in Ficksburg were organized under the umbrella of the group known as Meqheleng Concerned Citizens (MCC). This group was formed after three teachers became aware of the growing dissatisfaction among community members over a number of concerns. Subsequently, in what would lead to the birth of the MCC, the three teachers invited other community members. Only 20 community members turned up at this first meeting, where it was decided to take up the demands of the community in a more organized manner. In an attempt to provide justification as to why they had lost faith in the ANC, the Chairperson of MCC explained, "After that meeting, word about the formation of MCC spread like a Chinese whisper. We are all ANC members, however, we were left to develop our solutions in dealing with the genuine concerns of the community" (Interview, March 15, 2013). Another MCC leader also noted that it was not easy to bring about change from within any of the existing participatory structures, as anyone who posed critical questions was chastised as maintaining an oppositional stance.

A few weeks later, the MCC called another community meeting, which was well-supported, to inform residents about the way forward. By then the MCC had become an important vehicle to champion the concerns of the community. According to another MCC leader, about 15 grievances – all unresolved from past attempts by different fragmented groupings within the community – were tabled. Four central grievances that were highlighted at the meeting were the erratic supply of water to households, maladministration of municipal funds, sewerage spillage along roads, and the high unemployment rate, compounded, according to the MMC leaders, by the municipality's tendency to ignore the skills of locals when hiring. Other grievances included the poor condition of roads, leaking water meters, poor street lighting, a lack of recreational facilities, a lack of proper consultation about the IDP, and the demand for a 24-hour patrol along the border with Lesotho as a result of the high crime rate in the area (Interview, March 15, 2013).

The results of the survey conducted in Ficksburg show that 78.7% (n=157) of the respondents reported water, electricity and sanitation as their central service delivery concerns. The results furthermore reveal that 62.5% (n=125) of the respondents were satisfied with the manner in which the municipality engages with local residents, compared to 23.5% (n=47) who were not satisfied. As in the case of previous studies (Bernstein and Johnston 2007; Marais et al. 2008), the primary source of discontent of the respondents was poor water provision (78.7%, n=157).

As Simmons (2014:513) argued, "by studying grievances as not only materially but also ideationally constituted claims, scholars can gain analytical leverage on puzzles of social movement emergence and development". Thus, imbued by the support of the community, the MCC then engaged with the local municipality in what can be described as "a series of back-and-forth" submissions of letters by the community, followed by no response from the municipality. It became clear to the MCC that the tactic of engaging with the municipality through the writing of letters was not effective. Consequently, the MCC provided sufficient detail about their failed efforts to engage with the municipality, hence the decision to march to the municipality.

This legal protest – supported by several hundred residents - eventually took place on March 21, 2011, where a memorandum with a list of grievances was handed over to the Setsoto Municipality. The municipality was given 14 days to respond – standard practice in South African protest rhetoric. On the 15th day, the leaders of the MCC were called to a meeting with the municipal manager, but the municipality's response was once again rejected.

Braun (2016) has shown that distrust in representative political institutions is seen as a key source of protests. For example, in summing up the disappointment of the community, one resident remarked: "We were tired of being tired with the attitude of our local leaders". He continued, "I thought the time and energy we spent on this collective cause may, in time, help us all, but it seemed our efforts were in vain" (Interview May 30, 2014).

The following statements, which highlight the enduring attempts over a considerable time to engage the local municipality over community grievances - were common in my interviews with community members:

> I was the local chairperson of the SACP [South African Communist Party, which is in alliance with the ANC and COSATU] here. I was a very active citizen, chairing the Community Police Forum as well. But our local elected leaders see such activism in a different way. I was blamed by these leaders as having aspirations to become the local mayor. Actually, SACP members were only seen to be resourceful during elections. All vocal residents were often ignored in public meetings. The whole Tatane mess started when we questioned the ANC about the food parcels that are handed out to community members a few months before each election. These food parcels were handed out in the evening in some areas... The more you asked, the more you were labelled as "wanting to destroy the community" (Male community member, Interview May 30, 2014).

> Eish *broer* [brother]! I am a very patriotic South African and always supported my municipality, although I never really felt attached to the councillors imposed on us. We reached out to the municipality by engaging in the most humble terms of writing letters and repeated petitions, but each time we got an uninspired response. The municipality and our local leaders were deaf to the voice of the community yearning for nothing but basic services (Male community member, Interview May 30, 2014)

> The genuine concerns of the community were turned into inter-political party conflict by the municipality. Rumors spread through the community that we were being led by Tatane who is a member of COPE [the Congress of the People – one of the opposition parties in South Africa]. But we never cared as the MCC was apolitical and the cause it championed was on behalf of the community.... In fact, the response of the municipality- that the community should approach law enforcement agencies whenever we suspect corrupt activities - was a tacit signal to us that something was wrong with our democracy (Female community member, Interview May 30, 2014).

Other strong sentiments about the intransigent attitude of the municipality also came to the fore from interviews with community leaders. For instance, one local pastor said, "a local councillor was going around telling residents that they could complain until they turned blue, no one would ever listen to them" (Interview May 31, 2014).

And it was therefore no surprise to many residents when the MCC decided on another march to the municipality, citing continued distrust of the elected leaders in dealing with community grievances (this had by then grown to 29 items), and the apparent impunity of those responsible for corruption.

While extant scholarly literature has emphasized the purported role of the Internet and social media such as Twitter and Facebook as significant tools in a myriad of protests around the world (Enjolras, Steen-Johnsen, and Wollebaek 2012, Neyazi, Kumar, and Semetko 2016; Serafeim 2012), an important vehicle for the MCC in organizing and expressing dissent was a local radio station – Setsoto FM – Tatane used as a platform to openly criticize councillors and the municipality for poor service delivery. An added advantage for the mobilization of the community was that the local residents listened to and followed Tatane, as he was seen to be fearless (City Press 2011).

The action stage

According to the South African Human Rights Commission (SAHRC) Report (2011) on the death of Tatane, the protest march from Meqheleng Township to the Setsoto municipal offices in town was peaceful initially. The protest turned violent when enraged residents set fire to a public library, the Home Affairs office, and a storeroom at the municipality which then burned down completely. Then, police turned the tables on the violent protestors by using water cannons, rubber bullets, and teargas to disperse the crowd (SAHRC 2011). In the ensuing confusion, one resident said Tatane was attacked and killed by police officers when he tried to explain to them that there were elderly people taking part in the protest and that they should not use water cannons to disperse them (City Press 2011).

On May 13, 2011, a month after Tatane's death another protest erupted in Ficksburg. In the months that followed, amidst the government's attempt to resolve the impasse between the community and the local municipality, renewed protests broke out in Ficksburg in reaction to the results of an investigation undertaken by the Free State Provincial Government into corruption at the Setsoto municipality. Early that morning, Meqheleng residents began burning tyres, barricading roads and stoning police. The police retaliated by firing rubber bullets, and using stun grenades and tear gas to disperse the unruly crowd (Mail & Guardian 2011).

The aftermath of the Ficksburg protests

The residents were later addressed by the then provincial cooperative governance department head (and now municipal manager at Setsoto municipality) - Kopung Ralinkontsane. He announced that three directors and a manager from the municipality had been placed on special leave following allegations of corruption. The MCC insisted that they also wanted the mayor of the municipality to be put on special leave. The residents then left peacefully (Mail & Guardian 2011).

The aftermath of Tatane's death – a critical event in social movement literature (Opp 2009) – was predominantly marked by two significant changes: changes in the attitude of the municipality towards the grievances of the community, and the community towards the leaders of the MCC. Firstly, the event received a considerable amount of publicity in the local (national) and international media, increasing its potential impact on framing public opinion and exerting pressure on political actors to deal with the crisis. The widespread media coverage further thrust upon the municipality a greater responsibility in that it then had to deal with various external stakeholders, including provincial and national departments (as can be seen in the next sub-section on the municipality's response, various state institutions were tasked with dealing with the community's grievances). This media coverage could possibly have played a significant role in the protest action after the death of Tatane, as protest organizers might have been very conscious of the need to exploit heightened awareness about the plight of local citizens. It is known that both mainstream and online media are tools that, among others, lower the cost of participation, organization and recruitment for protest action (Tusa 2013; Wolfsfeld, Segev, and Sheafer 2013).

Secondly, the civil strife against the local governance figures in Ficksburg shifted to anger and suspicion directed towards leaders of the MCC. The fact that MCC leaders were having private meetings with the municipality and the Office of the Premier without providing any feedback to the community, which had grown accustomed to such feedback, ended up generating widespread resentment within the Meqheleng community. The result was that residents had begun to suspect that the MCC leaders "were setting themselves up for personal enrichment" according to one resident (Interview May 31, 2014). Other complaints about the MCC leaders ranged from them being selfish, to accusations that they were traitors or recipients of bribes:

We were thoroughly delighted when we started with the protest. At long last we had credible leaders who were putting the community first, we thought at the time. Ficksburg is not a sleeping town... We are not fools. How do you explain the sudden turn in the fortune of the MCC leaders? One was given a tender by the municipality at the peak of the protest. Another one is now working for the provincial government and two others at the local municipality. The others are now serving as ward committee members and have each received money from the province (Female community member, Interview May 30, 2014).

This is a wake-up call to all communities across South Africa. We trusted the MCC organizers, but since they returned from the cozy meetings with provincial government officials in Bloemfontein [capital city of the Free State Province], they have turned their backs on us. Tatane died in vain. The MCC leaders are now renovating their houses and others are now employed by the municipality (Female community member, Interview May 30, 2014).

I will find it very difficult to participate in protests in future. While our leaders are now exposed to the same patronage network that we fought against, active members of the ANC are now being threatened with the so-called political mortuary [rendered politically inactive] or "re tla kwala dipompo" [we will close the taps - in reference to preventing any business deals with the government]. I cannot believe that Tatane lost his life for a few people to benefit (Local businessman, May 29, 2014).

The Chairperson of MCC stressed however that the civic group was still functional, though they served as ward committee members at the time of the interviews. This, he said, was a much better way to represent the community. But when I asked him about this sudden change in strategy and whether the community supported the decision that the MCC leaders had taken, he noted:

> I was also labelled a traitor by the community when I started renovating my house and bought a new car. I applied for a loan at my bank, but I was told that I got the money from the government. I reckon the problem started when the Office of the Premier invited two MCC members to the State of the Province address in 2012. This was compounded when one of the fellow leaders of MCC was awarded a tender by the local municipality for the production of sandstone and another was allocated an open piece of land he had applied for. All these were interpreted as bribes (Interview March 15, 2013).

While I was interviewing the elderly resident who was captured on camera by the media holding a dying Tatane, he pointed to a man who had been standing across the street for a while and remarked, "He is one of them [MCC leaders] who have sold us out", he continued, "he now works at the municipality and is probably informing his superiors about you. I cannot blame people when they get opportunities, but this is a total white wash by our government". And with a whiff of anger he ended, "Well, money has muted our once fearless leaders" (Elderly community member, June 05, 2014).

I then approached the man across the street, who suddenly started walking away. All I could hear was his murmur, "I don't want trouble, and we know what you are up to. You are trying to incite this peaceful community". After a lengthy effort to convince him about my neutral role and responsibility in ensuring the anonymity of all participants – amidst his ranting about the ungratefulness of Meqheleng residents about the efforts made by the MCC leaders – I managed to pose one question and to get a response: There are widespread allegations that MCC leaders have been offered tenders, job opportunities and even money by the government to buy your silence? He responded:

My man, I cannot recall that anyone, I mean anyone in the community mentioned at the beginning when we started to mobilize that no one should ever work for the state. This is a democratic country, but I reckon since you are a researcher you will understand that in a country such as ours, a hungry stomach knows no allegiance... Yes, I was one of the leaders of the MCC and all I can say is my struggle was not in vain... I got something out of it. I got this job at the municipality after all the leaders were summoned to abandon the protest... Well, I had to decide between loyalty and bread on the table. Eish! It was a difficult one ... But in the end, the hunger pains ultimately took precedence over wider community concerns. I am now labelled as a sell-out (MCC leader, Interview June 05, 2014).

The survey also determined whether the respondents participated in any protests in Ficksburg at the time of the interviews or whether they would participate in future community protests. Slightly less than a third (31.5%, n= 63) of the 200 respondents indicated that they had not taken part in any community protests in Ficksburg before. Interestingly, though, almost half (46.5%, n=93) reported that they were willing to participate in future community protests. I now turn to the response of the municipality.

Response of the Setsoto Municipality

More often than not, a government faced with public discontent can respond in various ways. It can choose to accommodate the demands, repress the protestors, or devise means to divert attention from itself (Kreutz 2012). In an effort to understand the reaction of the municipality to the grievances and series of protests by the Meqheleng residents, I conducted an interview with the municipal manager. At the time of the interview (June 2014), the municipal manager had been in the position for more than two years, having been appointed in April 2012. I must also point out that the municipal manager had great insight into the Ficksburg protests as he was part of the provincial delegation which was tasked with investigating the concerns of residents.

According to the municipal manager, some of the major interventions by the Free State Provincial Government were to set up a multi-institutional intervention team consisting of the Department of Water Affairs, Office of the Premier and Bloem Water. Later, the Provincial Government established a Commission of Inquiry led by an employee of the provincial COGTA Department. The mandate of both intervention initiatives was to investigate the issues listed in the Meqheleng community's memorandum of demands and make recommendations to the Member of Executive Council (MEC) – Mamiki Qabathe. "Interestingly", the manager noted, "out of all the grievances listed, the provincial team could only identify erratic water supply, sewerage spillage, and the eradication of the bucket system as genuine service provision issues.

A main reason for the protest, it emanated from the interview, was erratic water supply. In what seems to be an illustrative example of what Schensul and Heller (2010) call the spatial legacies of apartheid, the manager noted:

> What was painful when I arrived here, was the observation that indeed the community had a genuine concern about water and sewerage spillage. There are two reservoirs in Ficksburg. The one is in the predominantly white neighborhood and the other in Meqheleng. A standard practice here was to pump the water from the treatment plant first to the reservoir in the predominantly white neighborhood and only when it was 80% filled, was the water directed to the reservoir in the black neighborhood. This resulted in the erratic supply of household water to the Meqheleng community. We cannot condone such a situation where citizens are treated differently. It was also sad to see sewerage spillage all over Meqheleng and, at times, to see children playing in the mess (Interview June 02, 2014).

When further describing the spatial legacies of apartheid, the manger indicated a combination of factors. Firstly, white communities had always had a waterborne sewerage system while the neighbouring black community used buckets. Secondly, the maladministration of money allocated by the national government to address the sewerage problem and accelerate the bucket eradication process was another factor. For example, between the years 2006 and 2010, the National Government allocated more than R185 million (13,567,415.76 USD) to Ficksburg's Bucket Eradication Programme. However, the municipality used the money for other budgeted items. Thirdly, many construction companies who had been contracted took advantage of the lack of technical inspection of projects by delivering poor quality work.

The municipal manager also pointed out a number of barriers that contributed to the tension between the municipality and the Meqheleng community. A major concern for the manager in the aftermath of the protests was the demand by the MCC that the municipality should write off the municipal bills of residents who were in arrears, which totalled more than R200 million (14,668,738.66 USD). Another concern noted was despite the government's purported goal of being people-centred, there was no vibrant interface between the municipality and the community. While the manager was satisfied with his progress over the two years since he had taken over, he provided advice to South Africans.

> I believe South Africans love themselves more than they love their country. When a municipality is charged R230 (16.8686 USD) for a basic plate of rice and curry by catering companies, there is a serious problem. Furthermore, lack of information may easily fuel protests. I received funding from the Local Government Small Enterprise Development Agency (SEDA) Fund to train 20 municipal employees and 15 external people as fire fighters. I had to strictly follow the conditions set out by SEDA, but that did not prevent some residents from stating that the municipality is corrupt. This was apparently for training the 20 municipal employees. I then realized the danger of lack of information. But above all, there is a complete myth about the notion of "The People Shall Govern". Municipalities are constantly in a catch-22 situation where they have to deal with municipal employees demanding higher wages, but pull their weight when they are supposed to work, as well as (deal with) communities demanding better services, yet (these communities) do not want to pay for the services.

Ganyesa – recurrent protests

A year after the eruption of the first community protests in post-apartheid South Africa, Ganyesa experienced its first protest on December 09, 2005, one which would serve as the beginning of spreading and recurring protests. During the first protest, residents were burning teargas and hurling stones during a demonstration after a series of memoranda had been handed to the council, complaining of corruption in the municipality and lack of service delivery (News24 2005).

Grievance and mobilization stages

The next protest – which centred on the demand that the poor 22km gravel road between one village (Tlhakgameng) and Ganyesa should be tarred - took place in May and July 2010. At the time, four schools were set al.ight in the village, forcing the Department of Education to close 19 others to ensure the safety of teachers and learners. Following the protest, the provincial branch of COSATU issued a statement condemning the destruction of community property, "We agree with the education department that this anti-revolutionary programme of burning and damaging community and government properties is politically motivated" (IOL 2013). Just before the schools reopened after the holidays in July 2010, the Basic Education Minister, Angie Motshekga, sent a high level delegation to the North West to assess the situation that led to the closure of 19 schools in Tlhakgameng Village.

A month earlier, on June 3, 2010, six members of the Ganyesa Residents' Forum (GRF) were arrested and held in custody until 8 June 2010, when they were released on bail. They were later tried for public violence in the Regional Court in Ganyesa, but were acquitted. The Forum members then decided to sue the Minister of Safety and Security for damages for their alleged unlawful and wrongful arrest and detention. More than three and a half years later, the court that heard the civil claim charge ruled in favour of the plaintiffs and awarded them an amount of money that was just slightly below a quarter of a million South African Rand (Southern African Legal Information Institute 2013).

> Legalamitlwa testified that he was the leader and member of a committee of the residents' forum at Tlhakgameng. The other plaintiffs were also committee members. He was present at the cross roads where a crowd had gathered. He was approached by W/O Masala to select a delegation to meet with the municipality. The committee was meeting in a Kombi parked nearby when shots rang out. The SAPS had fired rubber bullets at the crowd. Later, public buildings were burnt. At a much later stage Legalamitlwa met with Municipal officials (Southern African Legal Information Institute 2013).

This court case reflects the agency of organizers of protests, who strategically calculate the risk and benefits involved in achieving their collective goals. The court case may have brought a temporary halt to the protests in Ganyesa, The fickleness of the swinging pendulum of trust, as stated in Chapter 2, could have played a significant role in framing local residents to act against the dropping levels of political distrust.

The results of the survey show that 56.4% (n=141) of the 250 Ganyesa respondents reported that they were satisfied with the channels available to them regarding participatory local governance, compared to 20.4% (n=51) who were dissatisfied.

Action stage

The court case was therefore not the end of the protest action in Ganyesa. Two years later, on May 9, 2012, renewed protests, which drew a few thousand demonstrators, broke out over the unresolved demand for a tarred road. This time, the community protest affected nine villages and the schools in the Ganyesa region. The outraged residents burned businesses and a community hall in one village and looted and vandalized a wholesaler in another. Three houses belonging to a ward councillor and a principal were also torched in Manokwane village. Roads were also blockaded with rocks, tree branches and wreckages.

In some areas, trenches had been dug to block police and other vehicles from accessing the villages. Meanwhile, a woman lost her life while waiting for an ambulance that was prevented for more than two hours from entering one of the villages by its residents. Later, 144 residents were arrested and charged with public violence, malicious damage to property, arson and robbery (News24 2012).

Fitzgerald and Wolak (2016:132) concluded that "people's evaluations of local government are substantive rather than symbolic, reflecting the considerations beyond simply a predisposition to be trusting or mistrustful". Likewise, the protest organizers in Ganyesa reported that residents had reached a point of exasperation with the local municipality and the political system that treats them with disdain. The protest organizers believed that the municipality was adopting delaying tactics by making promises about tarring the road during each episode of protests, only to become arrogant afterwards. The GRF leaders then pointed out that they were of the view that some residents, especially those who had children in Grade 12, were growing impatient with the leaders for disrupting schools with each protest. Subsequently, the GRF decided at a community meeting to put to the test the veiled attempt on the part of North West Provincial Department of Public Works, Roads and Transport to ignore their demands by changing their protest strategy. As one protest organizer remarked, "We realized that our campaign had proved to be ineffective and we had to go back to the drawing board before losing the support of the community" (Interview June 03, 2014).

Meanwhile, in 2014, the North West Provincial Government implemented several road projects across the province, including in some villages in Ganyesa (Maje 2016). The interviews with several residents in Ganyesa and surrounding villages reveal that many residents supported the demand for a tarred road, and they were satisfied that the government was at least doing something about the roads. However, there was widespread condemnation of the destruction of schools and of the preventing of learners from going to school during protests. Most residents were of the opinion that during the reign of Lucas Mangope - the former Bophuthtswana homeland leader – schools were never the target of communities. Some downhearted residents summed up the level of hopelessness among parents during the peak of the protests.

> But all that we were praying for was that this conflict be resolved amicably for the sake of our children. It was sad to be treated as mere spectators by these young protest organizers. They were very arrogant and often threatened parents who complained about the destruction of schools. I reckon this is the democracy that we have all yearned for (Elderly woman, Interview June 04, 2014).

> Why can't we learn that a school has nothing to do with the demand for services or roads? In our case, I never joined these protests because I realized that some of these unemployed youth leading the residents have no future…. They are now planning to destroy the future of our children. When will this end? Roads are now being constructed, but I really don't know if this [these protests] will ever end. There are rumors that previous protest organizers have received jobs at the municipality and in other government projects. What message is the government sending to protestors? This will never end as each new leader wants to outshine the former… (Middle-aged man, Interview June 04, 2014).

My discussions with young residents further reveal a wide range of issues including the community's agency, and the nature of the sometimes complementary and sometimes contradictory protest tactics of the different village activists. These similar and disparate tactics of the diverse groupings of activists, despite all belonging to the GRF, was a challenge for the constellation of activist identities and strategies. "There is great comfort to be found in the fact that we [the youth] take our cue from the class of 1976 [in reference to the 1976 Soweto uprisings]", a youth put it.

Previous research indicates that community protests or insurgent practices are both "ambiguous and contradictory in their implications for citizenship and democracy" (Von Holdt 2011:7). For instance, residents interviewed complained about high levels of intimidation and the use of intimidation to recruit people to participate in protest action. However, protest organizers refused to take responsibility for actions conducted in the name of the civic organization.

Asked why they target schools, another young resident stated, "We never take a decision to destroy schools and public facilities. The destruction of property often occurs in the heat of the moment" (Interviews June 04, 2014). It later emerged from several other interviews that over the past 10 years, more often than not, the protest turned violent when the police tried to suppress the protest action or acted abusively towards the protestors. Other factors that fuelled the spread of violence during protests included politicians making pronouncements in the media that all was well in Ganyesa and surrounding villages, or when government officials did not arrive in time for their scheduled meetings with the community (Interviews with residents June 04, 2014).

The latest outbreak of protests occurred on October 24, 2015 in Southey village near Ganyesa. This protest, it can be contended, is the result of the how the GRF managed to successfully engage and form interdependent teams with the leaders of various villages around Ganyesa to find agency and achieve their goal. In addition, the vigorous associational life, as Swain (2010) describes it, in the villages, motivated residents to become more brazen with each passing protest action. However, in what signalled that their voices had finally been heard, the construction of some roads began in Ganyesa and a few villages between 2013 and 2014.

Clearly, no political leader would like to be associated with failed public projects, but the account by MEC for Public Works, Madoda Sambatha, which follows reveals inadvertently, a series of lost opportunities for politicians to resolve the impasse with citizens. Additionally, it also underscores how the process of road construction is fraught with legal and implementation challenges. For example, the latest protest action was as a result of the communities' dissatisfaction with the delay in completing the construction of roads that three contractors had abandoned after non-compliance by the state regarding payments. The MEC was quoted as saying that the department had no funds to begin the construction of roads that had been approved for the 2015/2016 financial year, and had hence approached the national treasury over the delayed projects. Some of the delays, the MEC noted, were caused by both contractors and residents. In the case of Ganyesa, the lengthy delay in the construction of other roads in the villages was caused by construction companies that had filed petitions in court challenging the awarding of contracts by the provincial government. Secondly, residents demanded water drainage plants only after some road construction projects had started. Thirdly, some residents prevented constructors from paving their gravel roads, citing concerns about the durability of such roads (Montsho 2015; Myburgh 2015).

Ironically, the latest community protest as a direct response to the suspension of a road construction project did not last long but had far reaching consequences: despite being very brief, it brought learning and teaching to a halt for three weeks in 17 schools in 21 villages in Ganyesa (Montsho 2015; Myburgh 2015). According to Myburg (2015), the North West Department of Education intervened by moving Grade 12 learners from Ganyesa to safe camps at other schools in the province. This was to ensure that the learners could write their final examinations without the threat of being interrupted. It was only later after meeting the Portfolio Committee on Public Works and Roads on Friday 30 October and being informed that the contractor appointed for the construction of the road had returned to work, that the community decided that schoolchildren should return to school (Maje 2016).

Aftermath

In the aftermath of a 10-year struggle against the state – a struggle which is likely to continue, I believe - some gravel roads around Ganyesa and villages have been tarred and some are still being tarred (Montsho 2015). These road constructions form part of the North West Province major infrastructure development drive, including efforts to upgrade the province's road infrastructure. In acknowledging the effect of protests on the image of the province, the Premier of North West, Supra Mahumapelo, stated in his 2014 State of the Province Address, "Brand North West has suffered major reputational damage due to the bad conditions of most of our roads. We are going to do everything possible with the limited resources available to government, to improve the general conditions of our roads" (SA Government 2014).

A recurring theme in many of the press statements by provincial government leaders about the closure of schools during protests was one of disappointment. For example, the North West MEC for public works cautioned protesting communities:

> We have seen many communities using pupils as their tool to embark on picketing. We really condemn that because the education department was forced to ferry Grade 12 pupils to various areas because of unrest.... We urge our people to engage with provincial government if there are issues. If they decide to burn schools then service delivery will be affected. The future of the pupils will be bleak. And the aim of this government is to change the lives of our people. ... Let us always think about the future of our children. They must get the opportunities that we were denied by the apartheid government. So let us be more responsible and think before we act (Maje 2016).

Similarly, the North West Education MEC, Wendy Matsemela, said:

> It is always a pity that whenever there are protests in communities, learners become victims. We are pleading with our communities that when there are protests learners be protected (Montsho 2015).

Residents' reactions to the protests were rather mixed. For the majority of young residents, the protest tactic of disrupting schools was effective. However, older residents, though satisfied with the construction of roads in some villages, remain sceptical of the GRF undertaking to suspend the protests. They were also outraged at the local municipality and provincial government for their lacklustre response to the grievances of the community. Some even called for "much harsher measures to be taken against residents who destroy schools". Others have come to believe that a crackdown on protestors who destroy public facilities was long overdue.

The results of the survey show a huge gap between the respondents who have participated in at least one protest action in the past in Ganyesa (26.4%, n=66) and those who have not (73.6%, n=184). Of the 250 respondents, 48.4% (n=121) stated that they were willing to participate in community protests in Ganyesa in future.

Grabouw – ethnic and inter-party political contestations

Grabouw, as could be seen from the earlier exposition of the socio-economic status of the cases, is known for its agribusinesses. As a result, jobseekers from across South Africa, particularly the Eastern Cape, move to towns such as Grabouw to seek work in factories. It is commonly known, as it will be seen later, that the new arrivals expect to find a job, accommodation and other basic amenities. However, this leads to several social problems. In sum, these social problems as well as the high dependency ratio of 45.9 of Grabouw could possibly affect the levels of trust in local authorities. For example, a recent study noted that there is an inextricable link between trust in local government and the quality of life in communities (Fitzgerald and Wolak 2016).

Grievance and mobilization stages

In response to the question why the Elgin Grabouw Civic Organization (EGCO) was created, four long-serving officials reported that the organization was created by resident leaders from various neighbourhoods in Grabouw to provide an apolitical civic response to the inadequate municipal service delivery in the town. Later, these leaders became the officials of the organization. EGCO was created in 2005, when the ANC was in control of the Theewaterskloof municipality. The first community protest erupted in 2006 due to unhappiness over a lack of housing in the area. This was a peaceful march to the local offices of the municipality. The outcome of the protests was that the municipality started building houses, and the EGCO "sort of became inactive till 5 years later in 2011 when the DA took over the municipality", one leader remarked (EGCO officials, interview June 30, 2015).

Several residents confirmed that the EGCO became active again in 2011 when the DA announced their local ward councillors and ward committees. One resident summed up the community's concern about the EGCO at the time:

> At first the municipality was run by the ANC. People could approach the municipality; we also had vibrant and active ward-based committees which allowed us to meet our councillor on a regular basis. However, we had several problems with the EGCO. It was created by disgruntled ANC members who were not nominated for senior positions within the local branch. When they began to mobilize the community, we wanted to know its purpose. We know what SANCO [South African Civic group] stands for... But this one [EGCO]... All I can say is that if you want to play dirty politics, then do not look further than the EGCO. It is nothing, but a factional organization. If the EGCO says something, the community just has to jump..... They are power hungry (Local ANC member, interview March 26, 2015).

The Grabouw residents took their anger to the streets again for the second time in March 2012. The main trigger to this was set off "when the school in the coloured neighbourhood was completed, while black children continued to attend school at an old army barracks" (EGCO official, interview June 30, 2015). According to another official of EGCO, the District Department of

Education promised in 2009 that the construction of the Umyezo Wama Apile School in the predominantly black neighbourhood would be completed in 2014. Interestingly, a community leader reported that the delay in the construction of the school was partially as a result of the meddling of the EGCO in the construction process. He further noted that EGCO officials wanted to become part of the adjudication process to decide on the successful bidding construction firm, as well as dictating which local residents had to be employed by the firm awarded the tender to build the school (Community leader, interview March 26, 2015).

A major trigger, which highlights the delicate and decisive ethnic sentiments in the Western Cape in general, and Grabouw in particular, was when the school in the coloured neighbourhood was completed. In an article titled, *Violent protests over school in Grabouw*, Isaacs (2012) reported that thousands of Grabouw residents from black neighbourhoods took to the streets in protest over "broken promises" to end overcrowding at the local school, Umyezo Wama Apile Combined School. The school had about 1 900 pupils, most of whom were forced to sit on the floor as the classrooms had no chairs and desks. The protestors demanded to be addressed immediately by the Western Cape MEC for Education – Donald Grant. At the time, residents of the two informal settlements temporarily blockaded the N2 highway (Isaacs 2012).

According to the DA, the protest in Grabouw and the Theewaterskloof municipal region were part of a well-orchestrated ANC campaign to destabilize DA-led municipalities through any means necessary. The *modus operandi* of the ANC, the DA leader said, was to make bribery attempts to persuade DA councillors and coalition partners to sign motions of no-confidence in the council leadership, thus forcing by-elections and providing the ANC with the opportunity to resume control of the municipality. When such attempts failed, it was reported, then local residents are co-opted to foment violence under the guise of "service delivery protests". Affidavits filed at the Caledon police station over a month before the violence in Grabouw detail how senior provincial ANC officials used a local ANC affiliate to facilitate the attempted bribery of DA councillors (Botha 2012).

An official of the Western Cape Provincial Department of Local Government also confirmed in an interview that they had communicated with the residents of Grabouw about the causes of the delay in the construction of the school. According to the official, the majority were satisfied with the efforts made by the provincial government, although a small group of politically motivated people continued to hold schools to ransom each time the community embarked on protests (Provincial Government Official, Interview June 28, 2015).

Notwithstanding the political dynamics, the survey results indicate that 42.6% (n=149) of the 350 Grabouw respondents were satisfied with the participatory local governance channels, compared to 35.4% (n=124) who were dissatisfied. In respect of service delivery-related grievances, a lack of housing (52%, n=182) was one of the foremost grievances among the respondents.

Action stage

The most notable feature of the *action stage* of the protest action in Grabouw was the closure and destruction of schools, as well as high levels of ethnic polarization within the civic organization and between local citizens at large. Thus, in stark contrast with the three other cases in predominantly black communities, the Grabouw protestors not only had to deal with the trust deficit between citizens and the local municipality, but with the increasingly low levels of intraorganizational trust. According to Shaw (1997), intraorganizational trust helps organizations attain success and cope with periods of high stress, uncertainty, and rapid change.

During the March 2012 protest in Grabouw, two classrooms at the Umyezo Wama Apile Combined School were set on fire, a third ransacked, and the school hall vandalized. To increase their leverage, the protestors also instituted a stayaway. One resident recounts his experience: "Protest organizers did not think about the consequences of their actions. They do not know the importance of education. Why do they involve schools in their battles?" (Male resident, Interview March 26, 2015).

This view was echoed by a former leader of EGCO who stated, "To the community's disbelief, an organization which is supposed to advance our needs is in fact destroying the future of our children". The leader expressed the view that the straw that broke the camel's back was the seemingly lax attitude of the majority of residents who allowed EGCO to continue with its "relentless campaign against poor service delivery, while actually driving political agendas" (Former EGCO leader, Interview June 30, 2015).

The centrality of participation fatigue has been noted in the literature. For example, Craske (1999) argues that new strategies and a shift in the agendas of municipalities make it difficult for civic organizations to keep people mobilized. This is also aptly illustrated by the Grabouw case. When asked why they are no longer active members of EGCO, another former EGCO leader provided three reasons: ethnicity, competition for leadership positions, and the violent protest tactics employed.

> I was among the core leaders of the EGCO when it was created. At first, we were all treated with respect. Later, though, I realized that critical decisions are often taken by the coloured leaders. Again, there were constant tensions between the coloured group and members of the SACP over key positions in the organization. This created animosity and suspicion between blacks and coloureds. The leader of the EGCO is a prominent ANC member and he ensured that he received all the praise for the efforts made by the forum. Unfortunately, there was no acknowledgement of the role we played... I also did not, and still do not, support the tactic of handing over a memorandum to the municipality, and then inciting the community. Most challenges can be addressed peacefully. We are ANC members. Our ward councillor should deal with our demands, not the DA ward councillors (Former EGCO leader, Interview June 30, 2015).

The next phase in the escalation of the sustained mobilization of Grabouw residents was what an EGCO leader calls "ward-based" protests: ward-specific grievances. For instance, in ward 13 (Siteview), the residents' demand - which was not supported by EGCO – was for the municipality to replace the asbestos roofs of their houses with corrugated iron. In the informal settlements, the main demand was about the disconnection of illegal electricity connections. An issue that cut across ethnic lines and ward borders in Grabouw, the protest organizers stated, was that of housing (EGCO leader, Interview June 30, 2015).

It was therefore no surprise when about 1 000 residents marched to the Grabouw municipal offices to complain about lack of housing, poor and expensive electricity supply, and bad road conditions on August 20, 2014. This time, protestors set the veld along the N2 highway on fire and poured oil on the surface of the highway that evening. This protest was followed by another one, which lasted three days, almost a month later (September 15), to show the community's dissatisfaction with the response to the memorandum delivered on August 20. As a result, the highway was closed to traffic for three consecutive days, but the other protestors also targeted alternative routes by throwing stones at passing motorists. The protestors also threw stones at police, who battled to contain the situation due to the darkness.

Later, some foreign-owned shops were looted (SAPA 2014). During the third day of the protest, the angry protestors set a local fire station alight – this being only one of the horrific scenes related to the protests shown on national television (ENCA 2014).

During this three-day protest action, more than 5 000 children from 12 local schools were yet again prevented from going to school. This took place at the time matric examinations were being written. One matric learner, quoted in Marus (2014) summarized the grave consequences of the protest: "I'm so confused because I needed to write two papers and I didn't. But how can I because our school is closed? People don't seem to think of the consequences, they are playing with my future here".

Aftermath

In the *aftermath* of the protests in Grabouw, on one hand, the municipality and provincial government kept on berating residents for the violence. On the other hand, the reaction of the community with regard to the protests was mixed. Some residents emphasized that causing mayhem during protests elicits a speedy response from state authorities. Others stated that despite serious attempts by the DA-led municipality to address community grievances, the ANC-led EGCO would continue to embark on violent political protests disguised as "service delivery protests".

Some community members, from both predominantly coloured and black neighbourhoods, indicated that they did not take kindly to the violent protest tactics of EGCO, but continued to suffer in silence for fear of victimisation. Another major refrain of the residents in Grabouw was that although some community grievances were genuine, EGCO had nothing concrete and constructive to offer, except to foment violence and intimidation. In fact, as I was driving through the predominantly black community in Grabouw, I observed several illegal power connections from poles in the formal neighbourhoods leading to several informal settlements. Several fatalities have already been reported as a result of these illegal electricity connections (Interviews, June 30, 2015).

Another local resident and ANC member stated that the illegal electricity connections are a direct outcome of the "siege mentality and free reign" that protest organizers have entrenched in Grabouw. The resident believed that EGCO is a factional organization of influential ANC figures. According to the resident, "These leaders decide who forms part of the school governing body, and who gets employed in community development projects". She continued: "If they do not get their way, then the community is dragged along in these silly protests. And it does not help to complain to regional or provincial ANC officials. They are in cahoots with the local officials". (Local ANC member, interview March 26, 2015).

However, a prominent EGCO committee member and ANC supporter were cited in *Business Day Live* (2014) that they "were tired of all the forums being created". They further continued to say that people wanted to see action within their communities. At the time, the EGCO secretary reported that she was satisfied with the outcome of the meeting with the Western Cape Provincial Government and other local stakeholders. During an interview with some EGCO leaders, they echoed that, in many respects, the protests in Grabouw represented the unresolved demands of residents identified as recurring lightning rods: a lack of housing, lack of consultation by local authorities, and poor electricity supply (EGCO leader, Interview June 30, 2015). We now turn to the response of the Western Cape Provincial Government.

According to the survey results, 42.9% (n=150) of the 350 respondents in Grabouw reported having participated in at least one protest action in the past, compared to 57.1% (n=200) who had not. The results further show that 54.9% (n=192) of the respondents reported their willingness to participate in any future community protests in the area.

Response of the Western Cape Department of Local Government

In the aftermath of the September 2014 protest, the provincial government responded by convening a meeting of more than 50 people from various sectors, including the municipality, protestors, police, civic groups and the Grabouw Taxi Association. The provincial official stated that it was evident that local politicians who had no interest in the needs of communities, and little information, were some of the drivers of the protests (Provincial Government Official interview, June 06, 2015).

Furthermore, a review of the provincial government's response to the Grabouw protests highlights several intervention strategies directed towards community protests in the province. According to the provincial official, "Technically it is difficult for us [the Provincial Government] to have first-hand information about community protests until incidences are reported by local municipalities". The province also depends on Thusong centres (a public communication and information system formerly known as Multi-Purpose Community Centres) to extend and integrate government services into outlying areas. The Thusong centres provide face-to-face interaction between government and the citizens. In addition, the province has also established a 24-hour Disaster Management Centre in Cape Town, which deals with all crises in the province. However, with a tinge of disappointment, the official reported that Grabouw, as with many other similar areas in South Africa, attracts many migrant jobseekers. The town also serves as an entry point to Cape Town. The presence of these jobseekers has a knock-on effect: the demand for housing and municipal basic services increases (Provincial Government Official interview, June 06, 2015).

Kuruman – The 'No Road, No School' protests

The origins of the protests in Kuruman and surrounding villages can be traced to community protests in Olifantshoek (an Afrikaans name meaning "elephants' corner"), a relatively small town about 80 kilometres south-west of Kuruman. The protests in Olifantshoek were organized by Olifantshoek Concerned Residents (OCR), formed by five active members of the local ANC Youth League (ANCYL) in 2009.

The grounds for the protests in Olifantshoek were laid when the OCR complained about local ANC members being exploited by ANC leaders for personal gain during elections, and alleged corruption within a community development trust. The trust was, the OCR stated, led by the chairperson of the local ANC branch. Going beyond these original concerns, the central grievance of the OCR in 2012 was the demand for the resignation of the Mayor of Gamagara Municipality. The mayor was accused of displaying great disrespect towards the community, and making empty promises about jobs, bursaries, and infrastructure projects.

The final precipitating factor that led to the violent protests and the closing down of schools for more than eight months in 2012 occurred when the OCR leaders were asked to provide evidence to corroborate the allegations made in their submission to the Public Protector who was investigating the municipality at the time (Focus group discussion with leaders of OCR, March 01, 2013). In a turn of events that would become a sad part of the history of protest behaviour in South Africa, the community forcefully shut down three schools, affecting 2583 learners.

Grievance stage

The same protest tactic of closing schools would later spread to several areas in the Northern Cape Province. In Kuruman, only five villages were involved initially in the protest action over the demand of tarred roads in 2012. A major protest tactic at the time was the blocking of the N14 road with stones, and burning barricades, which resulted in the closure of the road. Ten residents were later arrested. This set the tone for the two-year (2012-2014) long strife by the protest organizers, aptly referred to by the South African media as the 'No Road, No School' Forum (the Road Forum).There were two years of the recurrent eruption of protests in the area between 2012 and 2014.

In spite of the condemnation by the government, religious and civic groups, who likened the protests to human right abuse, the Road Forum maintained in an interview that their reaction was a direct response to a litany of failed attempts to get the attention of the municipality and the provincial government. According to the Road Forum, the villages around Kuruman have a long history of clashing with the state over the cross-border municipal areas that used to straddle between the Northern Cape Province and the North West Province of South Africa (Interview, Road Forum Committee, July 28, 2014).

A central grievance of the residents since 2012 has been that the government should tar the 720km stretch of gravel road to link 200 villages to the N14 midway between the towns of Kuruman and Vryburg. The Chairman of the Road Forum noted that they were encouraged when they met the local Municipal Manager for the first time at a community meeting on June 20, 2012. The Municipal Manager advised them to form one group as he was receiving numerous memorandums from various splinter community organizations. Immediately after the meeting, the Joe Morolong Road Forum was established, which unified all the concerned groups from the different villages.

Three months later, the Road forum was informed by the municipal manager that at least 130 kilometres of the road would be tarred. One committee member said: "After a series of meetings, we were shown the design of the road that would be tarred in 2013. We targeted the municipality because it was not entirely transparent on this issue" (Interview, Road Forum Committee. July 28, 2014).

When asked why they were demanding tarred roads and not any other services, mixed responses were provided by the Road Forum and residents. According to the Road Forum, many schools are 10 kilometres away from the villages. Due to the poor road conditions, children are forced to walk to school as the villagers with vehicles struggle to maintain their cars. The local taxi industry has also been affected by the poor roads and fewer and fewer taxi owners were keen to operate in the villages (Interview, Road Forum Committee. July 28, 2014).

This was corroborated in a report in the *Sowetan*, a leading South African newspaper, wherein residents complained about the effects of the gravel roads: ambulances not getting to them on time, or even breaking down before reaching them (Macupe 2016). Furthermore, the Chairperson of the Road Forum was adamant that a tarred road would have significant spinoffs for the residents, including the municipality. For example, he mentioned that residents would spend less time travelling, less money on the maintenance of vehicles, and tarred roads would enhance the safety of learners (Interview, July 28, 2014).

The results of the survey show that the majority (70.9%, n=283) of the 400 respondents in Kuruman were not satisfied with local participatory governance channels. In addition, 54.5% (n=218) reported bad road conditions as one of their main grievances. This was followed by lack of potable water, electricity and sanitation (28.5%, n= 114) and perceived corruption/nepotism at the local municipality (15.5%, n=62).

Mobilization stage

We now examine features of the mobilization tactics of the Road Forum. The Road Forum depended on impromptu community meetings, organized at short notice. A major obstacle, mentioned repeatedly by the Road Forum committee members, was the difficulty of organising meetings at a central location due to the villages being so scattered. In most instances, the chairperson would update community representatives from the different villages via Facebook or WhatsApp. It was then the responsibility of these representatives to share the information with the village (Interview 28 July 2014).

It now became evident that in all the other cases, the low levels of trust in local municipalities were compounded by the perceived high systemic tolerance for delays in responding to citizens' grievances. Likewise, the soaring promises made by the municipality in Kuruman raised the expectations among local citizens that the gravel road would be tarred soon. However, the failure of the municipality and the Northern Cape Provincial Government to fulfil this promise destroyed the trust of the community.

Action stage

During the *action stage*, the strife against the municipality for the Road Forum (which was acting as the voice of residents of the predominantly black villages around Kuruman) began in 2012 when the municipality repeatedly failed to fulfil its promise of starting to tar the roads as promised. This led to the closure of schools for more than six months, affecting about 15 000 learners (Mail & Guardian, September 20, 2012). The government responded by moving matriculants (final year school learners) to education camps elsewhere in the province (City Press, September 1, 2012).

In what seems to be a repeat of the 2012 protest, the so-called `no road no school` protestors barred about 16 000 learners, including almost 500 matriculants, and staff in 54 schools from going to school for several months in 2014 to get the attention of the authorities (City Press, September 22, 2014). The trust of residents in political actors and political systems seems to have been damaged by several factors including, among others, renewed unfulfilled promises, questionable decision-making, and intimidation tactics by the state. The following statements from the Road Forum members (Interview, July 28, 2014) capture their frustration:

> Subsequent to the 2012 school closures, we spent the entire 2013 running from one meeting to another about our request about the tarring of the road. What happened to the money the mines donated through the community trust? We got tired of promises.
>
> Everything was planned in detail. We even saw the preliminary design work done. In February [2014] we were told that the contractor would be on site by April. This did not happen... The next month were visited by the Deputy President of the ANC and the country during his election campaign. He also promised that our demands will be addressed immediately after the [General] elections. The elections came and passed and, suddenly, the tune of the ANC also changed. We were henceforth told that the ANC never promised us roads. It is a farce which we are expected to tolerate.

A major factor in the indifferent relations between the Road Forum and the state, which eventually led to the closure of schools and the burning of three, was when the Northern Cape Member of the Executive Council (MEC) of Roads and Public Works failed to arrive to receive the memorandum from the Road Forum leadership on June 5, 2014 (Kathu Gazette, June 12, 2014). The resolute leaders of the Road Forum noted that they had no regrets about the protest tactic and would employ it again should the opportunity present itself. In this regard, two leaders noted:

> It pains us to see our children not attending school. The government says that "education is key", so the schools are our only weapon against a system that thinks they can play bingo with our concerns.

> We saw how the might of violence in Khutsong [an area embroiled in long and protracted violent protests against the provincial demarcation of their municipality in 2007] and other towns elicited quick and positive responses from a very arrogant government. We were misled by the Vice President. He had the time to visit us before the elections because his political career depends on communities like ours. And we have a Premier who blames us in the media, but ignores our genuine demand.

In describing the response of the state, participants were highly conscious about the ways authorities handle protests. There was agreement that several attempts have been made by local leaders and municipal officials to destabilize the Road Forum by "making promises of jobs to members in exchange for leaving the group". Other state responses included generic strategies such as indiscriminate use of force by the police, and illegal and arbitrary arrests. In what ostensibly further contributed to the lack of trust in the state, one leader noted:

> We were very surprised when our water supply was stopped by the municipality. Apparently, all other state agencies were also instructed not to supply services to our village. As a result, state pension recipients were not paid and even ambulances did not arrive when called. These developments were a clear attempt by the state to turn the villagers against the protest.

Aftermath

To better understand the *aftermath* of the protests and the challenge of building mutual trust between municipalities and the residents in Kuruman, it is important to look at media headlines. These headlines exhibit the mixed impacts of the protests. For example, headlines such as "No road, no school protest costs Kuruman pupils a year" (City Press, September 11, 2014), "Education Department deregisters 500 Kuruman matrics" (Eyewitness News

2014), and "Where homework is a crime" (City Press, August 10, 2014), depicts the disappointment of various stakeholders in respect of the education of local children. In fact, the DA took a step further by laying criminal charges against protesters, saying children's constitutional rights to education were being violated (Business Day, August 18, 2014).

In May 2016, construction on the highly contentious gravel road started. This is supposed to be a positive outcome of the enduring community protest, however, several mainstream media reported that residents have threatened to boycott the local government elections if their demand that a 130 kilometre stretch of tarred road be completed is not met (City Press 2016; Sowetan 2016). However, the fact that thousands of learners missed out on a year of schooling is already showing negative effects according to various respondents: some refused to return to school, high levels of ill-discipline is reported at schools, as well as an increase in alcohol and drug abuse among teenagers.

The survey reveals that 54.5% (n=218) of the 400 respondents in Kuruman reported that they have participated in at least one protest action in the area. This is the highest proportion of participants compared to the other three cases: 42.9% in Grabouw, 31.5% in Ficksburg, and only 26.4% in Ganyesa. Furthermore, slightly more than half (55.5%, n=222) of the respondents in Kuruman indicated that they would not participate in any future community protests in the area.

Response of the Joe Morolong Local Municipality and Northern Cape Provincial Government

The Municipal Manager of Joe Morolong Municipality mentioned several challenges faced by municipalities in general and their municipality in particular. He stated that municipalities are part of three spheres of government, however, despite the explicitly different mandates of theses spheres, local municipalities bear the brunt of all levels of governance. A major challenge for rural municipalities, he noted, is the lack of capital. As a result, such municipalities are dependent on grants. More specifically, he reported that Joe Morolong consists of 15 completely rural wards, each with its own demands. The municipality does not provide services such as refusal removal, or electricity, and "water scarcity is a serious problem in the area and residents are sometimes without water for more than two weeks" (Interview, Municipal Manager, April 23, 2015).

The Municipal Manager acknowledged that the residents' concerns about the gravel roads around the Kuruman villages were genuine. He mentioned the difficulty in accessing certain areas during heavy rains. For him, the protest organizers are quick-witted and resourceful, and able to quickly mobilize the community around a central grievance, yet they failed to respond to several invitations to meetings.

> When they [protest organizers] did turn up for meetings, they never raised any concerns, except to indicate that they understand the challenges that the municipality faces. My personal plea to the protest leaders was to educate the community about the different spheres of government and their respective mandates. We gradually educate our constituencies about our responsibility as a municipality. Lack of reliable information concerning any issue at hand, makes it difficult for the community to appreciate the efforts of the state and municipality in particular (Interview, Municipal Manager, April 23, 2015).

Furthermore accounts by the then Acting Premier, Grizelda Cjiekella, in response to the 2012 protests in Kuruman, show some of the inherent challenges in dealing with community demands. The province's view that "the Northern Cape has ... fallen victim to a number of protests by community members under the guise of service delivery protests", somehow indicates the government's attitude towards the protest. The Acting Premier added that the main reasons for "these often illegal protests" are the demands for access roads. However, due to high levels of intimidation, it was difficult for the province to intervene successfully in some areas. She summed up the Province's response:

> Immediately when the protests started, a delegation of MECs was sent in to assess the situation. Several meetings were held with the mayors, community liaison officers, community leaders and various ward councillors. The delegation also listened to the communities' unhappiness and their concerns and received a memorandum of demands. In collaboration with the North West Provincial government, the road has been given priority status.... We are currently faced with a situation where protesters have now gone as far as destroying infrastructure of Government and businesses in the area. This is the same group of people who claim that Government is doing nothing to resolve their grievances and that Government is not delivering in their area (South African Government 2012).

The focus now turns to the discussion of the findings.

Discussion and conclusions

This chapter profiles four diverse case studies in predominantly black communities that serve as a microcosm of community protests in South Africa. Broadly, the findings reveal that while 'genuine' municipal service delivery issues trigger community protests, grievances related to a diverse range of services including roads and housing (which are not the responsibility of municipalities) also serve as significant catalysts for community protests. In addition, the chapter not only illustrates the ambivalence and tensions inherent in the relationship between municipalities and citizens, but posits that the increasingly heightened levels of violence, intimidation, and protest tactics of vandalizing schools and preventing learners from attending school will have far-reaching implications for South Africa.

The chapter generates several conclusions about how the conduct of political actors and institutions at local government level, including other spheres of government as well; contribute to the prevalence of community protests. Similarly, the chapter further accentuates how the perceptions of communities and their representative civic groups, widely known as concerned residents' forums in South Africa, tilts the swinging pendulum of political trust to either an increasing path of trust-building distrust, and ultimately protest action. In this regard, Meyer and Hyde (2004:77S) emphasize that civic groups (they use the concept neighbourhood associations) are "often regarded as the most genuine form of civil society organizations". Meyer and Hyde further note that the primary goal of such associations, as well as the forums they provide, is to preserve or improve conditions in a geographically delineated area and are typically directed by local residents.

A number of more specific extrapolations can be made with reference to the case studies. First, civil strife against local municipalities is constructed when individual citizens with a similar set of grievances realize that they need to act collectively to advance their goals (Van Stekelenburg et al., 2009). The civic groups in the case studies were formed as a direct means of mobilizing residents around key locality-specific grievances. It should be noted that the existence of grievances does not necessarily translate into protests. A noteworthy explanation in this regard is provided by Van Stekelenburg and Klandermans (2013:886):

People – social psychologists never tire of asserting – live in a perceived world. They respond to the world as they perceive and interpret it. Indeed, this is what a social psychology of protest is about – trying to understand why people who are seemingly in the same situation respond so differently.

The findings in this chapter reveal that a major trigger is the response (or lack thereof) of local authorities, which often tilts the pendulum of political trust to an increasing path of distrust of the political system. For example, in Ficksburg, water was the main source of discontent. According to a recent study conducted by the South African Water Research Commission, which investigated community protests and water service delivery in South Africa, the majority of social protests associated with water service delivery tend to occur in working-class urban and peri-urban localities characterised by high levels of poverty, unemployment, marginalization between various stakeholders: water services development planning at municipal level and water users at local household and community levels (Water Research Commission 2016).

The main triggers of community protests in the Ganyesa and Kuruman cases were demands for tarred roads, and housing in Grabouw. The former two cases were part of the then Bophuthatswana homeland characterised by, as was the case with others, high levels of underdevelopment (du Plessis and Scheepers 2000), while the last is an agribusiness mecca (in South African terms), attracting large numbers of jobseekers (Theewaterskloof Municipality 2016). As the study by the Water Research Commission (2016) shows, the increase in population, changing demographic profiles and citizen expectations as a result of rapid transformation of urban and rural settings, have been identified as some of the main triggers of community protests in South Africa. In Grabouw, once jobseekers arrive, they need accommodation. The first option is, typically, to stay in an informal settlement. These informal settlement areas later place huge pressure on municipalities to provide basic services, including housing.

In all four case studies, I found a paper trail of evidence of strategies - captured in letters, memorandums and minutes of meetings - employed by civic groups to engage with local, regional, provincial or national political actors. Citizens around the world care a great deal about how they are being treated by the political actors entrusted with their interests. Should this sense of trust be affronted, it creates an environment conducive to protests. Still, someone visiting or making a telephone call to a municipality, for example, hopes for some kind of 'good' interaction with municipal officials, but reality rarely lives up to that expectation. Norris (2011:1) proposes two Weberian 'ideal types' of local government systems that "derive from fundamental differences around the world in citizens' understanding of the purpose of local government". The first ideal type is what he calls the 'managerial' type. Here, local government primarily fulfils the role of 'local administration' (the efficient delivery of services). The second is the 'governmental' type of local government. Under this type, local government service delivery is important, including a "wider role... both as the mouthpiece of shared community interests of a locality and also in making policy choices in its name within the wider body politic" (Norris 2011:4). In this regard, the power of empowered client-interface cannot be overemphasized. The key factor applicable here is to what extent municipal frontline staff have been empowered to deal diligently with each and every citizen enquiry. And as Brown (2015:49) correctly attests, it is "the relationships we build with local municipal service providers that shape citizen experiences of the state".

Fitzgerald and Wolak (2016), for example, describe the interesting point that the root of political trust in local government is based largely on perceptions of political performance. When citizens perceive existing grievance redress mechanisms within municipalities and other government entities as inefficient after a series of disappointments, this leads to a final loss of public trust in the political system. In the context of South Africa, a study by the research team from the University of the Witwatersrand is useful in explaining the efficacy of violence (including the burning of public and private facilities) in forcing political authorities to listen to their collective demands (Von Holdt et al., 2011). The use of violence subscribes to the eventful perspective of Bessinger (2002) and Della Porta (2014), with reference to the high degree of eventfulness of protest actions: experimentation with new tactics, creation of feelings of solidarity, consolidation of organizational networks, and the development of public outrage.

Several other South African studies (Alexander 2010; Anciano 2012; Marais et al. 2013; Matebesi and Botes 2011; Langa and von Holdt 2012; Ngwane 2012; Runciman 2014) have shown how the use of violence and intimidation has generated some government responsiveness. The findings, in this regard, raise serious concerns about the purported role of participatory local governance channels and instruments in building and maintaining effective state-citizen engagements.

The findings further demonstrate that the cases are also symptomatic of larger issues around community protests. These issues include, among others, perceptions about the benefits accrued by protest organizers, inter- and intra-party political dynamics, and inter-governmental relations. For instance, the results show that civic groups face challenges of their own in their attempts to keep residents mobilized. These challenges relate to suspicion towards the leaders or among leaders, as well as the ethnic polarization as indicated by the Grabouw case study. In all case studies, a common refrain was the alleged incentives offered to protest organizers during or in the aftermath of protests. In the case of Grabouw, court papers revealed the effect of inter-party political contestations between the ANC and DA at national, provincial and local level. The court case initiated by the DA revealed how both provincial and local ANC officials in the Western Cape Province have attempted to bribe local DA councillors in an attempt to change the leadership of the local municipality (Mackay 2012).

More generally, these opportunistic attempts by the political elite have unintended consequences. A study on civil war resolution and relapse indicates that the likelihood of recurrent wars is higher in areas with a prior history of civil war. Civil wars are vastly different from community protests, however, the case studies in Ganyesa and Kuruman reveal how the opportunities landed by former protest organizers served as a catalyst for remobilization into protests. Providing incentives to protest organizers in an era of what I call "politics of the stomach" is a worrisome trend, since it not only inhibits representative political institutions and actors from dealing with the fundamental triggers of civil strife against local municipalities, but increases the likelihood of the recurrence of more brazen and violent community protests.

A closer look at previous studies indicates the duality of community: internal struggles and intra-elite struggles within the ANC (Alexander 2010; Langa and von Holdt 2012). In this regard, Langa and von Holdt (2012:96) conclude: "the ANC, it seems, absorbs most things, and many things take place within it. It is the place where the local elite, activists, those with organizational ability, the talented and the ambitious congregate". Consequently, mobilizers invent and reinvent their frames and repertoires of contention, at times even engaging in the clandestine real in order to avoid any victimisation in the aftermath of protests. Closely related to the intra-party struggles are the "centrifugal forces" within the ANC (Atkinson

2015:32). Two of the four general conclusions drawn by Atkinson (2015) in this respect are of relevance here. Firstly, the availability of a reliable stream of revenue, has created an extensive network of patronage. Secondly, is the centrifugal dynamic created by the South African Constitution, whereby each province became the home of a provincial elite. More often than not, it is in the interests of these elite to remain in power. The rise of provincial elites has not only compromised the functioning of provincial governments (Atkinson (2015), but local government as well. Since the obsession with control is a dominant feature of intergovernmental relations (Atkinson 2007), it is not difficult to contend that municipalities are, to some extent, becoming the scapegoats for problems way beyond their control.

Still, in the majority of studies on community protests, there is little or no consideration given to the negative impact of the mobilization tactic of using schools as bargaining power. This major shift in the mobilization of residents in predominantly black neighbourhoods will have far reaching consequences for the learners, the community, and South Africa at large. For example, the report of the United Nations Children's Fund (2014) indicates that children in conflict situations are at risk of truancy, repeating grades, and tend to have lower educational aspirations and achievement levels than children who have not been exposed to violence. In addition, there may also be long-term economic consequences, such as increased rates of unemployment in adulthood and a greater likelihood of living below the poverty line. Clearly, emancipative societies such as South Africa need citizens who can uphold emancipative values. The damaging and burning down of schools during community protests, I believe, is not in keeping with the societal norms and values that the current generation of civic activists would want to thrust to the forefront of mainstream societal behaviour.

Chapter 5: Ratepayers' associations and the "cheque book" protests in predominantly white communities

Introduction

The previous chapter highlighted a variety of perspectives on community protests within four predominantly black communities of South Africa. This chapter evaluates the *civil strife* (protest dynamics) in four predominantly white communities across four provinces of South Africa. Internationally, the prominence of neighbourhood-based civic activism occurs in the form of, for example, Residents' Welfare Associations (RWAs) in India (Coelho and Venkat 2009), Area Forums or Committees in the UK (Farrelly 2009), and neighbourhood associations in Japan (Pekkanen, Tsujinaka and Yamamoto 2014). These neighbourhood organizations are in a unique position to influence not only local social justice issues, but a range of other issues that affect local citizens.

In the context of South Africa, as reported earlier, there is an abundance of extant research on community protests in predominantly black communities. However, the voices of residents in predominantly white communities in post-apartheid South Africa remain generally unheard. Given the socioeconomic differences between black and white neighbourhoods, ratepayer associations differ greatly from residents' forums in black areas. For instance, a major difference is that ratepayers' associations mobilize in sustained ways as opposed to the periodic ways of residents' forums. I argue that the strong financial support ("cheque books") enable this sustained mobilization on the part of ratepayers' associations.

The empirical data is derived from four case studies of ratepayers' associations based in De Aar (Northern Cape), Heilbron (Free State), Riviersonderend (Western Cape), and Sannieshof (North West). Using an interpretive qualitative research approach, the fieldwork was conducted between March 2012 and May 2015, consisting of in-depth interviews with leaders and members of the four ratepayers' associations. In addition, the data is supplemented where necessary, with findings from 30 other ratepayers' associations from across South Africa.

The chapter is divided into three sections. Section one reviews the findings of the other ratepayers' associations in South Africa. The next section focuses on the case studies. Finally, conclusions and suggestions are given in section 3. Generally, I argue the simple dismissal of ratepayers' associations as "anti-government" will prove unsatisfactory as this is fraught with misunderstanding. However, at the time of writing, the leader of the National Taxpayers Union (NTU) was actively involved in campaigns aimed at self-determination, which may lend credence to the assertion that ratepayers' associations regard South Africa under a black-led government as a "failed state". Notwithstanding, I argue that local authorities should explore the possibility of partnering with local civic groups to help improve relations with citizens.

Ratepayers' associations in South Africa

An evaluation of ratepayers' associations involves considering their link to the NTU - an umbrella body with more than 300 community ratepayers' associations across South Africa. As stated earlier, these ratepayers' associations are withholding rates and taxes from municipalities and, in some places, are providing particular municipal services themselves. The associations seem to follow four common steps in establishing their grievances. First, they document their efforts to resolve the problem through engagements with the local municipality in the form of meetings and grievance letters, amongst others. Secondly, if those efforts fail, they declare a dispute with municipalities in terms of existing legislation. Thirdly, they withhold rates and deposit their payments into an interest-bearing account. Fourthly, they provide detailed accounts of these deposits to the municipality" (Multi-Level Government Initiative 2011).

It is interesting to note that the ratepayers' associations which are functional in predominantly white communities are now forging links and supporting others in black communities. As the Chair of the Beacon Bay Ratepayers' and Civic Association (BBRCA) in the Buffalo City Metropolitan Municipality (BCMM) (Eastern Cape Province of South Africa) notes:

> At present there are ten ratepayers' associations [RPAs] in the BCMM area, with an eleventh one in the process of forming – all due to the fact that the residents of BCMM

> are completely fed up with the on-going shenanigans of those who are supposed to be looking after our interests, not to mention the drastic deterioration of our once beautiful seaside town, East London, as well as King Williams Town, Mdantsane, Gonubie and Beacon Bay which all now fall within the BCMM boundaries.... Of the ten RPAs at present, three are made up of residents in the so-called "black" areas, with the eleventh also from a so-called "black" area, so it is not only the whites in our area who are fed up. All the RPAs are non-political and non-racial (as per all our Constitutions) and we only want the services from BCMM to which we are entitled and for which we hand over our hard-earned monies to them each month (Email Interview, April 08, 2013).

The nature of service delivery protests in South Africa is essentially racially oriented. Similarly, culture has been identified by Brigg (2010: 329) as an aspect that matters for peace. He further states "the ways in which individuals and groups make meaning of their social and physical world, and the values, beliefs and processes that are reproduced through this meaning-making, have implications for how conflicts are waged and ... for the ideas and practices that constitute peace".

Considering the profound influence that race has on every aspect of South Africans, it is not surprising to observe the different perspectives and approaches to peacebuilding from different races. As mentioned earlier, the racial composition of the majority of civic groups exemplifies the paradox insofar as "the fight against human injustices of the state", in the words of one community member. In response to the question why protestors resort to violence, the following statements from ratepayers' associations capture the feelings and underlying racial prejudices that could create extreme tension, polarise and threaten the future orientation of civic groups at community level:

> We are not barbaric and hence we choose peaceful ways of finding solutions. But we are clearly not afraid to use violence should it become necessary (Western Cape Ratepayers' association, E-mail interview, April 08, 2013).

> Our culture differs and violence is not part of a civilized culture. We do not believe in violence, but we did protest against poor service delivery... Over the past decades, tax payers have paid for the establishment of expensive and essential infrastructure of our towns and cities for the benefit of everyone - also those who have been bussed in to come and vote. What is the logic of now trying to destroy that (so that everyone is) worse off afterwards? We don't understand the reasoning and actions of people who destroy their own facilities when they are dissatisfied. The laws of this country provide them with all the appropriate avenues to legally force authorities to address their concerns. Why they run into streets and burn down facilities is a mystery. It is barbaric to destroy public facilities that will eventually put you at a disadvantage. It looks like a

political smokescreen. They are destroying the future of their own kids... (Community Forum, Western Cape).

Another noteworthy finding is that there are differences in approaches towards dealing with service delivery protests between two national predominantly white civil society organizations: AfriForum and the National Ratepayers' Association. In the case of the former, their approach is to continuously engage municipalities until a mutually acceptable solution to poor service delivery is found. The latter civil society organization follows a similar approach, but if no solution is found, it declares a dispute with the municipality and then legally withholds money which is paid into a trust account:

> AfriForum is a citizens' organization with integrity and (which is) accountable to its members who always operate within the law and will denounce any action that is against the law. It will be an irreconcilable double standard to expect that local authorities should obey the law if we don't. The withholding of tax is illegal and we don't encourage such action. Our approach is to first establish branch structures in communities. The branches are then registered as interest groups. As soon as a structure has been established in a community, we then obtain inputs from it in respect of challenges in the town or city. We then organize meetings with the municipality where we discuss these challenges and try to set realistic objectives to solve them. We would only consider our constitutional rights when our discussions with the municipality fail. We would then assess what legal recourse we have and only then would we approach the courts (AfriForum, Email Interview, April 08, 2013).

> The National Taxpayers' Association declared a dispute at national level. Subsequently, each participating individual association also declared disputes (based on the national dispute) with municipalities with regards to the stipulations of the municipal legislation. This is an attempt to prevent municipalities, for example, from cutting off electricity to force us to pay the money withheld. Property tax and fixed monthly amounts payable for water and electricity are paid by participating community members into a trust account administered by the ratepayers' association. The association would then provide municipalities with all the necessary proof of payment. In towns where the electricity of members was disconnected, we obtained court orders against the municipalities to reconnect the electricity. In such cases, the municipalities had to pay the legal costs of the association (Chairperson NTU, Email Interview, April 08, 2013).

To preface the discussion of the modus operandi of ratepayers' associations in South Africa, the case of the Dullstroom Ratepayers' Association (DRA) is instructive:

> Dullstroom is a small town in Mpumalanga which exists almost entirely on tourism. In about 2006, the potable water provided by the municipality was extremely discoloured - on occasion it was darker than coffee! The DRA, with a little assistance from the local Chamber of Business, took the matter up with both the local and district municipalities. Later, after a series of meetings between various stakeholders, the

district municipality commissioned a study of the supply and quality of water. The study was conducted by BTW Consulting. The report of BTW indicated some major problems relating to the water treatment plant. To resolve this matter, it was added as an item in the integrated development plan of the municipality. Subsequently, the water treatment plant was upgraded in 2011. Since then, the local citizens have enjoyed potable water of a high standard. A member of the DRA regularly monitors the quarterly reports of the water treatment plant. This is one of the positive outcomes of our engagement with the municipality. However, we still have reservations about the skill levels and commitment of the staff and supervisors responsible for the water treatment plant.

I also asked the chairperson to describe the relationship between the DRA and the local municipality. The following response was given:

> Following a number of perceived irregularities and questionable actions by the municipality during the last few years, the DRA and local business organizations of the four main towns in our municipality formed an organization called the Emakhazeni Good Governance Forum (EGGF) in January 2012. Although the Municipal Council had formally agreed that an Advisory Committee be formed comprising members of the EGGF and the municipality, the municipality was not pulling its weight when dealing with us. As a result, the Advisory Committee became dysfunctional in 2012. At the time, we strongly believed that the Mayor and the Speaker of the Council were behind this. As a result, we requested the MEC for COGTA to intervene and lodged a formal letter of 'No Confidence in Emakhazeni Local Municipality' with them. Our concerns related to the misuse of municipal infrastructure grants, municipal staff pension and medical aid deductions being used by the municipality and not paid to the respective investment companies, numerous versions of the Municipal Budget and IDP documentation and a debtors' book of R85-million (6,234.360.72 USD). We were also concerned by the lack of municipal services in terms of road repairs, and essential stand-by equipment due to the municipality itself being significantly in debt. The situation has not changed! As at February, ELM owed Eskom R8-million (586,857.80 USD), the debtors' book has grown by a further R10-million (733,528.28 USD), there is frequently no diesel available for official vehicles and equipment, and so it goes on. We try to work with the municipality, but the lack of technical expertise among municipal workers has a negative impact on the ability of the municipality to perform optimally. When people ask me why I spend so much time engaging or fighting the municipality, the only valid response I can provide is that the day my colleagues and I decide to keep our mouths shut, things will get worse here (DRA Chairperson, E-mail interview, 08 April, 2013).

Emthanjeni Ratepayers' Association – De Aar

De Aar – the third largest town in the Northern Cape Province of South Africa – is located in the Emthanjeni Local Municipality. The town has a population of 23,760 inhabitants and is renowned for its central location on the main railway line between Johannesburg, Cape Town, Port Elizabeth and Namibia. According to Statistics South Africa (2011), De Aar has a dependency rate of 60, and relatively high basic municipal service coverage. For example, 95.9% of the households have a flush toilet connected to sewerage, 94.2% weekly refuse removal, 73.1% piped water in dwelling, and 95.6% electricity for lighting. In respect of its economy, De Aar has the largest abattoir in the Southern Hemisphere and supplies all the major centres throughout the entire country with the famous "Karoo" lamb and mutton. The Emthanjeni Municipality (2015) reports that the water used in the town comes from boreholes, hence the large number of wind pumps.

The Emthanjeni Ratepayers' Association (ERA) is one of the weaker associations in respect of activism and support from local residents. The association was formed on 10 August 1993 as a result of the widespread practice where local business chambers join hands with other local structures to form a ratepayers' association. The main purpose of the association was to serve as a bargaining forum for the town. An invitation was also sent to the predominantly black community of Nonzwakazi to join the ratepayers' association. However, the chairperson of the De Aar Civic Association – which operates in the black community – indicated that they were already organized and in alliance with the ruling ANC. A marked difference from other ratepayers' associations is that during this infancy stage of the ERA, the local ANC officials made an undertaking to attend all future meetings from October 1993. They attended only two meetings, but later "disappeared" (Chairperson ERA, Interview February 12, 2014).

The main drivers that led to the decision to withhold rates and taxes in De Aar, the chairperson noted, was evidently the incompetence of the local municipality, as well as the deteriorating relationship between residents and the local municipality about several concerns, including the quality of water, dirty streets, sewerage spillage, and the pollution of the river on the outskirts of the town. The Chairperson of ERA reported that, during the early stages of their contestation around 2009, ERA had the support of a large section of the residents. At the time, most residents had lost confidence in the ability of the local municipality to deal with the sewerage spillage and quality of drinking water. He further averred, "I reckon we got the support of the community at the beginning because of the fear that our welfare was at risk". He continued, "Residents did also not take it lightly when they received incorrect bills from the municipality. We actually saw the poor provision of basic services as the failure of local governance" (Chairperson ERA, Interview February 12, 2014).

Concerns about the health hazard posed by the sewerage plant in De Aar was confirmed by the Green Drop Report. The Green Drop is an incentive-based regulation which was introduced by the Department of Water and Sanitation (DWS), previously DWA (Department of Water Affairs) in 2008. The Green Drop measures and compares the results of the performance of Water Service Authority as well as their Water Services Providers and subsequently rewards and/or penalizes the Municipality upon evidence of their excellence and/or failures according to the minimum standards or requirements that has been defined by DWS. The Green Drop measures performance on a percentage scale: 90-100% excellent; 80-<90% good; 50-<60% average; 30-<50% poor; and 0-<30 critical state (Department of Water and Sanitation 2013). In fact, the report also lamented that the sewerage plant was a "high risk" to local water resources and public health. At the time, the Water and Environmental Affairs Minister, Edna Molewa, was greatly concerned about the situation: "I am actually concerned, as political head, that we still have in South Africa … a situation where some of the municipalities are still struggling to get to a level of accounting on the quality of water … in the Eastern Cape,… and in other poorer provinces" (Business Day 2011).

ERA cited a continued distrust of the municipality after it responded erratically to letters and requests for meetings. A common refrain of the municipality in respect of the pollution of the river caused by sewerage spillage was often, according to ERA, "that the impact is not known as no studies have yet been undertaken" or that the "fact of the matter, no municipality in South Africa has control over when main sewer pipes will clog" (Volksblad 2009).

In a letter written in Afrikaans to the ratepayers' association dated June 17, 2008, a local businessman states his anger with the local municipality and the local tourist office, which is wholly funded by the municipality, for being incompetent and arrogant. It is interesting to note that the gist of the complaint was about the website of the local tourist office despite the huge amount of money spent on a private consulting company. According to the businessman, he complained to the municipality about the incorrect information that the tourism office fed to the public, "But to date, which is already six months later, I have only received an acknowledgment of receipt". And he added: "This is how white ratepayers are being treated" (Letter to ERA, 2008).

In response to the question why ERA is supportive of the protest tactic of withholding rates and taxes, in what is evidently an admonition of the mobilization of activists in predominantly black communities, the chairperson points out:

> We are not barbarians, hence, we prefer peaceful means to find solutions. But we are definitely not afraid to use more violent means if it necessary. Despite the almost cynical manner in which our concerns are been dealt with, we strongly believe that withholding rates and taxes is the best legal weapon we can use. Violence is not part of our culture (Chairperson ERA, Interview February 12, 2014).

Thus far, it seems that attitudinal reasons limited the municipality from active engagement with ERA. The official version of the municipality, which absolves it of any wrongdoing, was questioned by ERA. It is in fact, the persistent failure of ERA to obtain any favourable response from the municipality which contributed to disillusionment on the part of some residents, who are no longer as actively involved in the association as before. Nonetheless, ERA continued to seek accountability from the Emthanjeni Municipality and ensure that all residents are treated fairly by municipal officials, regardless of their race and political affiliation.

In 2014, plans by Transnet – a state-owned company that operates as a corporate entity - to dump more than 520 000 tons of asbestos used in railway tracks and quarry mines 300 metres from De Aar were met with anger by the local community and ratepayers' association. ERA claimed that besides the fact that the residents were not properly consulted about the plan, the area has strong winds and Transnet could not guarantee the safety of residents. According to the SABC (2014), the municipality indicated that it did not support the plan. We now look at the Heilbron case.

Heilbron Landowners and Residents' Association (HLRA)

Heilbron has a total population of 5,486, and a dependency ratio of 64,6. Moreover, less than half of the households (45.9%) had flush toilets connected to sewerage, 58% weekly refuse removal, 22.2% piped water inside dwelling, and 63.1% for lighting (Statistics South Africa 2011). Heilbron is part of the Ngwathe Local Municipality, led by the ANC. Broadly, the municipality has the worst unemployment rate within the Fezile Dabi District at 32.3%, a figure which is also above the provincial rate. Most of the affected people are youths. Their GDP growth rate is very slow at an average of 1.7%. The economy of the town is supported by industries such as Clover SA (a leading dairy company) and agriculture yields such as dairy products, maize, sorghum, wheat, sunflowers, beef and mutton. The town further boasts the Riemland wine route with several wine cellars where wine tasting and other activities can be undertaken (Ngwathe Local Municipality 2015).

The Heilbron Landowners and Residents' Association (HLRA) was established in 1993, but only became much more active in 2008. HLRA followed in the steps of its predecessor, Action Heilbron, which was established in 2001. Action Heilbron has also, on several occasions, brought to the attention of the Municipal Manager, the Mayor and the Unit Manager of Heilbron, the problems regarding the performance of the Municipality in Heilbron, without any success. HLRA is a diverse and apolitical organization, "formed with the aim of not being confrontational, but supportive of the local municipality", according to its leader. The association consists of various arms, including the ratepayers' association (which already existed during the apartheid political dispensation), a law association (which focuses primarily on hawker regulations and municipal-related matters), culture and arts, wine tasting, and marketing (responsible for beautifying the town). The association has an annual day-long town festival where all the different arms of the civic association participate in different activities. Sadly, many of the other arms have disintegrated and only the ratepayers' association remains active (Chairwoman HLRA, Interview March 31, 2014).

In December 2008, HLRA declared a dispute with the Ngwathe Municipality because of poor service delivery. Other grievances cited in the memoranda and letters of the HLRA included potholes in roads, lack of maintenance of public spaces and gardens, increasing numbers of illegal informal hawkers on the pavements of the central business district, casual jobseekers who do not have access to ablution facilities, the inability of the sewerage system to cope with the present load, and the non-maintenance of electricity infrastructure. The dispute was declared after HLRA notified the municipality in writing in November 2008 about the grievances of the residents and demanded an action plan, failing which the association would continue with its planned legal action. In part the Dispute Declaration letter states:

As appears from the above [reference to previous unsuccessful discussions between the residents and the municipality], no progress was made over the last seven years to attend to the concerns, complaints and problems of the inhabitants of Heilbron. This failure has led to the formation of the Heilbron Landowners' and Residents' Association. The Association accordingly hereby directs an urgent request to the Municipality to immediately attend to the above concerns and to furnish the Association with a written plan of action as to how the Municipality intends to attend to the grievances of the inhabitants of Heilbron before 28 November 2008. Please note that a Local Government is by Law compelled to render services to the inhabitants of its area. Service Delivery is not an optional responsibility of a Council but a legal requirement with which a Council must comply. In our opinion Ngwathe Municipality is clearly not achieving this (HRLA Letter dated November 04, 2008).

Instead of responding to the letter of the HRLA, the municipality stated that "we can cooperate, but cannot co-rule", according to the association. The municipality nonetheless convened a meeting with HLRA in February 2009, where it tabled a reaction plan – titled Action Plan: Service Delivery – as a response to the dispute declaration. Subsequently, "an Action Steering Committee consisting of various community stakeholders and the municipality was formed to implement a Rehabilitation Plan, which is based on the municipality's Action Plan: Service Delivery" (HLRA Committee member, Interview March 31, 2014).

The Chairwoman of HLRA emphasized that when the implementation of the Rehabilitation Plan was due to begin in April 2009, they realized that the municipality did not have the money to fund the different projects. In what would be met with fierce disapproval by the municipality, the association attempted to source funding by organising meetings with representatives of the then national Department of Water Affairs and Forestry, the municipality, and the councillors as observers. At the beginning of the meeting in May 2009, the Municipal Manager incorrectly declared that since it was a political meeting, he and his delegation were leaving. As a direct result of the attitude of the municipality, HRLA then expanded its original dispute declaration by citing that its members would, henceforth, pay the total money owed to the municipality into a trust account. HLRA would then only pay over the portion for services charged to the municipality, but withhold the money for rates and sanitation. HLRA then planned to use this money to implement the Rehabilitation Plan. The municipality once again did not respond (Interview March 31, 2014). "Since then", another HLRA member stated, "The municipality has been treating us as a white organization obsessed with finding fault with a black government" (HLRA Committee member, Interview March 31, 2014).

In the ensuing five-year long *strife* against the municipality (at the time of the interviews in March 2014), dominated by attempts by the ratepayers' association to implement the Rehabilitation Plan, the municipality responded by using intimidation tactics such as switching off the electricity supply of residents who had not paid the full amount on their municipal bills. The association took this matter to court and won an interdict against the council to prevent electricity cut-offs in the case of disputes. The legal costs that the municipality had to pay were almost R100 000 (7,336.19 USD). At the time, the response of the national Department of Co-operative Governance and Traditional Affairs was that, "Withholding rates was illegal" and that "Such action is illegal but the department has taken the route of engaging with the associations" (Masondo 2011).

Interestingly, there has been a drastic decline in the number of households that support the HLRA. For instance, in 2009 more than 130 households were members of HLRA, this decreased to 110 in 2012, and ultimately 50 households in 2014. When asked what could be the possible reason for this sharp decline in the support of the ratepayers' association, the Chairwoman remarked, "We are a legal organization that does not believe in throwing stones and destroying facilities and properties. Many residents were not patient enough, and may have thought that it was a waste of time to engage an obviously intransigent institution" (Interview March 31, 2014).

In response to the question of in what ways the HLRA has been successful, the Chairwoman of the association stated that the HLRA has proven that it is not a safe haven for rate defaulters as it does not accept any application for membership from residents whose municipal accounts are in arrears. Some of the major successes of the association, according to its leaders, are that the Ngwathe Municipality had no choice but to acknowledge that their inept, incompetent and unsatisfactory service does not meet with the residents' approval, the rebuilding of Long Street (a main street in Heilbron), financed by the Provincial Government, the upgrading of the sewerage works, and the recovery of the leaking water reservoirs in Heilbron, financed by Rand Water Board.

Moreover, the ratepayers' association managed to raise awareness of the concerns of both white and black residents as various regional, provincial and national government units have started to deal with some of the most pressing concerns of residents. There is also a real sense of urgency on the part of the municipality in dealing with potholes, unlike in the past when this took more than two years.

Riviersonderend Ratepayers' Association

Riviersonderend is an Afrikaans word meaning "river without end". The area is named after the Sonderend River at the foot of the Sonderend Mountains, and the settlement is a small farming village with a peaceful rural atmosphere, situated on the main Garden Route, approximately 160 km away from Cape Town. , and surrounded by farms. The town has a population of 5,245 and a dependency ratio of 54.5. The town has a high basic service delivery record: Flush toilet connected to sewerage (93.6%); weekly refuse removal (98.7%), piped water inside dwelling (88%), and electricity for lighting (94%).

The emergence of the Riviersonderend Ratepayers' Association

The Riviersonderend Ratepayers' Association (RRA) saw the light after numerous complaints by residents who raised concerns about the general deterioration of the town from disrepair to downright degradation. The chairman of RRA believes that as more and more residents became aware during "their gossip sessions over coffee" – an inescapable character of small towns – that their concerns were widespread, and so a decision was taken that these concerns should be tackled in a collective manner. The civic group contributes R1 000 (73.3720 USD) annual membership fee to the National Taxpayers' Union, taken from the contributions made by local members (Chairperson RRA, Interview March 26, 2015).

At the time, one of the main grievances that the RRA wanted the local authorities to address were, first and foremost, the dispute about the gap between the revenue received from residents of Riviersonderend and the amount of money spent on the development of the town. According to the chairperson of RRA, the town has a 96% rate of payment compared to the average of 14% for Grabouw (one of the case study areas discussed in the previous chapter). Thus, the RRA concluded that the local residents were subsidizing the development of poor paying areas such as Grabouw. The latter town was also blamed for being a haven for jobseekers from other provinces, resulting in the constant creation of new informal settlement areas.

A major concern for the RRA in this regard was the dumping of sewerage into the river by the informal settlers, with the resultant negative impacts on farming and the ecosystem in the region.

A second major grievance was the alleged "deliberate failure by the local municipality to maintain infrastructure until it becomes a budget item". This was apparently a ploy to ensure that tenders were available to the existing patronage system of the local and provincial political elite. The third grievance, and one of the causes of much outrage among residents, was the dirty water provided to households. In fact, the RRA blamed the high prevalence of cancer among residents in the town on the high chlorine content of the water. In spite of various attempts over a considerable period of time to get the municipality to address the issue about the quality of water, including a request to the South African Public Protector and the Human Rights' Commission, the matter remained unresolved (Committee member RRA, Interview March 26, 2015). The following excerpts aptly capture the animosity between the ratepayers' association and the municipality:

> In the complaint on water quality in Riviersonderend, Clive Sandenbergh, chairman of the ratepayers' association, submitted test results which show that in 2011 water tested from the Sonderend pump station contained high levels of E.coli and coliform – both dangerous bacteria. According to Sandenbergh sewerage spills from towns upstream filter into the town's drinking water along with animal manure from nearby farms. However, the town's second water source, the Olifants River, is not being used because of a damaged pipeline. The R1.6 million (73,802.96 USD) allocated for repairing it has allegedly been used for other projects. Sandenbergh has also complained that the flocculent which is being used to settle silt in the Sonderend River contains aluminium. "Unfortunately, the aluminium ends up in our drinking water. Prolonged exposure, longer than a year, has been implicated in chronic neurological disorders such as dementia and Alzheimer's", he says. However the municipality denies that there is any problem with the water. "We can honestly confirm that we have not received any complaints from the Human Rights' Commission and we are not aware of any water problems in Riviersonderend. We will investigate and respond to the Human Rights' Commission as soon as we receive such written complaints from them", said municipal spokesman Stiffie Cronje (Hawker 2013).

Subsequently, the RRA were sent from "pillar to post" by the municipality. The local municipal officials' response to the demands of RRA ranged from, "You think you are governing this town" to "Attention-seeking murmurs from an old age home" (in an apparent sarcastic reference to the high number of pensioners in the town). Of particular concern to the RRA, was that the attitude of the Theewaterskloof Municipal and Provincial Government officials had proven that the "DA is a diluted version of the ANC with regards to the handling of the grievances of citizens". According to the chairperson of the RRA, the attitude of the municipality could be summarised as a local authority that shifted from "a position as provider of basic services to a parasitic relationship where the local political elite enrich themselves by exorbitant salaries and above-inflation annual increases" (Committee member RRA, Interview March 26, 2015).

Echoing the above, the Chairperson of RRA stated:

> We know that we are a poor community, but do we really have to be reminded of this each time we approach the municipality to assist us to initiate poverty alleviation projects? This is a difficult story to swallow especially when our Municipal Manager receives a salary of R143, 000.00 (10,493.26) per month. Note I said 'receives' and not 'earns' because he does not deserve that. He is paid more than the President of Japan ... But we are 'a poor municipality'. This is the foremost reason behind the widespread dissatisfaction among residents. It is actually a case of Rome burns while Nero plays his violin... (Chairperson RRA, Interview March 26, 2015).

Notwithstanding the RRA's lofty goal of making Riviersonderend attractive to tourists passing through the town and ensuring safe water provision to residents, the civic group never planned to undermine the authority of the municipality. The group's chairperson cited that there is a real problem with the way community voices are being heard by the political elite. The attitude of the local municipal officials and municipal manager, the chairperson, noted, is against the "the fundamental cornerstones of community trust-building by failing to fulfil their duties". Seemingly, the toxic relations with the municipality worked to the advantage of the RRA. The RRA used the unresponsiveness of the municipality in its mobilization strategy to frame apathetic residents. As a result, the membership of the civic group rose from 20 members in 2008 to 250 members in 2015 (Chairperson RRA, Interview March 26, 2015).

From the RRA's point of view, withholding rates and taxes is based on the common law principle that if one party does not perform, the other party does not need to perform. However, the group regards itself as consisting of law-abiding citizens of South Africa who have faith that the Constitutional Court will support their plight should they approach it. Should this attempt fail, then the community will have to look to alternative means to "protect our own rights", a RRA Committee member noted. She continued, "We see violence only as a last option. A lot of money is recklessly squandered by the destruction of equipment, vehicles and buildings during protests in other areas. It is taxpayers who will have to fund the replacements" (Committee member RRA, Interview March 26, 2015). The chairperson added, "We are mostly a community with a Christian Calvinistic background. We believe in the inherent goodness of all people. However, if we are once again told we are wrong, we will simply have to proceed to the barbaric and uncivilized option to expel the municipality by force".

The RRA claims that thus far (at the time of interviews in March 2015), they had "only received crumbs from the municipality in an attempt to appease the displeasure of residents". For example, the chairperson stated that he was representing the white community of the town in a ward committee consisting of ten members. However, all his suggestions are often ignored during meetings without due consideration. I further observed from several documentations of the civic group, and as confirmed during the interviews as well, that the RRA will continue to proactively engage the municipality in three related areas of concern. These areas of concern are citizen participation, municipal responsiveness, and equitable spending on the local development of the various towns within the municipality.

According to the RRA, "the biggest problem we have with Theewaterskloof Municipality is that the system is driven by politics". A possible solution for many of the challenges faced by municipalities across South Africa, according to the RRA, is that building trust between municipalities and the citizens they serve can only be achieved when the power to make decisions at local government level is transferred from political parties to taxpaying local citizens. The next case is of Sannieshof in the North West Province of South Africa.

Sannieshof Residents and Ratepayers' Association

Sannieshof is a small train stop and farming town in the middle of the North West Province's maize farming belt, in a vast rural area called the 'Stellaland' (Star Land) or 'Platteland' (Flat Land), and is known for its massive bank of grain silos and plant nurseries. The town, which started as a post office to serve the farms in the district, was named in honour of the first postmaster, John Voorendijk's wife Sannie, and now forms part of the Tswaing Local Municipality. The main economic sectors are agriculture and small-scale mining. Furthermore, the town has a population in excess of 11 000, a dependency rate of 71.2, flush toilets connected to sewerage (57.9%), weekly refuse removal (55%), electricity for lighting (67.2%), and an extremely low connection of piped water inside dwellings (22%) (Statistics South Africa 2011). Of special note, is that most of the Sannieshof households are not connected to the sewerage system. The municipality is expected to extract the sewerage at least once a week.

The emergence of and grievances of the Sannieshof Residents and Ratepayers' Association

Sannieshof Residents and Ratepayers' Association (SRRA) is one of the more acclaimed ratepayers' associations due to its pioneering role in the mobilization of residents in predominantly white communities of South Africa. The association is popularly known by its Afrikaans acronym, SIBU (Sannieshof Inwoners en Belastingbetalers Unie). For this reason, I am using the acronym SIBU, instead of SRRA.

The initial footprints of SIBU can be traced to mid-2005. At the time, the local Afrikaans Business Chamber served as an organization that promoted the interests of local residents. Long before the formation of SIBU, the concerns in the town were about the local municipality's apparent inability to deal with challenges related to the local water purification plant, the provision of safe and reliable supply of household water, and the erratic sewerage extraction from households. Similarly, potable drinking water and sanitation issues dominated the concerns of SIBU (Gouws et al. 2010).

During its infancy stages, SIBU was led by what the media described as "a dynamic woman" Carin Venter. SIBU was formally established in April 2008 after residents of the town had been exposed to an unbearable smell due to the high number of sewer blockages since 2004.

Mobilization stage

A critical event that would set the mobilization machinery of SIBU in motion was when the municipality's tractor used for the extraction of sewerage from household septic tanks broke down in 2005. Sannieshof residents were repeatedly without sewerage services, with the longest period lasting more than seven weeks. The sewerage system disintegrated and, consequently, sewerage bubbled from septic tanks and even flowed from toilets. Drinking water and boreholes became contaminated as a result (Chairperson of SIBU, Interview March 02, 2012).

The sewerage crisis was followed by another one: the erratic supply of potable due to problems with water pipes which the municipality claimed it did not have the money to fix. The residents then decided they need to take proactive action through SIBU, which was provided office space by the local business chamber (SIBU member, Interview March 02, 2012). At this stage, a complete breakdown in trust between the residents and the local municipality was already evident. What later ensued would be a nine-year long strife by SIBU against the local municipality. The strife of the ratepayers' association was dominated by writing letters, and organising meetings with various government entities, including going the legal route on two occasions.

As indicated earlier, the protest tactic in the predominantly white community was primarily that of withholding (or the refusal to pay) municipal rates and taxes directly to the local municipality, as legally required. In November 2007, together with two other ratepayer associations of neighbouring towns, SIBU declared a legal dispute with the municipality (Gouws et al. 2010). This was the culmination of several failed meetings, and formal correspondence about the quality of drinking water, corruption, and faulty municipal accounts, was all of which had been repeatedly ignored by the municipality (Slabbert 2008).

Henceforth, SIBU's members paid their municipal bills directly into a trust bank account managed by the group. SIBU then pays only the water and electricity bills of each member directly to the municipality, whilst the portion for rates and taxes was retained in the trust account. In what would resemble a parallel municipality, SIBU used a portion of the funds in its trust account to finance essential municipal services, appointed its own employees to clean the town streets, maintain graveyards, and repair street lights. The five employees were supported by a team of volunteers, whilst the streets of the town have been kept clean by a local garden cleaning Service Company hired by SIBU. Between November 2007 and February 2013 an amount of approximately R1 million (73,362.94 USD) was withheld. SIBU's chairperson avers, "We have respect for the rule of law, but for us, this is the only peaceful means available to us" (Chairperson of SIBU, Interview March 02, 2012).

As the impasse intensified, an interesting debate between the former Chairwoman of SIBU and the Director of Technical Services at Tswaing Municipality, was published in an online Afrikaans journal. This debate is indicative of the growing gulf and trust-deficit between the ratepayers' association and the municipality. The debate in part reads:

> **SIBU**: This is about work that needs to be done, workers who are hardly at work, tractors have not been present, tractors and suction dredgers which are constantly left broken in workshops, water pumps which are not constantly maintained due to years of neglect, garbage that is not removed.... And sewerage that is only extracted once residents pay bribes to municipal workers, reporting broken water and electricity meters over a period of 8 years without any response, and the perennial leakage of water through pipes that are hardly repaired...the list could continue .... SIBU tried to work with the Director for a year, but he was negative from the outset about our involvement and action. ... On the contrary, why is our work in and around the town suddenly a problem? The outstanding bills we paid on behalf Tswaing, water pumps, tractors, wagons that we fixed, the garbage we removed daily .... This was acceptable over a period of 18 months... Similarly, the municipal manager undertook to repay SIBU the money it paid for the new pump of the sewerage works - it never happened.

> **Municipal Director:** The fact of the matter is that Mrs. Carin Visser openly 'declared war' during the trespassing court case against her and (is) doing everything in her power to prove her point in the media. If she was really so worried about the state of affairs, which had already been out of order five years ago, then it is clear that I am not being provided the opportunity to resolve their problems ... They were requested several times not to take the law into their own hands, because I was frantically working towards addressing their concerns (Roodt 2009).

Meanwhile the municipality started to threaten residents whose accounts were in arrears with legal action. This never occurred, but the former chairperson of SIBU was later arrested and charged for trespassing on municipal property after she went to acquaint herself with the situation at the local water and sewerage treatment plant. The case was dismissed in court and SIBU remained steadfast in their approach. For instance, the current chairperson noted:

> There cannot be any doubt about our approach as we declared a legal dispute. Our action is legal because we declared our dispute in writing. In fact, it is unconstitutional to expect us to pay for services that we do not receive. We, however, pay the money individual members owe over to the municipality. We are not an organization of defaulters. This community trusts us because we have a reliable system. Our books are kept by people with accounting skills (Chairperson of SIBU, Interview March 02, 2012).

In response to the questions of why this specific protest tactic was used and not the widely known public protests used in predominantly black communities, the current chairperson avers:

> Politics used to be a topical issue that dominated almost all conversations in the past in South Africa. These days we do not talk politics. Instead, we are asking questions. And one of the most pertinent questions asked is, where is this country going? If the ANC

does a good job in governing this country, led them rule for as long as they can. But when weak local government institutions are failing communal life, it creates the context for protest action. The culture of white South Africans is this: 'If you have a car and it is not broken, you will not go and deliberately devise means to break it. This is where we differ from other communities. We don't break what we have built' (Chairperson of SIBU, Interview March 02, 2012).

Discussions and conclusions

A peculiar feature of the South African local government system is its stable legal and institutional environment. Moreover, over the past two decades, core municipal systems and processes for delivering basic services have been established and consolidated. Today, it seems the local government's key challenge is not a lack of legislation or policies, but their implementation.

This chapter highlights how ratepayer associations in predominantly white communities amplify and channel the concerns of residents. Race, it appears, remains a contentious and ambiguous issue in the relationship between municipalities and ratepayer associations. In the context of this chapter, race as Peens (2012; 38) noted, "is materially embedded in people's experience of place". Thus, the actions of ratepayers' associations in predominantly white communities have led to heavily antagonistic relations with the government. In fact, these civic groups are generally regarded as groups of white people who are openly showing disrespect to a democratically elected black government.

While I acknowledge the potential strain that ratepayers' associations can put on the budgets of municipalities, this is actually not true, as the official response from various municipalities asserts that ratepayers' associations are primarily driven by the race-based ideology of undermining a so-called "black government". In fact, I contend that insufficient attention has been given to the plight of these civic groups in general, and their potential further contributions, in particular.

Furthermore, even if some of these groups may still harbour rather romanticized attachments to the old political dispensation in South Africa, the evidence presented here, illustrates the enduring strife of residents in predominantly white communities, as in the case of black communities, over the quality of potable water, sanitation, and broadly, the general deterioration of areas in which case studies were conducted.

Unlike civic groups in predominantly black communities, ratepayers' associations have access to both financial capital (albeit out of their own pockets) and a strong support base. For example, by affiliating to the National Taxpayers' Association, local associations receive vital publicity and support. Since most of these associations are led by "gifted" professionals, they also manage to generate significant media interest.

The experience of these cases also shows us that ratepayer associations have much more choices available once the pendulum of trust has tilted towards complete distrust at local government level. For example, in the case of Riviersonderend, the ratepayers' associations used the Promotion of Access to Information Act 2000 to pressurize the municipality to provide it with access to several forms of documentation it initially refused to release. Similarly, in the Heilbron case study, the association remained steadfast in its fight to ensure that the municipality implement the Rehabilitation Plan agreed upon after winning a court case against them.

Broadly, though, the foregoing arguments should be treated in the context that municipalities are facing serious challenges. A useful lesson for ratepayers' associations seeking to lobby and engage with local authorities is to be aware of the political environment that exists.

Yet despite the fact that the rise and prominence of ratepayers' associations has generated tensions at local government level, they are useful for several reasons. Here, the Sannieshof case – where SIBU has paid for the repair of equipment – demonstrates the positive contribution ratepayers' associations could make.

It would be reasonable to conclude that proactively engaging and building rapport with ratepayers' associations will provide municipalities with more opportunities to resolve local issues. However, the race 'blame game' not only blunts this opportunity, but compounds the historical and racial stereotypes in South Africa. Furthermore, the study of ratepayers' associations may contribute to the debates in international literature on nonviolent community strife as exemplified in studies by Chenoweth and Stephan (2011) and Nepstad (2011).

Chapter 6: Conclusions: The implications and future of community protests in South Africa and beyond

Introduction

The post-apartheid history of the South African local government system has always been fraught with difficulties. Some of the well-known initial challenges faced by the system post-apartheid was to transform the former, fragmented system into a much more representative one. Undoubtedly, the responsibilities and challenges faced by local municipalities have also changed profoundly since 1994. These responsibilities and challenges ranged from decentralization, to poverty eradication, to improving citizens' quality of life (Gordon, Roberts and Struwig 2015).

Today, municipalities are at the coalface of an era characterised by widespread attempts by the political elite to advance or safeguard their interests. Against this backdrop, this concluding chapter provides a synopsis on the dynamics of community protests in South Africa. Twelve years since the outbreak of the first community protests in 2004, there have been significant shifts in the mobilization tactics of civic groups in their strife against municipalities for better services. Similarly, government responses to community protests are highly diverse across provinces. At national level, the shift is more glaring: from the non-negotiable approach involving police who acted brutally against protestors during the Thabo Mbeki era, to the various attempts to enhance the current Jacob Zuma dispensation (Duncan 2012).

Broadly, this chapter draws connections between the chapters of the book. It underscores how civic actors in predominantly black communities are labelled as agent provocateurs aimed at destabilizing the country. Conversely, it further shows how ratepayers' associations are perceived as groups of white elitists undermining the ANC – led government. I conclude that civic groups can offer valuable support to municipalities, however, the trend of closing down schools or even burning them down during community protests in predominantly black communities should be condemned.

Civic groups – similar grievances, but different mobilization tactics

The growing influence of neighbourhood activism marks a transition in the political culture from a milieu where political actors and institutions take decisions on behalf of their constitutions, to the realization that building lasting relationships of trust with local communities is the way to go. In practice, civic groups exhibit several similarities and differences. In respect of similarities, the shared identities (set of economic and sociodemographic structural conditions) and distinctiveness of residents in both predominantly black and white communities provides them with what social movement scholars (Libach 2003) refer to as the basis for organizational mobilization.

Generally, community protests in South Africa in comparison to protests in, for example Armenia, Burundi, Brazil, Japan, and Venezuela (Carothers and Youngs 2015), are relatively small-scale events focusing on locality-specific micro-level issues. Yet they not only constitute a highly significant event but have far-reaching effects as well. However, the question still remains: What incentives motivate community groups with a fundamentally similar set of grievances to embark on completely different protest tactics?

The answer lies in both the structure and resources available to the civic groups. This is summarised in the following table.
Table 3 shows that ratepayers' associations in South Africa are highly structured and coordinated; and with a clearly defined leadership. In respect of mobilization resources, ratepayer associations have access to much more extensive resources, ranging from financial support, some skilled professionals as members, and the support of a national association. These resources provide the means and impetus for effective mobilization. Perhaps, this support base, together with the "voluntarist" engagement, as Coelho and Venkat (2009:358) note, are possible reasons for the longevity of ratepayer associations in South Africa. Conversely, several studies of community protests in South Africa (Alexander 2012; Langa and von Holdt 2012; Matebesi and Botes, forthcoming; Ngwane 2012) suggest that residents' forums in predominantly black communities are more sporadic.
And as Carothers and Youngs (2015) note, evidence from this study also suggests that in a few cases, for example in Sannieshof and Heilbron, the ratepayers' associations built on the organizational work of existing civic bodies such as local business forums. Conversely, residents' forums in predominantly black communities (which are largely localities of frugal existence), are more spontaneous, highly fragmented; with weak authority struc-

tures.

Table 3: Structure and mobilization tactics of civic groups in South Africa

Variable	Ratepayers' Associations	Residents' forums/Concerned groups
Community Structure	Predominantly white communities. Highly structured and coordinated. Clearly defined leadership. Affiliated to a national body.	Predominantly black communities. Spontaneous. Highly fragmented. Weak authority structures.
Leadership	Strong leader ties increases survival	Weak leader ties
Goals	Demands for basic municipal service provision, including a range of other services.	Demands for basic municipal service provision, including a range of other services.
Mobilization	Weakly tied networks coordinated through well-developed communication networks. The latter offsets the weakly tied networks.	Dense networks provide channels for recruiting participants for collective action.
Tactics	Nonviolent: Letters, petitions, engaging with Provincial and National Government Departments, Chapter Nine Institutions, or courts of law.	Nonviolent to violent: Nonviolent: Letters, memorandums, protest marches, engaging with Provincial and National Government Departments, Chapter Nine Institutions. Violent: Using or involving the use of physical force to cause harm or damage to someone or something, including high levels of intimidation, forceful closure of schools, the destruction of public and private properties, and shooting of police at protestors.

Source: Author's material

It is also interesting to consider the violent nature of community protests in South Africa. Historically, between 1976 and 1991, black South Africans had no rights to public assembly due to a blanket ban on all open-air gatherings. "Nevertheless demonstrations and protests by the black community", Jarman et al. (1998) contend, "were widespread and frequently ended in violent confrontation with the South African Police Force". Currently, there is a growing chorus of proponents who claim that violence has become endemic in community protests in black neighborhoods. Von Holdt (2011:7), along with others, argues about "the use of violence in political and social disputes to buttress local power".

A recent report by the South African Research Chair in Social Change at the University of Johannesburg provides useful insights into the protests in general in South Africa. The reports note that protests in this country are not necessarily more violent than in others. This report, however, is based on analysis records of the South African Police Services Incident Registration Information System (IRIS) (Runciman et al. 2016). The IRIS system, I contend, records all protest actions which are beyond the scope of the notion of community protests in the context of this book.

Undoubtedly, community protests have now become overt actions that affirmatively encourage violence, as well creating a political environment at local level that promotes a discourse of distrust and social disintegration. As frustration sets in among the politically awakened citizens of the 21st century, more radical tendencies grow within the organizations. The radical leanings, among others, of the citizens are informed by what Jakes (2015:102) calls "life's default settings". He further notes that societies are caught in a dysfunctional default setting of violent engagement – a cyclical trap that is endured by generation after generation".

Seemingly, as evidence from this study suggests, a new cyclical trap embedded within community protests in black communities is the disruption of schools and the explicit preventing of learners from attending school. This trend is a cause for concern and, as with all social pathologies, arresting this trend requires an active citizenry. However, it is encouraging to note that the South African Human Rights' Commission (*see text box below*) recently held three days of hearings on the impact throughout the country of community protests on the right to access basic education (South African Human Rights Commission 2016).

Political trust, participatory local governance and community protests

The level of political trust in local governance political actors and institutions is a key outcome related to direct experiences with the political system. As noted in chapter 2, a major difference between the two dominant theoretical traditions of political trust - institutional and cultural theories – is that trust is regarded as a thoroughly cognitive phenomenon that depends on the knowledge and beliefs citizens have about particular institutions and actors (Kong 2014 Shaleva 2015) in the case of the former, while cultural theories emphasize that trust is based on attitudes regarding values learned early in life (Putnam 2000). A major convergence of both traditions is that trust is framed as a response to direct experience with political actors and institutions.

Determinants of political trust at community level

Community protests are situated within an intricate nexus of trust, actors (political as well as civil), and institutions. In an economic and racially segmented society like South Africa, the trust/ties will be different. For instance, one group of residents may exhibit higher levels of trust towards local political actors and institutions, while others might have strong distrust due to ethnic affiliation or racial differences. However, here the pendulum will usually be applicable to the people with low levels of trust in the political system: their views of the system change due to a lack of service delivery.

Another determinant of trust is immigration. According to Putnam (2000), when there is migration on a large scale, it not only breaks the trust between migrants and hosts, but also among the host population. The impact of large scale urbanization is well known. For example, the Grabouw case study shows how the rapidly growing backlogs due to substantial migrant jobseekers play a role in ethnic tension and community protests. Similarly, Brosché (2015:4) claims that major drivers of communal conflicts in which thousands of people have been killed in three Sudanese regions (Darfur, Eastern Sudan and Greater Upper Nile) are not only based on ethnic and religious identity, but the "dividing line between the 'original' inhabitants of an area and more 'recent' settlers.

A third determinant of political trust and, later on, community protests is grievances. Grievances alone, however, are not enough to motivate communities to embark on protests. Karl-Dieter Opp's (2009) structural-cognitive model discussed in chapter 2 suggests that care must first be taken to translate the individual grievances of residents (a micro cognitive phenomenon that something is wrong or needs to be addressed) into collective action (a macro activity). I argue, cautiously though, that the political opportunity structure, which is an important component in the mobilization process (Della Porta 2015), in South Africa is more conducive to popular participation. However, this situation may change, as also predicted by Duncan (2012), as soon as community protests constitute a real threat to the political status quo.

One of my overarching premises is that community protests are not sudden events "helicoptered" into local communities. Together with an array of locality-specific grievances (with access to and the quality of potable water and roads taking centre-stage), it is often a heightened sense of collective grievance due to low levels of trust in the abilities and willingness of local authorities to deal with their concerns over basic needs and conditions of dignified living, that leads to community protests.

What is of consequence is when residents distrust local political actors and institutions. This distrust manifests itself over a considerable period; as exemplified by the documentary evidence of attempts to engage with the political system by the various case study groups, and as a result little to no attention is given to citizens' concerns. It is only "when the smoke calls" (Von Holdt et al. 2011) that the state responds. In such situations of distrust, citizens are less likely to cooperate with public actors or institutions (Gordon et al. 2015).

A novel finding in respect of political trust that needs further research is the association between the perceived bias of political actors in availing crucial opportunities to certain powerful protest organizers and recurrent community protests. A possible explanation behind this, as will be seen later, is the desire to decrease the threat that some protest organizers pose. Thus, the aftermath of the protests in the Ficksburg case has engendered a wave of suspicion and distrust among community members that the silence of the leaders of the civic organizations has been bought by the local municipality. On the other hand, a common refrain among protest organizers in the Ganyesa and Kuruman cases was that they were motivated by previous protest leaders who have subsequently been employed by the local municipality.

It should be noted, though, that there are two distinct schools of thought on the linkage of civic group leaders and the polity during or in the aftermath of protests. The first, supported by McAdam (1999), believe that social movements use their pre-existing networks to pursue their transformative agenda by working closely with government leaders and their programmes. The proponents of this school of thought argue that cooperation, as in the case of the Community Councils in Venezuela (Bean 2015), the indigenous and peasant organizations in Bolivia (Shoaei 2012), and the unemployed "*piquetero*" movements in Argentina (Miettunen 2015), captures the political significance of the pressing survival needs of civic actors: a response to the concrete material demands of their constituents.

The second school of thought has many constructs but a notable consensus among its different proponents is that cooperation with the government and inclusion in political structures are signs that civic groups are losing their transformative and reformist agenda. For instance, neutralization is known as the type of cooptation where protest leaders are recognized but do not obtain benefits for their individual leaders or their constituents. Overall, the term may also imply that the leaders are "sell-outs" and easily duped (Lapegna 2014).

While each school of thought has merit and evidence to support its claims, this study shows that the lack of trust in protest leaders is a potential driver of recurrent protests. This lack of trust, Chen (2015) argues, is due to a large extent to the special position that protest leaders are usually situated in: among others, they inspire commitment, mobilize resources, frame demands and influence outcomes. As Chen (2015:133,-134) further notes, protest leaders:

> Need to assume high risk and costs. And at the same time (they) are often rewarded for their leadership role. While high rewards can attract potential leaders and activists to take the leadership position, they can also possibly raise their followers' suspicions…. Such mistrust can severely damage the momentum of popular mobilization.

The problem of political power and political trust

Municipalities are often stymied by the power of local, provincial, and national levels of government. Local municipalities have limited financial resources and are thus over-dependent on grants from the central government. Consequently, there is some allegiance to the national government. The same can be said about provincial governments. This study found that on the days of protests, provincial government officials will often visit the affected community and address protestors. At times promises are made without the knowledge of the local municipality. When these promises are not met, residents target the local municipality.

You may recall that I mentioned earlier about a general concern about the annual audit reports of municipalities by the Auditor-General in South Africa. At the beginning of June 2016, the Auditor-General, Kimi Makwetu, released the consolidated general report on municipal audit outcomes for the 272 South African municipalities. Makwetu emphasized the benefits of good governance, including proper financial controls and debt collection in the administration of local government. Responses that laud the report, for example one by SALGA, that "we are beginning to see positive changes"

(Selebano 2016:2) are disheartening. For example, the leader of the Mountain View/Suiderberg ratepayers' association in the Western Cape Province of South Africa cautions:

> The Government must act tougher (sic) and acknowledge that (there are) cadres in senior positions in local municipalities. The Ministers of Local Government and National Treasury should stop ignoring complaints that are accompanied by evidence, but press charges against municipal officials who are involved in corrupt activities. They should have the conviction to actually take action. We get the feeling that they [the Ministers] hope that things will get better without them having to act against wrongdoers. They do not have the courage to act... The utter disdain for financial prudency shown by local councils will never cease as long as the laissez faire attitude of the government and the bullying of municipal officials by politicians do not end. Downplaying serious cases of financial mismanagement is a central element of political impunity. A government that does not want to recognize the implications of this on local livelihoods is nothing but a shame (E-mail interview, 08 April, 2013).

Qualified audit reports are nothing but euphemisms for the blatant flaunting of the Public Financial Management Act (PFMA). This endemic characteristic of local government finances is also not an oversight. It is a conscious ploy to maximize the personal financial interests of political and executive actors in the short-term, regardless of the long-term damage to the image of local governance in general, and the inability to transform the lives of local residents. This situation might have been acceptable during the early stages of the post-apartheid era, however, in an era of characterised by rising expectations, trust in local authorities cannot be warranted when local councils fail to monitor the budgets of municipalities regularly. The significance of this is that "trust that is warranted contributes to the foundation of a good society. It helps people to thrive through healthy cooperation with others and to be morally mature human beings" (McLeod 2015).

A remarkable fact about the responsibility of higher tiers of government towards local governments is the intricate link between fiscal resources of provinces and patronage relationship at this level. While the functioning of political elites who, according to Atkinson (2015:51) "relish their role as national king-makers and regional potentates ... does not necessarily prefigure administrative collapse", there are several implications on both the polity and civil society. First, officials at provincial and municipal level as well as partisan members with aspirations of leadership or senior positions within the political system often jostle to appease provincial elites. This situation is further perpetuated by the elitists who have positioned themselves as purveyors of a specific set of moral values. Second, this creates an environment where political subordinates are bludgeoned to toe the line or else be thrown into the 'political mortuary' (rendered politically obsolete). I contend that in such a highly partisan milieu, the attitude of provincial political elite shapes how local officials deal with the concerns of residents. Should senior provincial officials deny and deflect the grievances of communities, this can potentially create complacency at local level. This complacency, in turn, leads to a lack of empathy among local authorities when dealing with local residents. This becomes more problematic once citizens – with a less trustful image of local authorities - reach out to more noninstitutionalized platforms of engagement.

Government attempts to enhance state-citizen relations

The South African Government's response to community protests is highly diverse, ranging from statutory enactments to practical initiatives. In acknowledging trust in government as a fundamental element of the democracy, the South African Presidency has explicitly pledged to improve citizens' trust in government. As a result, the Presidency set up a telephone hotline and social networking page in 2010. The main purpose of the two initiatives was to engage with communities, assess their service-delivery issues, and to enforce accountability among public servants in the country (Managa 2012).

Another key initiative from the highest office in South Africa is the Presidential Local Government Summit. The second summit in post-democratic South Africa took place in 2014. The main focus of the summit was on strategies to help government address issues relating to service delivery and improving living conditions of citizens. In this regard, President Zuma noted:

> Every single individual in our three sphere dispensation must know his or her responsibilities to make local government function better. We must go back to the basics in the real sense. We must commit to ensuring that municipalities are able to provide water, electricity, parks, street lighting, refuse removals, repairing of potholes, dealing with the frustrating interruption of services and billing problems affecting households. Going back to the basics also means a recommitment to provide these services in a professional and caring manner which recognizes each resident as a valuable client. Going back to the basics therefore will mean that each municipality will actively interact with the community and promote ongoing two-way communication in every ward. Municipalities must ensure that all programmes which

are implemented at local level are clearly communicated and reported to communities. Going back to the basics means reviewing tendering systems and dealing with corruption systematically within the supply chain system in local government (The Presidency of the Republic of South Africa 2014).

The Local Government Turnaround Strategy (LGTAS) approved in 2009 has two primary aims. The first is to increase the confidence of the majority of our people in our municipalities, as the primary delivery vehicle of the developmental state at local level. The second relates to re-building and improving the basic requirements for a functional, responsive, effective, efficient and accountable developmental local government. The LGTAS are currently managed through a National Coordinating Unit in the Department of COGTA, which serves as a *"Nerve Centre"* for implementation (COGTA 2014).

Scholarly evidence reveals that the impact of the LGTAS in the case of local municipalities has not been significant in improving community participation and service delivery (Monakedi 2012). A possible explanation for this could be that municipalities are dominated by partisan agendas, with less of a focus on the interests of citizens. The Local Government Municipal Systems Amendment Act No 7 of 2011, which forms part of government's LGTAS, seeks to prohibit political cadres from holding senior municipal management jobs and also bans the employment of top municipal managers who do not have basic skills (Government Gazette 2011). This is an unprecedented Act and, surprisingly, came from within the ranks of the ruling ANC.

There is also evidence that provinces have recognized the importance of formulating strategies to deal with community protests. For instance, the Free State Provincial Government has established a Priority Committee on Stability to monitor community protests. This forum is chaired by the Provincial COGTA Department, and is composed of Security Managers from local municipalities, security agencies, SALGA South African Local Government Association (SALGA), and other key sector departments. Furthermore, the Free State COGTA Department has developed Guidelines for Management of Memorandums, and the establishment of Petition Management Committees. These guidelines stipulate the turnaround time for dealing with memorandums submitted by communities to municipalities (Free State COGTA Department, E-mail interview June 28, 2016).

Concluding remarks – a call to value education

Community protests around issues to do with the provision of basic municipal services as well as a wider spectrum of concerns, have intensified in the last five years in South Africa. The protests are embedded within the wider socio-political contexts of the country. While the protests highlight the growing influence of civic actors and civic groups, essential importance is attributed to the notion of political trust: a factor that influences the opportunities for cooperation, according to Brosché (2014).

A key feature of community protests in South Africa is that they are nonpartisan and waged by ordinary citizens to voice their rights and demands. However, a prevalent narrative on community protests in predominantly black communities in South Africa is the alleged involvement of a third force trying to effect regime change. This narrative is conceived for and by ruling class interests and serves as a major impediment to effectively dealing with genuine community concerns.

In addition, the view among the polity that ratepayers' associations represent white elitism tends to miss the situated agency of these civic groups. For instance, the Sannieshof and Heilbron cases, to some extent, provide evidence of how ordinary citizens can positively contribute to service delivery at municipal level. Yet, I contend that the involvement of the National Taxpayers' Association in efforts related to self-determination, no matter how legal and morally justifiable, will lend credence to the scepticism about the purported goal of ratepayers' associations in South Africa.

Broadly, though, despite a vibrant political representative system and an arsenal of participatory governance tools ranging from ward-based committees, ward councillors, integrated development planning, budgeting, to municipal performance management processes, the local government system in South Africa still faces the wrath of the repertoire of dissenting voices from citizens. The biggest challenge, by far, remains the dichotomy between the rhetorical zeal about the representative nature of South African participatory local governance and existing practice: a system in which elitism is entrenched by residing actual decision-making within the polity.

Hence, it is recommended that the South African local government system should be geared towards maximizing the influence of civic groups to yield the radical reduction in the trust-deficit between municipalities and local citizens. Participatory governance systems that are context-specific and accountable, together with the adoption of minimum uniform norms and standards for municipalities in dealing with community grievances and community protests, will go a long way towards arresting the strife against local governance. This will have a profound impact on good governance. In this regard, good governance can in turn engender and strengthen trust in local government. Citizen trust in local political actors and institutions remains an important predictor of citizen support beyond partisan lines. It remains to be seen whether the strategies developed by several provincial governments and SALGA will generate greater state responsiveness.

I cannot help but lift my hands from the desktop for this particular contribution by reflecting on my interaction with a complete stranger. It was an early winter morning in July 2015 when I decided to quickly grab something to eat at a petrol filling station. As I entered the shop, I saw a man with a partially concealed handgun in the holster on his right-hand side. He had just completed his purchase and was turning. I started to raise my hands - and maybe I should not have – while starring at the stranger's gun and said: 'Eish, let me put up my hands. One can never be too certain about one's safety in *Mzansi* (South Africa)". He stopped and gave me a wry-looking smile and retorted:

> *Broer* [brother]! I know how you feel... It is an all too common feeling that I understand. Many South Africans are currently too despondent about the future. But remember, we defeated the biggest monster of them all – apartheid. No one thought it was possible... Whatever our current experience, it too shall pass...

I borrow from this anecdotal description to remind us that South Africa is in a unique and fortunate position. The country has a sad history of disorder and political unrest associated with resistance to apartheid (Centre for the Study of Violence and Reconciliation 1998). There are pockets of local governance excellence in South Africa which need a coordinated approach. In fact, Africa has shown that dialogue, albeit with mixed results, enhances trust and has contributed to harmonious relations in countries such as the Central Republic of Africa, Democratic Republic of Congo, Mali, Somali, and South Sudan. Thus, South Africa, and Africa in general, have the opportunity to learn from their own mistakes and those made by other developing countries on how to deal with community protests.

More specifically, the need for effective ways to influence citizen perception of municipalities is critical. Municipalities should have dedicated communication experts who conduct proactive outreach strategies aimed at the dissemination of key information about municipal programmes. The premise of such communication strategies should not only focus on enhancing the image of the local municipality, but map out effective grievance redress, transparency, and accountability mechanisms. In this regard, as a South African noted almost a decade ago, there is a crucial need for sectoral departments at national and provincial level to prioritize municipal capacity-building (Atkinson 2007).

In conclusion, we need to remain cognizant of the pitfalls posed by the brazen mobilizing tactic of civic groups in predominantly black communities to disrupt learning and teaching, and destruct school buildings during community protests. I reckon this is not the type of norms and values South African parents want to perpetuate into the future. In the words of the late and former President of South Africa, Nelson Mandela, we seem to have forgotten that "education is the most powerful weapon to change the world".

References

Abers, Rebecca. 1998. From clientelism to cooperation: local government, participatory policy and civic organizing in Porto Alegre, Brazil. *Politics and Society* 26(4):511-537.
Adler, Nanci. 2012. "The bright past", or Whose (Hi)story? Challenges in Russia and Serbia Today. *Filozofija I Društvo* XXIII (4): 106-118.
African National Congress. 2007. Strategy and tactics: building a national democratic society. Retrieved March 24, 2015 (http://www.anc.org.za/docs/pdf).
Ahmad, Muhammad Shakil and Talib Noraibi Bt. Abu. 2013. Local government systems and decentralization: Evidence from Pakistan's devolution plan. *Contemporary Economics* 7(1):33-44.
Alexander, Peter. 2010. Rebellion of the poor: South Africa's service delivery protests – a preliminary analysis'. *Review of African Political Economy* 37(123):25–40.
Amaechi, Kingsley E. 2013. A comparative and social movement study of Boko Haram and MEND. Masters dissertation. Oslo: MF Norwegian School of Theology. Retrieved January 24, 2014 (https://brage.bibsys.no /xmlui//bitstream/ id/13541-2/AVH5035-kand-nr-6077masteravhandling-Amaechi-navn.pdf).
Anciano, Fiona. 2012. Agents of change? Reflecting on the impact of social movements in post-apartheid South Africa. In: Dawson, Marcelle and Sinwell Luke (eds.). *Contesting transformation: popular resistance in twenty-first-century South Africa*. London: Pluto, pp.143-165.
Arce Moises and Mangomet Jorge. 2012. Competitiveness, partisanship, and subnational protest in Argentina. *Comparative Political Studies* 46(8): 895-919.
Armed Conflict Location and Event Dataset. 2013. Real-time analysis of African political violence. *Conflict Trends,* 10:1-10. Retrieved June 28, 2014 (http://www.acleddata.com/wp-content/uploads/2013/01/ACLED-Conflict-Trends-Report_No-10_January-2013.pdf).
Arnstein, Sherry R. 1969. A ladder of citizen participation. *Journal of the American Institute of Planners* 35(4):216-224.
Atkinson, Doreen. 2015. Provinces as bulwarks: centrifugal forces within the ANC. *Transformation: Critical Perspectives on Southern Africa* 87:32-54.
Atkinson, Doreen. 2007. Taking to the streets: has developmental local government failed in South Africa?" In: Buhlungu, Sakhela, Daniel John, Southall Roger, Lutchman Jessica 9eds.). *State of the nation. South Africa 2007*. Cape Town: HSRC Press, pp.53-77.
Auditor-General of South Africa. 2015. MFMA 2013-14 Media release. 3 June. Retrieved August 12, 2015 (https://www.agsa.co.za/Documents/Auditreports/MFMA2013 2014.aspx).

Aulich, Chris. 2009. From citizen participation to participatory governance in Australian Local Government. *Commonwealth Journal of Local Governance* Issue 2: January, Retrieved January 24, 2016 (http://epress.lib.uts.edu.au/ojs/index.php/clg).

Ballard, Richard, Habib Adam and Valodia Imraan (eds.). 2006. *Voices of protest: social movements in postapartheid South Africa*. Pietermaritzburg: University of KwaZulu-Natal Press.

Barichievy, Kelvin, Piper Laurence, and Parker Ben. 2005. Assessing 'participatory governance' in local government: A case-study of two South African cities. *Politeia* 24(3):370-393.

Barr, Bobb. 2016. Has Latin American populism spread to US? *Mobilizing Ideas*. Retrieved April 15, 2016 (https://mobilizingideas.wordpress.com/2016/04/08/has-latin-american-populism-spread-to-the-us/).

Barvosa, Edwin. 2011. Inner contradiction to immigration quagmire: A response to Rogers Smith. *Perspectives on Politics* 9(3):559-565.

Bean, Anderson M. 2015. Venezuela, human rights and participatory democracy. *Critical Sociology* April 30, doi:10.1177/0896920515582093.

Bean, Clive. 2001. Party politics, political leaders and trust in government in Australia. *Political Science* 53:17-27.

Benford, Robert D. 1997. An insider's critique of the social movement framing perspective. *Sociological Inquiry* 67(4):409-430.

Bernstein, Ann and Johnston Sandy. 2007. *Voices of anger: protest and conflict in two municipalities*. Johannesburg. Centre for Development and Enterprise.

Bifulco, Lavinia. 2013. Citizen participation, agency and voice. *European Journal of Social Theory* 16(2):174-187.

Bond, Peter. 2001. *Debates in local economic development policy and practice: reversing uneven development and reactivating the state in a 'post-Washington' epoch*. Municipal Services Project, Research Series Occasional Paper. Johannesburg: University of Witwatersrand.

Booysen, Susan. 2015. *Dominance and decline: The ANC in the time of Zuma*. Johannesburg: Wits University Press.

Booysen, Susan. 2009. Beyond the ballot and the brick: continuous dual repertoires in the politics of attaining service delivery in South Africa?' In: McLennan, Anne, and Barry Munslow (eds.). *The politics of service delivery*. Johannesburg: Wits University Press, pp.104-136.

Booysen, Susan. 2007. With the ballot and the brick: the politics of attaining service delivery. *Progress in Development Studies* 7(1):21–32.

Boulding, Carew, and Brown David S. 2015. Do political parties matter for turnout? Number of parties, electoral rules and local elections in Brazil and Bolivia. *Party Politics* 21(3):404-416.

Botes, Lucius, Lenka Molefi, Marais Lochner, Matebesi Sethulego, and Sigenu Kholisa. 2007. *The new struggle: service delivery-related unrest in South Africa*. Bloemfontein: Centre for Development Support (University of the Free State).

Bovens, Mark. 2003. A framework for the analysis and assessment of accountability arrangements in the public domain. Retrieved October 12, 2014 (http://www.qub.ac.uk/polproj/reneg/contested_meanings/Bovens_Public%20Accountability.connex2.doc).
Brancati, Dawn. 2014. Pocketbook protests: Explaining the emergence of prodemocracy protests worldwide. *Comparative Political Studies* 47(11):1503-1530.
Braun, Robert. 2016. Historical legacies of contention and clandestine resistance to violence. *Mobilizing Ideas*. Retrieved May 01, 2016 (https://mobilizingideas.wordpress.com/2016/02/10/historical-legacies-of-contention-and-clandestine-resistance-to-violence/#more-8754).
Brewer, Paul R, Gross Kimberly, Aday Sean, and Willnat Lars. 2004. International trust and public opinion about world affairs. *American Journal of Political Science*, 48(1):93-109.
Brown, Julian. 2015. *South Africa's insurgent citizens: On dissident and the possibility of politics*. Pretoria: Jacana.
Burawoy, Michael, and von Holdt Karel. 2011 *Conversations with Bourdieu: The Johannesburg moment*. Johannesburg: Wits University Press.
Business Day. 2011. Eastern Cape sewage works 'pose health risk'. Retrieved February 23, 2015 (http://www.businessday.co.za/articles/Content.aspx?id=147341).
Brosché, Johan. 2015. Causes of communal conflicts- Government bias, elites, and conditions for cooperation. Dissertation Brief Series 06. Retrieved March 29, 2016 (file:///C:/Users/matebsz/Documents/!%20aSocial%20Protests/2016/Chapter%203/DDB-2015-6-Johan-Brosche_web.pdf).
Brown, Justin. 2016. SA's rating neither down nor out. *City Press*, May 08, p.9.
Burns, Danny, Hambleton Robin, and Hoggett Paul. 1994. *The politics of decentralisation: Revitalising local democracy*. London: Macmillan.
Byrne, Elaine. 2013. Deliberative democracy might offer a remedy for the extremely low levels of political trust in Ireland. *LSE European Politics and Policy (EUROPP) Blog* (18 Jan 2013). Retrieved May 01, 2016 (http://blogs.lse.ac.uk/europblog/2013/01/18/deliberative-democracy-political-trust-ireland-elaine-byrne/).
Camaerts, Bart. 2012. Protest logics and the mediation opportunity structure. *European Journal of Communication* 27(2):117-134.
Camay, Phiroshaw and Anne Gordon. 2000. Sandton rates dispute: local government restructuring and financing of equitable services. *South African Civil Society and Governance Case study no 5*. Retrieved May 24, 2015 (https://www.google.com/-search?q=sandton+rates+dispute&ie=utf-8&oe=utf-8).
Carlin, Ryan, and Love Gregory. 2013. The politics of interpersonal trust and reciprocity: an experimental approach. *Political Behavior* 35(1):43-66.
Carothers, Thomas, and Youngs Richard. 2015. The complexities of global protests. Retrieved May 24, 2016 (http://carnegieendowment.org/files/CP_257_Youngs-Carothers-Global_Protests_final.pdf).
Carothers, Thomas. 2006. Confronting the weakest link: Aiding political parties in new democracies. New York: Carnegie Endowment for international Peace.

Castells, Manuel. 1983. The city and the grassroots. A cross-cultural theory of urban social Movements. Berkeley: University of California Press.
Centre for the Study of Violence and Reconciliation. 1998. *The Policing of Public Gatherings and Demonstrations in South Africa 1960-1994*. Paper commissioned by The Commission on Truth and Reconciliation (TRC) Research Department, May. Retrieved March, 14, 2014 (http://www.csvr.org.za/index.php-?-option=com_content&id=1483%3Athe-policing-of-public-gatherings-and-demontrations-in-south-africa-1960-1994&Itemid=2).
Chan, Joseph M, and Lee Francis LF. 2005. Mobilization and protest participation in post-handover Hong Kong. A study of three large scale demonstrations. Occasional Paper No 159. Retrieved November 10, 2014 (http://www.cuhk.edu.hk/hkiaps/publications/op/OP159-text.pdf).
Chen, Le, Dean Janice, Frant Jasper and Kumar Ranchana. 2014. What does "service delivery" really mean? Retrieved May 24, 2015 (http://www.worldpolicy.org/blo-g/2014/05/13/ what-does-service-delivery-really-mean).
Chen, Xi. 2015. Cooptation and protest leadership during industrial restructuring in China. In: Dong, Lisheng, Kriesi Hansper, and Kűbler Daniel (eds.). *Urban mobilizations and new media in contemporary China*. London and New York: Routledge, pp.133-150.
Chikerema, Arthur F. 2013. Citizen participation and local democracy in Zimbabwean Local Government System. *IOSR Journal of Humanities and Social Science* 13(2): 7-90.
Christensen, Henrik S. 2011. Political trust and political consumerism as individualized collective action – Are political consumers less trustful? Retrieved July 04, 2016 (https://www.abo.fi/fakultet/media/23741/henrikserupchristensen.pdf).
Chulu, Jimmy. 2015. *Decentralization: Is it a blue print for local governments in developing countries?* Social Science Research Network (SSRN). December 13, 2015. Retrieved March 04, 2016 (http://ssrn.com/abstract=2701497).
City Press. 2011. Tatane's death a hit. Retrieved August 12, 2015 (http://www.news24.com/Archives/City-Press/Tatanes-death-was-a-hit-2015042-9).
Coelho, Karen and Venkat, T. 2009. The politics of civil society: Neighbourhood associationism in Chennai. *Economic and Political Weekly* 44(26/27):358-367.
Cormley-Heenan, Cathy, and Devine Paula. 2010. The 'us' in trust: Who trusts Northern Ireland's political institutions and actors? *Government and Opposition* 45(2):143-165.
Craske, Nikki. 1999. *Women and Politics in Latin America*. Cambridge: Polity Press.
Essoungou, André-Michel. 2011. African elections – work in progress. Retrieved April 24, 2015 (http://www.un.org/africarenewal/magazine/august-2011/african-elections-works-progress#sthash.d2RiX2de.dpuf).
Exadaktylos, Theofanis, and Zahariadis Nikos. 2013. The lack of public trust in political institutions is a massive obstacle to public policy change in Greece. Re-

trieved April, 01(http://blogs.lse.ac.uk/europpblog/2013/01/17/greece-trust- institution).
Davis, Junior R. 2006. Evaluating and disseminating experiences in Local Economic Development: Observations on Integrated Development Programmes of the Free State, Republic of South Africa. Kent, UK: Natural Resources Institute.
Della Porta, Donatella. 2015. Target choices and intense times. Mobilizing ideas, June 10. Retrieved January 10, 2016 (https://mobilizingideas.wordpress.com/2015/06/10/target-choices-in-intense-times/).
Della Porta, Donatella, and Reiter Herbert, 2012. Desperately seeking politics: political attitudes of participants in three demonstrations for worker's rights in Italy. *Mobilization* 17(3):349-361.
Della Porta, Donatella and Piazza Gianni. 2008. *Voices of the valley, voices of the straits: How protest creates communities.* New York: Berghahn Books.
Denters, Bas. 2002. Size and political trust: Evidence from Denmark, The Netherlands, Norway and the United Kingdom. *Environment and Planning C: Government and Policy* 20(6):793-812.
Department of Cooperative Governance and Traditional Affairs. 2014. *Back to Basics.* Retrieved May 24, 2015 (http://www.cogta.gov.za/sites/cogtapub/Pages/back-ground. aspx).
Department of Cooperative Government and Traditional Affairs. 2009. State of Local Government in South Africa. Retrieved May 24, 2015 (http://www.gov.za/sites/-/www.gov.za/files/state-local-gov-rpt1.pdf).
Donnelly, Lynley. 2016. Guptas become too hot to handle. *Mail & Guardian.* Retrieved April 12, 2016 (http://mg.co.za/article/2016-04-08-guptsa-become-too-hot-to-handle).
DPLG (Department of Provincial and Local Government of RSA). 2008. *Integrated Development Plan (IDP) Format Guide.* Retrieved May 24, 2015 (www.cogta.gov.za%2Findex.php%2F2014-04-29-10-00-8%2Flocal-government-frameworks-1%2Fguidelines-frameworks-1%2F315-1-idp-format-guide-2008-)
Druckman, James N, Peterson Erik, and Slothuus Rune. 2013. How elite partisan polarization affects public opinion formation. *American Political Science Review* 107(1):57-79.
Duncan, Jane. 2010. Voice, political mobilisation and repression under Jacob Zuma. Paper presented at 'A Decade of Dissent: Reflections on Popular Resistance in South Africa, 2000-2010', symposium, University of Johannesburg, School of Tourism and Hospitality, November 12-14. Retrieved (https://www.ru.ac.za/med-ia/.../Duncan_Dissent_Under_Zuma.docx*).*
Du Plessis, Willemien, and Scheepers Theo. 2000. House of Traditional Leaders: Role, problems and future. *PER/PELJ* 3(1):73-95.
Duvsjö, Jennifer K. 2014. *What is affecting political trust? A comparative study on Europe.* Doctoral dissertation. Department of Political Science, Linnaeus University. Retrieved March 25, 2016 (http://lnu.diva-portal.org/smash/get/diva2:788098/FULLTEXT01.pdf).

Eagan, Jennifer L. 2016. Deliberate democracy: political theory. Retrieved July 05, 2016 (https://global.britannica.com/topic/deliberative-democracy).
Eiermann, Martin. 2016. "In the land of Uncle Sam": Populism and race in the United States. *Mobilizing Ideas*, April 8. Retrieved April 15, 2016 (https://mobilizingideas.wordpress.com/2016/04/08/in-the-land-of-uncle-sam-populism-and-race-in-the-united-states/).
Ekman, Joakim, and Amnå Erik. 2012. Political participation and civic engagement: towards a new typology. *Human Affairs* 22(3):283-300.
Emthanjeni Local Municipality. 2015. Review of the IDP 2015/16. Retrieved April 15, 2016 (*nc.spisys.gov.za/Final%20IDP%20Review%202015.do*).
Enjolras, Bernard, Steen-Johnsen Kari, and Wollebaek Dag. 2012. Social media and mobilization to offline demonstrations: Transcending participatory divides? *New Media & Society*, pp. 1-19. doi:10.1177/1461444812462844
Epstein, Barbara. 1991. *Political protest and cultural revolution: nonviolent direct action in the 1970s and 1980s*. Berkeley: University of California Press.
Erlanger, Steven, Castle Stephen, and Gladstone Rick. 2016. Iceland's Prime Minister steps down amid Panama Papers scandal. *New York Times* http://www.nytimes.com/2016/04/06/world/europe/panama-papers-iceland.html?_r=0
Farrelly, Michael. 2009. Citizen participation and neighbourhood governance: analysing democratic practice. Local Government Studies 35(4):387–400.
Fitzgerald, Jennifer, and Wolak Jennifer. 2016. The roots of trust in local government in Western Europe. *International Political Science Review* 37(1):130-146.
Friedman, Steven. 2009. People are demanding public service, not service delivery. Business Day Live, 29 July, Retrieved October, 14, 2014 (http://www.bdlive.co.za/articles/2009/07/29/people-are-demanding-public-service-not-service-delivery).
Fukuyama, Francis. 2000. *Social capital and civil society*. International Monetary Fund Working Paper WP/00/74. Retrieved March 29, 2014 (https://www.imf.org/external/pubs /ft /wp/2000/wp0074.pdf).
Fukuyama, Francis. 1995. *The social virtues and the creation of prosperity*. New York: Free Press.
Ganuza, Ernesto, Nez Héloïse, and Morales Ersnesto. 2014. The struggle for a voice: tensions between associations and citizens in participatory budgeting. *International Journal of Urban and Regional Research* 38.6, pp. 2274-2291. DOI:10.1111/1468-2427.12059
Good Governance Africa. 2016. Special focus: South Africa GGA's national survey on quality of government Municipalities: our Government Performance Index. *Journal of Good Governance* Issue 3 (March).
Gordon, Steven L, Roberts Benjamin J, and Struwig Jarè. 2015. Trusting the coalface: Public trust in South African Local Government and the Millennium Development Goals. *Millennium Development Goals (MDGs) in Retrospect* 58 (Social Indicators Research Series):63-80.

Government Gazette. Municipal Systems Amendment Act 7 of 2011. *Government Gazette* Nop 34433. Retrieved May 14, 2016 (http://www.dta.gov.za/cgta_2016/-wp-content/uploads/2016/06/MUNICIPAL-SYSTEMS-AMENDMENT-ACT-2011.pdf)

Greffrath, Wynand and Duvenhage, Andre. 2014. South Africa and the 2014 national election: A shift to the left? *Journal/Joernaal* 39(2):196-224.

Gundersen, Adolf G. 2000. Deliberative democracy and the limits of partisan politics: Between Athens and Philadelphia'. In: Portis Edward B, Gundersen Adolf G and Shively Ruth L (eds.). *Political theory and partisan politics*. New York: State University of New York, pp.97-116.

Guo, Hai D, and Neshkova Milena I. 2013. Citizen input in the budget process: When does it matter most?" *The American Review of Public Administration 43(3)*:331-346.

Gutto, Shadrack. 2001. *Equality and non-discrimination in South Africa: The political economy of law and law making*. Cape Town: New Afrika books.

Guwa, Nontando. (2008). Confronting challenges of public participation. *Local Government Transformer* 14(1):6-8.

Haider, Huma. 2011. State-society relations and citizenship in situations of conflict and fragility. Governance and Social Development Resource Centre. Retrieved March 29, 2014 (http://www.gsdrc.org/docs/open/con88.pdf).

Hawker, Dianne. 2013. Deluge of water complaints to SAHRC. March 03, 2013. Retrieved May 15, 2014 (http://www.iol.co.za/news/south-africa/deluge-of-water-complaints-to-sahrc-1479699).

Harvey, Davey. 1989. From managerialism to entrepreneurialism: The transformation in urban governance in late capitalism. *Geografiska Annaler* 71(1):3-17.

Heese, Karen and Allan Kevin. 2016a. Mashaba's promises and plans may clash with Johannesburg's realities. *BusinessDay Live*. Retrieved September 02, 2016 (http://www.bdlive.co.za/opinion/2016/09/02/mashabas-promises-and-plans-may-clash-with-johannesburgs-realities).

Heese, Karen and Allan Kevin. 2016b. Stress test for political blocs. *BusinessDay Live*. Retrieved August 08, 2016 (http://www.bdlive.co.za/opinion/2016/08/08/stress-tests-for-political-blocs).

Held, David. 1999. *Global transformations: Politics, economics and culture*. Stanford, Calif: Stanford University Press.

Herriman, Jade. 2011. *Local government and community engagement in Australia*. Working Paper No 5. Australian Centre of Excellence for Local Government, University of Technology Sydney.

Hess, Steve. 2015. Foreign media coverage and protest outcomes in China: The case of the 2011 Wukan rebellion. *Modern Asian Studies* 01(January):177-203.

Hetherington, Marc J, and Rudolph Thomas J. 2015. *Why Washington won't work: polarization, political trust, and the governing crisis*. Chicago: Chicago University Press.

Holland, Travis A. 2015. Social networks as sites of e-participation in local government. *Global Media Journal - Australian Edition* 9(1):1-8.

Holston, James. 1998. Spaces of insurgent citizenship. In: Sandercock Leonie (ed.). *Making the invisible visible. A multicultural planning history*. London: University of California Press, pp.37-56.
Hlongwane, Nkulu T. 2011. Evaluating the Integrated Development Plan (IDP) as a performance management system for a selected Kwazulu-Natal municipality. Retrieved May 12, 2016 (http://ir.dut.ac.za/bitstream/handle/10321/700/Hlongwane_2011.pdf?sequence=1&isAllowed=y).
Hutter, Swen, and Braun Daniela. 2013. *Trust in representative democracy and protest behavior. A multilevel analysis of European democracies*. European University Institute: Max Weber Programme, EUI Working Paper MWP 2013/14.
Idasa. 2010. *The state of local government and service delivery in South Africa: Issues, challenges and solutions*. Report submitted to the Portfolio Committee on Co-Operative Governance and traditional Affairs (COGTA) for public hearings: Co-ordinated service delivery. Pretoria: Idasa.
Independent Electoral Commission of South Africa. 2016. More about municipalities. Retrieved May 12, 2016 (http://www.elections.org.za/content/Elections/2016-Municipal-Elections/More-about-municipalities/).
Independent Electoral Commission of South Africa. 2015. 2016 Municipal Elections Handbook. Retrieved May 12, 2016 (www.elections.org.za/%2Fcontent%2FDocuments%2FPublications%2F2016-Municipal-Elections).
Inglehart, Ronald, and Welzel Christian. 2009. How development leads to democracy: What we know about modernization. *Foreign Affairs* 88(2):33-48.
Inglehart, Ronald, and Catterberg, Gabriela. 2002. Trends in political action: the developmental trend and the post-honeymoon decline. *International Journal of Comparative Sociology* 43:300-316.
Inglehart, Ronald. 1990. *Culture shift in advanced industrial society*. Princeton NJ: Princeton University Press.
Inglehart, Ronald. 1997. *Modernization and postmodernization: cultural, economic, and political change in 43 societies*. Princeton, NJ: Princeton University Press.
IOL. 2013. Nineteen schools closed after arson. Retrieved May 04, 2015 (http://www.iol.co.za/news/south-africa/nineteen-schools-closed-after-arson-489-0).
Isaacs, Laure. 2012. Violent protest over school in Grabouw. Retrieved June 04, 2014 (http://www.iol.co.za/news/south-africa/western-cape/violent-protest-over-schoo-l-in-grabouw-1249863).
Isotalus, Pekka, and Almonkari Merja. 2014 Political scandal tests trust in politicians: the case of the Finnish Minister who resigned because of his text messages. *Nordicom Review* 35(2):3-16.
Jacobsen, Georg. 2011a. Macro factors and public opinion: An investigation of economic left–right attitudes in advanced industrialized democracies. PhD thesis. Norwegian University of Science and Technology Faculty of Social Sciences and Technology Management. Retrieved May 04, 2015 (http://www.divaportal.org/smash/get/diva2:437046/FULLTEXT02.pdf).

Jacobsen, Georg. 2011b. Education and the Zeitgeist: Government positions and public opinion on income distribution. *European Political Science Review* 3(1):103–124.
Jakes, Thomas D. 2015. *Destiny: Step into your purpose.* New York: TDJ Enterprises.
Jansen, Jonathan. 2012. Seven dangerous shifts in public education crisis. Politicsweb. Retrieved May 24, 2015 (http://www.politicsweb.co.za/news-and-analysis/seven-dangerous-shifts-in-the-public-education-cri).
Jarman, Neil, Bryan Dominic, Caleyron Nathalie, and de Rosa Ciro. 1998. Politics in public: Freedom of assembly and the right to protest. Report No. 8. *Democratic Dialogue.* Retrieved June 14, 2015 (http://cain.ulst.ac.uk/dd/report8/report8.htm).
Kanyinga, Karuti. 2014. *Kenya: Democracy and political participation.* A review by AfriMAP, Open Society Initiative for Eastern Africa and the Institute for Development Studies (IDS), University of Nairobi. Nairobi: Open Socity Foundations.
Khanna, Akshay, Mani Priyashri, Patterson Zachary, Pantazidou Maro, and Shqerat Maysa. 2013. The changing faces of citizen action: a mapping study through an "unruly" lens. *IDS Working Paper* 423, June. Retrieved January 04, 2016 (http://www.ids.ac.uk/files/dmfile/Wp423.pdf).
Klandermans, Bert. 1997. *The social psychology of protest.* Oxford: Blackwell.
Klandermans, Bert. 1984. Mobilization and participation: Social-psychological expansions of resource mobilization theory. *American Sociological Review* 49:583–600.
Klenk, Nicole L, and Hickey Gordon M. 2010. A virtual and anonymous, deliberative and analytic participation process for planning and evaluation: The concept Mapping Policy Delphi. *International Journal of Forecasting* 27: 152-165
Kleven, Øyvin. 2015. Voter turnout in local elections in Norway. Lower voter turnout than Sweden and Denmark. Samfunnsspeilet 2/2015. Statistisk sentralbyrå.
Kreutz, Joakim. 2012. *Dismantling the conflict trap: Essays on civil war resolution and relapse.* Doctoral thesis. Department of Peace and Conflict Research. Upsala: Uppsala University.
Knysna Municipality. 2015. Final IDP Review 2015/2016 – Knysna Municipality. Retrieved June 24, 2015 (www.knysna.gov.za/wp-content/uploads/.../2015-2016-IDP-Review-29-May-2015.pdf).
Koma, Samuel B. 2014. *Developmental local government with reference to the implementation of the local economic development policy.* Doctoral thesis. School of Public Management and Administration. Pretoria: University of Pretoria.
Kong, Dejun T. 2014. Perceived competence and benevolence of political institutions as culturally universal facilitators of political trust: Evidence from Arab countries. *Cross-Cultural Research* 48(4):385-399.
Krishna. Anirudh, and Shrader Elizabeth. 2000. Crosscultural Measures of Social Capital: A Tool and Results from India and Panama. World Bank Working Paper No. 21. Retrieved May 12, (http://www.worldbank.org/socialdevelopment).
Langa, Malose, von Holdt Karel. 2012. Insurgent citizenship, class formation and the dual nature of a community protests: A case study of 'Kungcatsha'. In: Dawson,

Marcelle and Sinwell Luke (eds.). *Contesting transformation: popular resistance in twenty-first-century South Africa*. London: Pluto, pp.80-100.
Lapegna, Pablo. 2014. Pitfalls of "co-optation". Retrieved June 22, 2015 (http://participationanditsdiscontents.tumblr.com/post/77071378901/pitfalls-of-cooptation).
Laser, Julie A, and Leibowitz George S. 2009. Promoting positive outcomes for healthy youth development: utilizing social capital theory. *Journal of Sociology & Social Welfare* (XXXVI)1:87-102.
Leblas, Andrienne. 2011. *From protest to parties: party-building and democratization in Africa*. Oxford: Oxford University Press.
Leduka, Modieli. 2009. *Participatory budgeting in the South African local government context: The case of Mantsopa Local Municipality*, Free State Province. Retrieved May 24, 2015 (www.scholar.sun.ac.za>handle).
Lekvall, Anna. 2013. *Development first, democracy later*? Stockholm: IDEA.
Letsoalo, Matuma. 2016. Zuma escapes the chop again as ANC leaders blame poor performance on NO 1. Retrieved August 16, 2016 (mg.co.za/article/2016-08-15-zuma- escapes-the-chop-again-as-ANC-leaders-blame-poor-performance-on-no-1).
Letsoalo, Matuma. 2015. ANC seeks new grass-roots leaders. *Mail & Guardian*, April 17, p. 12.
Levi, Magaret, and Stoker laura. 2000. Political trust and trustworthiness. *Annual Review of Political Science* 3(1):475-507.
Lewis-Beck Michael.S, Nadeau Richard, and Elias Angelo.2008. Economics, party, and the vote: causality issues and panel data. *American Journal of Political Science* 52(1):84-95.
Lichbach, Mark I. 2003. Contending theories of contentious politics and the structure-action problem of social order. *Annual Review of Political Science* 1(1):401-424.
Lipsky, Michael. 1965. *Protest and city politics*. Chicago: Rand McNally & Co.
Lobe, Thembeni. 2008. *An evaluation of Ward Committees and entrenching public participation within the Mangaung Local Municipality*. MA dissertation. Department of Political Science. Bloemfontein: University of the Free State
Machado, Fabiana, Scartascini Carlos, and Tommasi Mariano. 2009. Political institutions and street protests in Latin America. *Journal of Conflict Resolution* 55(3): 340-365.
MacKay, Moses. 2012. Bitter feud over DA defectors. SowetanLive, April 17, 2012, Retrieved August 14, 2014 (http://www.sowetanlive.co.za/news/2012/04/17/bitter-feud-over-da-defectors?filter=all_comments).
Macupe, Bongekile. 2016. Road of discontent finally gets tarred after lengthy protests. *Sowetan*, June 6, p. 8.
Magubane, Khulekani. 2016. Municipal demarcation protests in Limpopo worsen. Retrieved May 26 (http://www.bdlive.co.za/national/2016/05/04/municipal-demarcation-protests-in-limpopo-worsen).
Mail & Guardian. 2016. Limpopo: Another school burnt. Retrieved May 26, 2016 (http://mg.co.za/article/2016-05-24-limpopo-another-school-burnt).

Mail & Guardian. 2011. Police crack down as new protests rock Ficksburg. Retrieved August 24, 2013 (http://mg.co.za/article/2011-05-13-police-crack-down-as-new-protests-rock-ficksburg).
Maje, Obakeng. 2016. Road projects running smoothly, MEC says. The New Age online. Retrieved May 26, 2016 (http://www.thenewage.co.za/road-projects-running-smoothly-mec-says/).
Makhanya, Mondli. 2016a. The IEC must protect our X. City Press, Voices. Retrieved May 26, 2016 (http://city-press.news24.com/Voices/the-iec-must-protect-our-x-20160506).
Makhanya, Mondli. 2016b. All hail Chief Justice Mogoeng. *City Press*, April 3, p.13.
Managa, Azwifaneli. 2012. Unfulfilled promises and their consequences: A reflection on local government performance and the critical issue of poor service delivery in South Africa. *Policy Brief* No 76, Africa Institute of South Africa. Retrieved July 14, 2014 (http://www.ai.org.za/wp-content/uploads/downloads/2012/05/No-76.-Unfulfilled-promises-and-their-consequences.-A-reflection-on-local-government-performance-and-the-critical-issue-of-poor-service-delivery-in-South-Africa.pdf).
Marais, Lochner, Matebesi Sethulego, Mthombeni Mandla, Botes Lucius, and Grieshaber Deidre. Municipal unrest in the Free State (South Africa): a new form of social movement? *Politeia* 27(2):51-69.
Marrian, Natasha. 2015. Go back to the people, activist Makhura urges. *Business Day Live*, Retrieved May 26, 2016 (http://www.bdlive.co.za/national/2015/06/22/go-back-to-the-people-activist-makhura-urges).
Marris, Peter. 2008. Planning civil society in twenty-first century: An introduction. In: Douglas, Mike, and Friedman John (eds.). *Cities for citizens*. West Sussex: John Wiley & Sons, pp. 9-17.
Marus, Lia. 2014. The grave consequences of the Grabouw protests. Retrieved May 26, 2016 (http://www.hrpulse.co.za/news/231476-the-grave-consequences-of-the-grabouw-protests).
Masondo, Sipho. 2016. Top 6. *City Press*, April 03, p. 4.
Masondo, Sipho. 2011. Residents 'take over' three ANC-run towns. *Times Live*, April 10. Retrieved July 24, 2015 (http://www.timeslive.co.za/politics/2011/04/10/residents-take-over-three-anc-run-towns).
Masters, Jonathan. 2016 The U.S. Supreme Court and Obama's Immigration Actions. Retrieved April 23, 2016 (www.cfr.org/immigration/us-supreme-court-obamas-immigration-actions/p37630).
Matebesi, Sethulego, and Botes Lucius. Forthcoming. Party identification and service delivery protests in the Eastern Cape and Northern Cape Provinces of South Africa. *Journal of Southern African Studies*.
Matebesi, Sethulego, and Botes Lucius. 2011. Khutsong cross-boundary protests: the triumph and failure of participatory governance? *Politeia* 30(1): 4-21.
Matsilele, Trust. 2016. FNB declines to give reasons for closure of Guptas' accounts. Retrieved May 11, 2016. (www.cnbcafrica.com/news/southern-africa/2016/04/06/guptas-oakbay-fnb/).

Mbontsi, Dunyiswa K. 2010. *An analysis of the role of a community-based project on poverty alleviation: A case of Daantjie Bakery in the Mbombela Municipality, Mpumalanga Province.* Masters dissertation. Department of Public Administration. Port Elizabeth: Nelson Mandela Metropolitan University.

McAdam, Doug. 1999. *Political process and development of black insurgency 1930-1970.* Chicago. University of Chicago Press.

McLaren, Lauren. 2016. Immigration and the demise of political trust. Retrieved April 23, 2016 (www.the-plot.org/2016/02/16immigration-and-the-demise-of-political-trust/).

McLeod, Carolyn. 2015. Trust. *The Stanford Encyclopaedia of Philosophy* (Fall 2015 Edition). Zalta, Edward N (ed.). Retrieved January 12, 2016 (http://plato.stanford.edu/archives/fall2015/entries/trust/).

Meyer, Megan, and Hyde Cheryl. 2004. Too much of a "good" thing? Insular Neighborhood associations, nonreciprocal civility, and the promotion of civic health. *Nonprofit and Voluntary Sector Quarterly* 33(3 suppl):77S-96S.

Miettunene, Juuso V. 2015. Prefigurative politics: Perils and promise. Doctoral thesis. School of Politics and International Relations, The University of Kent. Retrieved April 14, 2016 (https://kar.kent.ac.uk/.../194PhD%20Dissertation%20%20Juuso-o%20 Miettunen_ hand.).

Mishler, William, and Rose Richard. 2001. What are the origins of political trust? Testing institutional and cultural theories in post-communist societies. *Comparative Political Studies* 34(1): 30-62.

Mngoma, Sibusiso. 2010. *Public participation in the informal trading by-laws amendment: the case of Johannesburg inner city.* Masters dissertation. Johannesburg: University of Witwatersrand.

Mnguni, Lukhona. 2016. Zuma is the antithesis of democratic values. *Sowetan*, April 6, p.15.

Mohamed, H. 2000. *Kerala's experiment in local democracy and development: Lessons and options for the Greater Bloemfontein Local Council.* Johannesburg: Planact.

Monaco Sara. 2008. *Neighbourhood politics in transition. Residents' associations and local government in post-apartheid Cape Town.* Upssala (Sweden): Acta Universitatis Upsaliensis.

Monakedi, Tshepo A. 2012. *Consolidating developmental local government through the Local Government Turnaround Strategy: The case study of Makhuduthamaga Local Municipality.* Masters dissertation, Faculty of Engineering and the Built Environment, University of the Witwatersrand. Retrieved December 14, 2015 (http://wiredspace.wits.ac.za/jspui/bitstream/10539/12863/1/MSc%20DP-%20T%20A%20Monakedi..pdf).

Montambeault, Françoise. 2016. *The politics of local participatory democracy in Latin America: Institutions, actors, and interactions.* Stanford: Stanford University Press.

Montgomery, Jacob. M, Smith Steven. S, and Tucker Patrick. D. 2015. Moving the unmoved mover? The origins and limitations of systematic individual-level

change in party identification. Retrieved October 14, 2015, Retrieved (https://pages.wustl.edu/montgomery/articles/13578).
Montsho, Molaole. 2015. Pupils in Ganyesa return to classes. Retrieved December 14, 2015 (news/south-africa/north-west /).
Moon, Chung-in, and Plott David. 2013. A letter from the editors. *Global Asia* 8(3):1.
Moreno, Luis. 2015. Catalonia's in(ter)dependence and Europeanization. Instituto de Politicas y Bienes Publicas. Working Paper 2015-07. Retrieved March 31, 2016 (www.digital.csic.es).
Moseley, Mason, and Moreno Daniel. 2010. The normalization of protest in Latin America. Americas Barometer Insight Series 42, Retrieved November 09, 2015 (http://www.americasbarometer.org/).
Mossberger, Karen, and Wu Yonghong. 2012. Civic engagement and Local E-Government: Social networking comes of age. Retrieved January 24, 2016 (http://ipce.uic.edu/interior/CELocalEGovSMFullReport2012.pdf).
Mubungizi, Betty C, and Dassah Maurice C. 2014. Public participation in South Africa: Is intervention by the courts the answer? *Journal of Social Science* 39(3):275-284.
Municipal IQ. 2016. Press Release: Gauteng and national service delivery protest figures fall. Retrieved March 12, 2016 http://www.municipaliq.co.za/publications/press/201602231 446112167.doc.
Municipal IQ. 2014. Press Release: Municipal IQ's updated Municipal Productivity, Compliance and Governance and Hotspots Monitor results. Retrieved March 12, 2016 (http://www.municipaliq.co.za/publications/press/201412031701396816.doc)
Murray, Christina. 2006. The Human Rights Commission et al: What is the role of South Africa's Chapter 9 Institutions? *PELJ* 9(2):122-147.
Myburgh, Daisy. 2015. DA applauds community's decision to send children back to school. Retrieved June 04, 2016 (http://www.dampl.co.za/2015/11/da-applauds-communitys-decision-to-send-children-back-to-school/
Nabatchi, Tina, and Leighninger Matt. 2015. *Public participation for 21st Century democracy*. San Francisco: Jossey-Bass.
Nandipha, Khuthala. 2013. IEC credibility in question after Tlokwe judgment. *Mail & Guardian*. Retrieved June 24, 2014 (http://mg.co.za/article/2013-09-18-00-iec-credibility-questioned-after-tlokwe-judgment).
Ndabeni, Khanyi. 2015. 4 years after Tatane's death, nothing has changed in Ficksburg. Retrieved June 12, 2015 (http://www.timeslive.co.za/sundaytimes/stnews/-2015/07/05/4-years-after-Tatanes-death-nothing-has-changed-in-Fiksburg).
Nepstad, Sharon E, and Kurtz Lester R. 2012. Introduction. In: Nepstad, Sharon E, and Kurtz Lester R (eds.). *Nonviolent Conflict and Civil Resistance (Research in Social Movements, Conflicts and Change)* 34:xi-xxvii.
Netshitenzhe, Joel. 2016. The principles of relations. *City Press*, May 29, p.5.
Newton, Kenneth. 1999. Social and political trust. In: Pippa Norris (ed.). *Critical citizens: Global support for democratic government*. Oxford: Oxford University Press, pp. 342-361.

News24. 2012. North West protest spread. Retrieved October 10, 2014 (http://www.news24.com/SouthAfrica/News/North-West-protests-spread-20120510).
News24. 2014a. Back to basics for local government – Zuma. *News24*. Retrieved October 10, 2014 (http://www.news24.com/SouthAfrica/News/Back-to-basics-for-local-government-Zuma-20140918).
News24. 2014b. Civil society must fight corruption – Madonsela. *News24*, November 24, 2014. Retrieved May 07, 2015 (http://www.news24.com/SouthAfrica/News/Civil-society-must-fight-corruption-Madonsela-20141124).
News24. 2002. 30 held after protests. Retrieved May 12, 2013 (http://www.news24.com/SouthAfrica/News/30-held-after-protests-20051209).
Neyazi, Taberez A, Kumar Anup, and Semetko Holli A. 2016. Campaigns, digital media, and mobilization in India. *The International Journal of Press/Politics* 21(3):398-416.
Ngwane, Trevor. 2012. Labour strikes and community protests: I there a basis for unity in post-apartheid South Africa. In: Dawson, Marcelle and Sinwell Luke (eds.). *Contesting transformation: popular resistance in twenty-first-century South Africa.* London: Pluto, pp.125-142.
Nhlabathi, Hlengiwe. 2016. SACP warns ANC to search its soul. *City Press*, April 03, p. 4.
Nickson, Andrew. 2011. *Where is local government going in Latin America? A comparative perspective.* Visby (Sweden): Swedish International Centre for Local Democracy. Retrieved October 10, 2014 (http://www.icld.se/pdf/icld_wp6_printerfriendly.pdf)
Nkosi, Bongani. 2012. Children held to ransom for services. *Mail & Guardian*, September 20, Retrieved May 2013 (http://mg.co.za/article/2012-09-21-children-held-to-ransom-for-services).
Norris, Pippa. (ed.). 1999. *Critical citizens: global support for democratic government.* Oxford: Oxford University Press.
Nyaguthii, E. and Oyugi L.A. 2013. Influence of community participation on successful implementation of constituency development fund projects in Kenya: case study of Mwea constituency. *International Journal of Education and Research* 1(8):1-16.
Nyalunga, Dumisani. 2006. The revitalisation of Local Government in South Africa. *Retrieved March 15, 2015 (*http://ddp.org.za/information/material/articles/The%20Revitalisation%20of%20Local%20Government%20in20Government%20in%20South%20Africa%20.pdf/view).
Nye, Joseph S, Zelikov Phillip D, and King David C. 1997. *Why people don't trust government.* Cambridge: Harvard University Press.
Oberschall, Anthony. 1996. Opportunity and framing in the Eastern European Revolts of 1989. In: McAdam, Doug; McCarthy John D; and Zald Mayer N (eds.). *Comparative perspectives on social movements: Political opportunities, mobilizing structures and cultural framings.* New York: Cambridge University Press, pp. 93–121.

Okuru, Mina and Armah-Attoh Daniel. 2015. Ghana's decentralization: Locally centralized decision making ill serves its public. *Afrobarometer Dispatch* No 23, April, 2015. Retrieved August 12, 2015 (http://afrobarometer.org/sites/default/files/publications/Dispatch/abr6dispatchn-o23.pdfz).

Olimat, Muhamad. S. 2014. Introduction: Democratization, Arab Spring and Arab women. In: Olimat, Muhamad S (ed.). *Arab Spring and Arab Women; challenges and opportunities.* London: Routledge, pp.1-16.

Olson, Mancur. 1965. *The logic of collective action.* Cambridge: Harvard University.

O'Neill, Onora. 2002. *A question of trust: The BBC Reith Lectures 2002.* Cambridge: Cambridge University.

Opp, Karel-Dieter. 2009. *Theories of political protest and social movements: a multidisciplinary introduction, critique, and synthesis.* New York: Routledge.

Opu, Eric. 2014. *Social networks and participatory governance of urban green commons: The case of Vuosaari District in Helsinki, Finland.* Masters dissertation, Department of Urban and Rural Development. Uppsala: Swedish University of Agricultural Sciences.

O'Regan, Kate. 2010. *Political parties: The missing link in our constitution?* Conference of Political parties in South Africa: The interface between law and politics. Keynote address. Cape Town, August 27. Retrieved August 19, 2014 (http://www.law.uct.ac.za/sites/default/files/image_tool/images/99/Political-Parties-in-the-Constitution-address-27-August-2015.pdf).

Osmani, Sddiqur. 2008. Participatory governance: an overview of issues and evidence. In: United Nations. *Participatory governance and the Millennium Development Goals.* New York: United Nations.

Pandeya, Ganesh P. 2015. Does citizen participation in local government decision-making contribute to strengthening local planning and accountability systems? An empirical assessment of stakeholders' perceptions in NEPAL. *International Public Management Review* 16(1):67-98.

Parramon-Gurney, Marie, Gilder Andrew, and Swanepoel Ernesta. 2012. South Africa's Municipal Integrated Development Plans. Retrieved January 08, 2016 (https://www.academia.edu/1228983/South_Africa's_Municipal_Integrated_Development_Plans).

Parkinson, Graig. 2015. *Pendulum of politics: Today's politics from yesterday's history.* Bloomington: Author House.

Paret, Marcel. 2015. Violence and democracy in South Africa's community protests. *Review of African Political Economy* 42(143):107-123.

Parnell, Susan, and Pieterse Edgar. 1999. Developmental local government: The second wave of post-apartheid transformation. *Africanus* 29(2):61-86.

Patel, Sejal, Sliuzas Richard, and Georgiadou Yola. 2016. Asian countries participatory local governance in Asian Cities: Invited, closed or claimed spaces for urban poor? *Environment and Urbanization Asia* 7(1):1–21.

Patel, Yusuf. 2001. *Integrated development planning: Improving governance and development.* Plan Press, pp. 2.

Pather, Ra'eesa. 2016. 'No one is going to tell us what to do' and other Hlaudi Motsoeneng-isms. *Mail & Guardian*, June 01, 2016, Retrieved June 29, 2016 (http://mg.co.za/article/2016-05-31-hlaudi-motsoeneng-continues-to-decree-unfavourable-policies).

Pekkanen, Robert J, Tsujinaka Yutaka, and Yamamoto Hidehiro. Translated by Tkach-Kawasak, Leslie. 2014. *Neighborhood associations and local governance*. New York: Routledge.

Pew Research Center. 2015. Beyond distrust: How Americans view their government. November 23, 2015. Retrieved January 08, 2016 (http://www.peoplepress.org/2015/11/23/beyond-distrust-how-americans-view-their-government/).

Pharr, Susan J, and Putnam Robert D (eds.). 2000. *Disaffected democracies: Whose troubling the trilateral countries*. Princeton (New Jersey): Princeton University Press.

Pilane, Pontsho. 2015. Looking ahead: The death of the rainbow and the rise of fallism. Retrieved March 05, 2016 (http://www.thedailyvox.co.za/looking-ahead-the-death-of-the-rainbow-and-the-rise-of-fallism/).

Pillay, Udesh. 2006. Issues of democracy and governance. In: Pillay, Udesh et al. (eds.). *South African social attitudes: changing times, diverse voices*. Cape Town: HSRC Press, pp.1-16.

Pintor, Rafael L, Gratschew Maria and Sullivan Kate. 2012. Voter turnout rates from a comparative perspective. In: Pintor, Rafael L, and Gratschew Maria (eds.). *Voter turnout since 1945: A global report*. Stockholm: International Institute for Democracy and Electoral Assistance.

Piper, Laurence and Nadvi Lubna. 2010. Popular mobilization, party dominance and participatory governance in South Africa. In: Thompson Lisa and Tascott Chris (eds.). 2010. *Citizenship and social movements: perspectives from the global south*. London: Zed Books, pp. 212-238.

Pithouse, Richard. 2012. South Africa: On the murder of Andries Tatane. In: Firoze, Manji and Sokari Ekine (eds.). *African awakening: The emerging revolutions*. Cape Town: Pambazuka Press, pp.180-183

Pithouse, Richard. 2011. 'The service delivery myth'. *Development in Focus* 1 (February):6–7.

Powell, Derek M, O'Donovan Michael, and de Visser Jaap. 2015. *Civic protests barometer 2007-2014*. Cape Town. Retrieved March 05, 2016 (www.mlgi.org.za).

Putnam, Robert D. 1993. *Making democracy work: Civic traditions in modern Italy*. Princeton, NJ: Princeton University Press.

Putnam, Robert D. 2000. *Bowling alone: The collapse and revival of American community*. New York: Simon and Schuster.

Ramphele, Mamphele. 2016. State capture: how 'liberation culture' damages SA's future. *Sunday Times*, April 10, p.21

Reddy, Purshottama, Maharaj Brij. 2008. Democratic decentralization in post-apartheid South Africa. In: Saito, Fumihiko (ed.). *Foundations for local governance: Decentralization in comparative perspective*. Heidelberg: Physica, pp. 185-211.

Republic of South Africa. 1997. Republic of South Africa. 2009. *Constitution of the Republic of South Africa*, 1996. Retrieved July 21, 2013 (http://www.info.gov.za/documents/const itution/).
Reuters. 2016. Rape gaffe could cost contender presidency. *Cape Argus*, April 19, p.10.
Robins, Steven. 2010. How deep is 'deep democracy'? Grassroots globalization from Mumbai to Cape Town. In Coelho Vera.S & von Lieres Bettina (eds.). 2010. *Mobilizing for democracy*. London: Zed Books, pp.143-156.
Robinson, James A., Torvik Ragnar, and Verdier Thierry. 2006. Political foundations of the resource curse. *Journal of Development Economics* 79(2):447–468.
Rogerson, Christian M. 2014. Reframing place-based economic development in South Africa: the example of local economic development. *Bulletin of Geography. Socio–economic Series* 24:203–218.
Rogerson, Christian M. 2010. Local economic development in South Africa: strategic challenges. *Development Southern Africa* 27(4):481–496.
Rogerson, Christian M. 2011. Tracking Local Economic Development Policy and Practice in South Africa, 1994 – 2009. *Urban Forum* 22(2):149-168.
Rogerson, Christian M. 2009. *Strategic Review of Local Economic Development in South Africa*. Retrieved September 04, 2015 (file:///C:/Users/matebsz/Downloads/LED_Strategic_Review.pdf).
Rogerson, Christian M. 2008. Consolidating Local Economic Development in post-apartheid South Africa. *Urban Forum* 19(3):307–328.
Rogerson, Christian M. 2004. Pro-poor local economic development in post-apartheid South Africa. The Johannesburg fashion district. *International Development Planning Review* 26(4):401-429.
Rogerson, Christian M. 2006. Local economic development in post-apartheid South Africa: a ten-year research review. In: Padayachee Vishnu (ed.). *The Development Decade? Economic and social change in South Africa, 1994–2004*. Cape Town: HSRC Press, pp.227–253.
Roodt, Dan. 2009. Verval van Sannieshof 'weens 10 jaar se wanbestuur. Retrieved July 24, 2015 (http://praag.co.za/?p=5131).
Rowe, Gene, and Frewer Lynn J. 2004. Evaluating public-participation exercises: a research agenda. *Science Technology Human Value* 29(4):512–556.
Runciman, Carin, Alexander Peter, Rampedi Mahlatse, Moloto Boikanyo, Maruping Boitumelo, Khumalo Eunice and Sibanda Sihlapi. 2016. Counting Police-recorded Protests: Based on South African Police Service Data. Johannesburg: Social Change Research Unit, University of Johannesburg. Retrieved June 29, 2016. (https://www.uj.ac.za/faculties/humanities/sarchi/Documents/Counting%20Police-Recorded%20Protests.pdf)
Runciman, Carin. 2014. Mobilising insurgent citizenship: forging local authority and everyday policing in Protea Court. *South African Review of Sociology* 45(1):29-44.
Runji, Nompumelelo. 2016. Polls must be free and fair – and be seen to be. *Sowetan*, May 19, p.11.

Sachikonye, Lloyd M. 2002. Democracy, sustainable development and poverty: Are they compatible? *DPMF Occasional Paper*, No. 2. Retrieved May 29, 2016 (http://dpmf.org/images/occasionalpaper2.pdf).

Schugurensky, Daniel. 2016. Democratic innovations and local governance: An international perspective. *Local Government Reconsidered*. Paper 4. Retrieved May 01, 2016 (http://digitalcommons.chapman.edu/localgovernmentreconsidered/strerengtheningdemocracy/papers/4).

Schlesinger, Batista. 2015. The power of participatory decision making. Retrieved May 01, 2016 (https://www.opensocietyfoundations.org/voices/power-participatory-decision-making).

Seekings, Jeremy. 2000. After Apartheid: Civic groups in the "New" South Africa. In: Adler Glenn, and Steinberg Johnny (eds.). From Comrades *to citizens. The South African civics movement and the transition to democracy*. London: Macmillan Press, pp.205–224.

Seekoei, Kamogelo. 2016. Makwetu lauds audit. *New Age*, June 2, p.1.

Selebano, Bonolo. 2016. SALGA condemns anarchy. *New Age*, June 2, p.1.

Serafeim, Katerina. 2012. The impact of social media on press freedom in Greece: Benefits, challenges and limitations. *Essachess* 5(9):163-192.

Setsoto Local Municipality. 2015. About us. Retrieved August 14, 2015 (http://www.setsoto.info/content.php?7-about-us).

Shabalala, Zandi. 2016. South African public prosecutor wants fund to probe Gupta-Zuma links. Retrieved May 14, 2016 (https://africajournalismtheworld.com/201-6/06/07/south-african-public-prosecutor-wants-fund-to-probe-gupta-zuma-links-/).

Shaker, Lee. 2014. Dead newspapers and citizens' civic engagement. *Political Communication* 31(1):131-148.

Shaleva, Anna. 2015. Culture or Institutions? A quasi-experiment on the origins of political trust in Europe. June 30, 2015. Retrieved March 25, 2016 (http://ssrn.com/abstract=2372930).

Shaw, Robert B. 1997. *Trust in the balance: Building successful organizations on results, integrity and concern*. San Francisco: Jossey-Bass Publishers.

Shi, Tianjian. 2001. Cultural values and political trust: A comparison of the People's Republic of China and Taiwan. *Comparative Politics* 33(4):401-419.

Shoaei, Maral. 2012. MAS and the indigenous people of Bolivia. Masters thesis, College of Arts and sciences, University of South Florida. Retrieved May 15, 2014 (http://scholarcommons.usf.edu/etd/4401).

Sibisi, Sinazo. 2009. Brushing against the grains of history: Making local economic development work in South Africa. Retrieved March 25, 2016 (http://www.dbsa.org/EN/About-Us/Publications/Documents/DPD%20No%20.-5.%20-Brushing%20against%20the%20grains%20of%20history%20Making%2-0local%20 economic %20development%20work%20in%20South%20Africa-.pdf).

Simmons, Erica. 2014. Grievances do matter in mobilization. *Theory and Society* 43(5):513-546.

Skocpol, Theda. 1999. Advocates without members: The recent transformation of American civil life. In: Skocpol, Theda. & Fiorina, Morris P (eds.). *Civic Engagement in American Democracy*. Washington, DC: Brookings Institution Press.

Smirnov, Oleg, Dawes Christopher T, Fowler James H, Johnson Tim, and McElreath, Richard. 2010. The behavioral logic of collective action: partisans cooperate and punish more than nonpartisans. *Political Psychology* 31(4):595-616.

Smith, Terence, and de Visser Jaap. 2009. *The role of ward committees in South Africa: Evidence from six case studies*. Cape Town: Salty Print

Smith, Rogers M. 2011. Living in promisedland? Mexican immigration and American obligations. *Perspectives on Politics* 9(3):545-557.

Snow, David A. 2013. Grievances, individual and mobilizing. In: Snow, David A, Della Porta Donatella, Klandermans Bert, and McAdam Doug (eds.). *The Wiley-Blackwell Encyclopaedia and Political Movements*, vol 3. Malden, MA. Wiley-Blackwell, pp.1200-1204.

Sotarauta, Markku, and Beer Andrew. 2016. Governance, agency and place leadership: lessons from a cross-national analysis. *Regional Studies*, DOI: 10.1080/00343404.2015.1119265

SABC (South African Broadcasting Corporation). 2014. N. Cape municipality halts Transnet asbestos dumping. Retrieved February 12, 2015 (http://www.sabc.co.za-/news/a/317fbc0042822bb4a62bfe56d5ffbd92/N.-Cape-municipality-halts-Tran- snet-asbestos-dumping-20141001.

South African Human Rights Commission. 2016. National hearing on the impact of protest-related actions on the right to access a basic education in South Africa. Retrieved July 04, 2016 (http://sahrc.org.za/index.php/sahrc-media/news-2/item/385-national-hearing-on-the-impact-of-protest-related-actions-on-the-right-to-access-a-basic-education-in-south-africa).

South African Human Rights Commission. 2011. Council for the advancement of SA Constitution vs. South African Police. Retrieved February 01, 2015 (http//:sahrs.gov.za/Dcuments/!%20aSocial%20Protests/2016/Chapter%204%20-Fidings/JUNE2_Report%20Comm%20%20SA%20Police%20Service%203010-12.pdf).

South African Government. 2014. State of the Province Address by Mr Supra Ramoeletsi Mahumapelo, the Premier of the North West Province, to the first session of the Fifth Legislature of the North West. Retrieved February 01, 2015 (htt-p-://www.gov.za/state-province-address-mr-supra-ramoeletsi-mahumapelo-premier-north-west-province-first-session).

South African Local Government Association. 2015. 15 Years Review of Local Government: Celebrating achievements whilst acknowledging the challenges. Retrieved January 21, 2016 (http://www.salga.org.za/Documents/Knowledge%20Hub-/Local%20Government%-/Local%20Government%20Briefs/15-YEARS-OF-DEVELOPMENTAL-AND-DEMOCRATIC-LOCAL-GOVERNMENT.pdf).

South African Local Government Association. 2013. About local government. Retrieved February 01, 2015 (http://www.salga.org.za/pages/Municipalities/About-Municipalities).
Southern African Legal Information Institute. 2013. Motshware and Others v Minister of Safety And Security (449/2011, 450/2011, 451/2011, 452/2011,453/2011, 454/2011) [2013] ZANWHC 74 (12 December 2013). Retrieved May 04, 2015 (http://www.saflii.org/za/cases/ZANWHC/2013/74.pdf).
Sowetan. 2016. New plan to fire Zuma. *Sowetan*, April 6, p.1.
Steyn, Ibrahim. 2012. The state and social movements: Autonomy and its pitfalls, *Politikon* 39(3):331-351.
Steyn, Ibrahim. 2007. *Towards transformative local participatory governance.* Retrieved March 15, 2015 (www.ddp.org.za>research-themes>download).
Surty, Fatima. 2010. The political/administrative interface: the relationship between the executive mayor and municipal manager. Masters dissertation. Community Law Centre, University of the Western Cape. Retrieved October 14, 2014 (http://etd.uwc.ac.za/xmlui/bitstream/handle/11394/1726/Surty_LLM_2010.pdf?sequence=1).
Swain, Ashok. 2010. Struggle against the state: Social network and protest mobilization in India. Surrey: Ashgate.
Swart, Ignatius. 2013. South Africa's service-delivery crisis: From contextual understanding to diaconal response. *Theological Studies* 69(2):1-16.
Talo`, Cosimo, and Mannarini Terri. 2014. Measuring participation: Development and validation of the Participatory Behaviors Scale. *Social Indicators Research*, DOI 10.1007/s11205-014-0761-0
Tapscott, Chris. 2010. Social mobilization in Cape Town: a tale of two communities. In Lisa Thompson and Chris Tapscott (eds.). *Citizenship and social movements: perspectives from the global south.* London: Zed Books.
Tau, Poloko. 2016. Councillor with a lot to lose. *City Press*, May 22, p. 10.
Tausch, Nicole, Becker Julia C, Spears Russell, Christ Oliver, Saab Rim, Singh Purnima, and Siddiqui Roomana N. 2011. Explaining radical group behavior: Developing emotion and efficacy routes to normative and nonnormative collective action. *Journal of Personality and Social Psychology* 101(1): 129-148.
Tahvilzadeh, Nazem. 2015. Understanding participatory governance arrangements in urban politics: idealist and cynical perspectives on the politics of citizen dialogues in Göteborg, Sweden. *Urban Research & Practice* 8(2):238-254.
Theewaterskloof Municipality. 2016. *Our towns.* Retrieved June 20, 2016 (http://www.twk.org.za/our-towns-0).
The Hunger Project. 2014. 2014 State of Participatory Democracy Report. Retrieved December 24, 2015 (http://www.thp.org/wp-content/uploads/2014/10/2014-State-of-Local-Dem-Report-The-Hunger-Project.pdf).
The Presidency of the Republic of South Africa. 2014. *Address by President Zuma on the occasion of the Presidential Local Government Summit 2014*, Gallagher Convention Centre, Midrand Retrieved December 24, 2015 (http://www.thepresidency.gov.za/pebble.asp?relid=18023).

Thornhill, Christopher. 2008. Local government after 15 years: issues and challenges. In: De Villiers Bertus (ed.). 2008. Review of Provinces and Local Governments in South Africa: Constitutional Foundations and Practice, *Konrad Adenhauer Stiftung Occasional Papers*. Johannesburg. Retrieved June 24, 2015 (http://www.kas.de/wf/doc/kas_15071-544-1-30.pdf?090204110937).

Thwala, Chitja. 2014. The causes and socio-political impact of the service delivery protests to the South African citizenry: A real public discourse, *Journal of Social Science* 39(2):159-167.

Tlhabi, Redi. (2011). Violent protests are microcosm of our society. Available at http://www.sowetanlive.co.za/columnists/2011/07/08/violent-protests-are-microcosm-of-our-society (retrieved 24 May 2015).

Torcal, Mariano, and Martini Sergio. 2014. Trust across political conflicts: evidence from a survey experiment in divided societies. Paper presented at European Consortium for Political Research (ECPR) General Conference, University of Glasgow 3 - 6 September 2014. Retrieved March 14, 2016 (https://ecpr.eu/Filestore/-PaperProposal/7d08e680-d33b-4118-9b33-b1586bf93bf3.pdf).

Tong, Yangi, and Shaohua Lei. 2014. *Social protest in contemporary china, 2003-2010: Transnational pains and regime legitimacy*. New York: Routledge.

Tshabalala, E. L, and Lombard Antoinette. 2009. Community participation in the Integrated Development Plan: a case study of Govan Mbeki Municipality. *Journal of Public Administration*, 44(2):396-409.

Tsubogo, Minoru. 2014. The role of civil society and participatory governance in Japanese democracy: Citizen activities and the concept of a citizen municipality. *Japanese Political Science Review* 2 (2014), 39–61

Tusa, Felix. 2013. How social media can shape a protest movement: The cases of Egypt in Retrieved June 14, 2014 (https://www.files.ethz.ch/isn/184966/201302-21104512_Tusa_Felix.pdf).

United Nations. 2015. Transforming our world: the 2030 Agenda for Sustainable Development. Retrieved June 12, 2015 (https://sustainabledevelopment.un.org/post2015/transformingourworld).

United Nations Children's Fund. 2014. *Hidden in plain sight: A statistical analysis of violence against children*. New York: UNICEF.

University of the Free State. 2016. Twenty years of the constitution of South Africa – cause for celebration and reflection. Retrieved May 28, 2016 (http://www.ufs-.ac.za/template/news-archive-item?news=7760)

Van Belle, Jean-Paul, and Cupido Kevin. 2013. Increasing public participation in local government by means of mobile phones: the view of South African youth. *The Journal of Community Informatics* 9(4). Retrieved January 24, 2015 (http://-ci-journal.net/index.php/ciej/article/view/983/1054).

Van der Waldt, Gerrit. 2014. Fostering Local Democracy. In: Van der Walt, Gerrit (ed.). *Municipal Management: Serving the people,* second edition. Claremont: Academic Press, pp.23-51.

Van Stekelenburg, Jacquelien, and Klandermans Bert. 2013. The social psychology of protest. *Current Sociology Review* 61(5-6):886–905.

Van Stekelenburg, Jacquelien, Klandermans Bert, and Van Dijk Wilco W. 2009. Context matters: Explaining why and how mobilizing context influences motivational dynamics. *Journal of Social Issues* 65(4):815–838.
Visser, Alison. 2016. Why Sweden is discussing Tess Asplund. *City* Press, May 08, p.8.
Vitale, Denise, and Lavalle Andrian G. 2014. Participatory governance and social protest in Brazil. Retrieved January 24, 2015 (http://www.chance2sustain.eu/fileadmin/Website/Dokumente/Dokumente/Publications/publications_2014/-   C2S-OPC2S_OP_No13_WP6_Participatory_Governance_and_Social_Protest_in_Brazil.pdf).
Vivier, Elmé, Seabe Dineo, Wentzel Marie, and Sanchez Diana. 2015. From information to engagement: exploring communication platforms for the government-citizen interface in South Africa. *The African Journal of Information and Communication* 15:81-92.
Von Holdt, Karl. (2013). South Africa: the transition to violent democracy. *Review of African Political Economy* 40(138): 589-604.
Von Holdt, Karl et al. 2011. *The smoke that calls: Insurgent citizenship, collective violence and the struggle for a place in the new South Africa. Eight case studies of community protest and xenophobic violence.* Johannesburg: Centre for the Study of Violence and Reconciliation/ Society, Work and Development Institute, University of Witwatersrand.
Waheduzzaman, Wahed, and Alam Quamrul. 2015. Democratic culture and participatory local governance in Bangladesh. *Local Government Studies* 41(2):260-279.
Walker, Richard M, and Andrews Rhys. 2013. Local government management and performance: A Review of evidence. *Journal of Public Administration Research and Theory Advance*. doi: 10.1093/jopart/mut038.
Wampler, Brian. 2012. Participatory budgeting: Core principles and key impacts. *Journal of Public Deliberation* 8(2):1-13.
Wampler, Brian, and McNulty Stephanie L. 2011. *Does participatory governance matter? Exploring the nature and impact of participatory reforms.* Comparative Urban Studies Project: Woodrow Wilson International Center for Scholars. Retrieved June 24, 2015 (https://www.wilsoncenter.org/sites/default/files/CUSP_1-10108_Participatory%20Gov.pdf).
Water Research Commission. 2016. *Exploring the link between social protests and water service delivery in South Africa.* Technical brief. Retrieved June 22, 2016 (http://www.wrc.org.za/Knowledge%20Hub%20Documents/Briefs/Briefs%2020 16/TB_2133_Social%20protests%20and%20water%20service%20delivery.pdf).
Watts, Jonathan. 2016. Dilma Rouseff: Brazilian congress votes to impeach president. *The Guardian*. Retrieved May 14, 2016 (https://www.theguardian.com/world/2016/apr/18/dilma-rousseff-congress-impeach-brazilian-president).
Wilcox, David. 1999. *A to Z of participation.* New York: Joseph Rowntree Foundation.
Wilkes, Rima P. 2015. We trust in government, just not in yours: race, partisanship, and political trust, 1958-2012. *Social Science Research* January (49):356-71.

William, Fox F, and Menon Balakrishna. 2008. Decentralization in Bangladesh: Change has been elusive. In: Martinez-Vazquez, Jorge, and Vaillancourt François (eds.). Decentralization in developing countries: *Global perspectives on the obstacles to fiscal devolution* (Studies in Fiscal Federalism and State–local Finance series). Cheltenham, UK and Northampton, MA, USA: Edward Elgar, pp.215-250.

Wallis, AJ. 2015. Tlokwe by-elections were not free and fair – ConCourt. Retrieved January 12, 2016 (http://www.politicsweb.co.za/documents/tlokwe-byelections-were-not-free-and-fair--concour).

Williams, John J. 2006. Community participation: Lessons from post-apartheid South Africaolice. *Policy Studies* 27(3), 197-217.

Winters, Matthew S, and Weitz-Shapiro Rebecca. 2015. Political corruption and partisan engagement: evidence from Brazil. *Journal of Politics in Latin America* 7(1):45-81.

Winters, Matthew S, and Weitz-Shapiro Rebecca. 2014. Nonpartisan protests in Brazil. *Journal of Politics in Latin America* 6(1):137–150.

Wolfsfeld, Gadi, Segev Elad, and Sheafer Tamir. 2013. Social media and the Arab Spring: Politics comes first. *The International Journal of Press/Politics* 18(2) 115–137.

Wong, Timothy K, Wan Po-san, and Hsiao H Michael. 2015. The bases of political trust in six Asian societies: Institutional and cultural explanations compared. *International Political Science Review* 32(3): 263-28.

World Bank. 2009. Linking citizens and the state: An assessment of civil society contributions to good governance in Cambodia. Geneva: World Bank. Retrieved June 12, 2015 (http://siteresources.worldbank.org/EXTSOCIALDEVELOPMENT/Resource s/244362-1193949504055/4348035-1296838689014/7712311-29-8494972121/ Assessment_CivilSocietyContributionsCambodia.pdf).

Worthington, Glenn. 2001. Political trust and social capital in Australia. Parliament of Australia: Parliamentary Library Research Note 12. Retrieved June 14, 2014 (http://apo.org.au/resource/political-trust-and-social-capital-australia).

Yilmaz, Serdar, and Venugopal Varsha. 2013. Local government discretion and accountability in Philippines. *Journal of International Development* 25(2):227-250.

Zittel, Thomas, and Fuchs Dieter (eds.). 2012. *Participatory democracy and political participation can participatory engineering bring citizens back in*? London: Routledge.

Zuern, Elke. (2011). *The politics of necessity: community organizing and democracy in South Africa.* Madison: University of Wisconsin Press.

Active citizens 34–35, 50, 62, 67, 73, 93, 147
African National Congress (ANC)
  partisanship 43–46, 55, 87, 151–55
  patronage 53, 55, 70–71, 80, 82, 96, 122, 136, 151
Alexander, Peter 7, 14, 79, 86, 121–22, 145
Arab Spring 1, 11
Atkinson, Doreen x, 70, 122, 151, 156
Auditor-General of South Africa 12, 54, 150
Back to Basics Campaign 11, 152
Ballard, Richard 5, 14
Bond, Peter 71
Booysen, Susan 5, 7–9, 14, 58, 68
Brazil 8, 38, 44, 63, 67, 75, 145
Chapter 9 institutions 12, 74
Christensen, Henrik S. 26–27
Citizenship 28, 57, 85, 103
  insurgent citizenship 1–2
  state-citizen relations 39, 55, 57, 61, 64–65, 121, 152–53
Civic associations 15–16, 132
Collective behavior 45
Community engagement 65
Cross-border municipalities 79, 113
Della Porta, Donatella 5, 48, 50, 82, 121, 148
Democratic Alliance (DA) 12–13, 77, 89, 90, 106–10, 116, 121, 122, 136
Departments of Cooperative Governance and Traditional Affairs (COGTA) x, 5, 73, 78, 90, 98, 128, 153
Dullstroom Ratepayers' Association (DRA) 127–28
Economic Freedom Fighters (EFF) 83
Elgin Grabouw Civic Organization (EGCO) 90, 106–7, 108–11
Europe 13, 15, 26, 37–39, 45
Extra-representational channels 48
Ficksburg 3, 20, 89–99, 117, 119, 149
Free State Province 3, 14, 71, 94, 96, 98, 153
Fukuyama, Francis 26
Ganyesa 20, 89–90, 99–105, 117, 120, 122, 149
Ganyesa Residents' Forum (GRF) 100–105
Gauteng Province 12, 14, 46, 79, 83
Ghana 13, 76
Grabouw 20, 89–90, 105–12, 117, 120–21, 135, 148
Grievance
  formulation 28, 32, 47, 88
  genuine 27, 110, 118
Heilbron 124, 131–34, 143, 145, 154
Heilbron Landowners and Residents' Association (HLRA) 131–34

Highly structured groups 50–51
Immigration 36–37, 38, 39, 148
Independent Electoral Commission (IEC) 69, 74–78, 83
Inglehart, Ronald 1, 2, 25
Institutions
  democratic 28, 35, 37, 55, 66
  formal 21
  international 25
  public 36, 87
  state 6, 27, 31, 33, 82, 95
Integrated Development Plan (IDP) 8–9, 58–60, 68–74, 92, 128
International Criminal Court 82
Jacobsen, Georg 34, 41
Jansen, Jonathan ix, 3
Joint Planning Initiatives (JPIs) 73
Kenya 66
Khutsong 79, 116
Klandermans, Bert 5, 30, 49, 119
Liberal 1, 5, 53
Local communities 58, 68, 72, 73, 131, 145, 148
Local Development Plans (LEDs) 69
Local Development Plans (LED's) 10, 70–74
Macro changes 5, 31
Malamulele 80
McAdam, Doug 49, 149
MENA region (Middle East and North Africa) 65, 66
Meqheleng Concerned Citizens (MCC) 91–98

Municipal Demarcation Board (MDB) 69, 78–81
Municipal IQ x, 12–15, 75, 80
Municipalities
  municipal services 2, 11, 13, 16–17, 87–89, 106, 118, 121, 125, 128–29, 140, 146, 154
National Taxpayers Union (NTU) 17, 125, 127, 135, 142, 154
Ngwane, Trevor 14, 17, 79, 121, 145
No road, no school protest 116
No Road, No School protest 112–18
No, Road, No School protest 3
Non-institutional space 4, 28
Non-state actors 6, 13, 25, 31, 33–34, 47, 50, 52, 56, 57
Nonviolent protest tactic 2, 146
North West Province 18, 22, 77, 89, 100, 102, 104–5, 113, 118, 124, 138
Northern Cape Province x, 3, 18, 22, 73, 90, 113–18, 124, 128
Occupy Wall Street 1
Olifantshoek 3, 112
Organizational networks 1, 121
Pakistan 13
Panama Papers 37
Pithouse, Richard 3, 7
Police 3, 11, 23, 27, 39, 51, 84, 91, 94, 95, 101, 103, 107, 109, 111, 116, 144, 146
Political participation 27, 30, 48, 56
Political protests 1, 110

Political structures 5, 31, 149
Political structures and processes 5, 31
Political system 1, 25, 27, 32, 34–35, 39, 44, 48, 49, 59–60, 84–87, 101, 115, 119, 121, 147–49, 151
Political trust
 trust-building 6, 31, 33, 47, 119, 137
 trust-deficit 33, 52, 140, 154
Political violence 52
Popular mobilization 2, 9, 58, 67, 150
Post-apartheid South Africa 3, 7, 8, 15–16, 21, 53, 58, 60, 91, 100, 124
Protest action 5–8, 21, 29, 50–51, 80, 88, 95, 101–5, 108, 110–11, 113, 117, 119, 141, 147
Protest movements 45, 57
Protest organizers 91, 95, 101–3, 108–10, 113, 117, 118, 121, 122, 149
Public space 1, 132
Putnam, Robert D. 25, 33, 147, 148
Riviersonderend Ratepayers' Association (RRA) 135–38
Rogerson, Christian M. 71–72
Runciman, Carin 2, 7, 28, 35, 51, 86, 121, 147
Sannieshof Residents and Ratepayers' Association (SIBU) 22–23, 139–43
Schools

bargaining power 16, 86
closure 23, 100, 105, 108, 115, 146
destruction 102, 108
Setsoto Municipality 89–90, 93, 94, 95, 89–90
Social capital 25–26, 33
Social media 84, 86, 94
Social movements ix, 6, 14, 28, 29, 44, 49, 149
Social networks 47–48, 63, 152
South African Broadcasting Corporation (SABC) 87, 91, 131
South African Local Government Association (SALGA) 5, 18, 150, 155
South African National Civic Association (SANCO) 16, 106
Spain 8, 15, 37, 45, 57
State-citizen engagement 39, 55, 57, 61, 64–65, 121
Structural-cognitive model (SCM) 5, 28–31, 34, 88
Swain, Ashok ix, 5, 36, 48, 49, 103
Swinging pendulum of trust 6, 20, 28, 31–33, 36, 55, 86, 101, 119
Theewaterskloof Municipality 89–90, 106–7, 120, 136–38
Uganda 13
United Nations (UN) 64, 72, 123
Von Holdt, Karl 4–5, 7, 18, 28, 36, 45–46, 51–52, 86, 103, 121–22, 145, 146, 149
Vuwami 80–81, 85

183

Western Cape Province x, 12, 18, 22, 73, 89, 107, 111–12, 122, 124, 126, 150
White Local Authorities (WLAs) 68
Zuma, Jacob 39–41, 53–54, 144, 152

GPSR Authorized Representative: Easy Access System Europe, Mustamäe tee
50, 10621 Tallinn, Estonia, gpsr.requests@easproject.com